The Timber Economy of
Puritan New England

Charles F. Carroll

The Timber Economy of Puritan New England

Brown University Press   Providence

Brown University Press, Providence, Rhode Island 02912
© 1973 by Brown University. All rights reserved
Printed in the United States of America
By Heritage Printers, Inc.   [by] Charles F. Carroll. Providence,
On Warren's Olde Style   Brown Univ. Press [1973]
Bound by The Delmar Companies   221 p.
Designed by Richard Hendel

Library of Congress Cataloging in Publication Data
Carroll, Charles F   1936–
   The timber economy of Puritan New England.
   1. Lumber trade—New England—History.   2. Forests
and forestry—New England—History.   3. New England—
Economic conditions.   I. Title.
HD9757.A1C35   380.1′41′490974   73–7122
ISBN 0–87057–142–7

To my mother

Contents

Contents

List of Maps

Preface

Almost forty years ago, Walter Prescott Webb's classic work *The Great Plains* made students of American history aware of the changes that took place when men first left the humid woodland of eastern Texas and developed a semiarid and treeless land. But the full story of man's first great encounter with a new environment in America has not been told.

The adventurers and Puritan exiles who came to America in the seventeenth century found themselves in unfamiliar surroundings, for there were no virgin forests in England, and many inhabited parts of Britain were almost completely stripped of forest cover. The giant trees of the North American forest created an environment quite different from the gently rolling countryside of England, and for men accustomed to work in well-kept fields and orchards, or to the amenities of university life, the hum of small commercial towns, or the bustle of the great metropolis of London, adaptation to life in a vast forest was profoundly difficult and disturbing.

But if Englishmen were unaccustomed to woodlands and dismayed by the prospect of living in a strange new environment, they were drawn to a land that could provide an abundance of one of the most important natural resources. Indeed, before the nineteenth century, nearly every human activity depended on timber. Until the axman felled the trees, most craftsmen could not follow their callings; crops could neither be sown nor harvested; houses could neither be built nor furnished; clothes could not be made; rooms could not be warmed; ships could not sail; rivers could not be crossed; the fires of industry could not burn; wars could not be fought; and the sick could not be healed. By the seventeenth century there was such a serious timber shortage in England that the timber resources of New England attracted many investors and settlers. And more than in any other section of the North American forest, large numbers of inexperienced colonists from the treeless English countryside were compelled by climate, terrain, and the poor condition of the soil to adapt to the forest quickly and completely, and to become hunters, trappers, and woodsmen who collected and processed forest products for markets in many lands.

The Puritan leaders of the 1630s had hoped to create a model Christian commonwealth isolated from what they thought were corrupt societies in Europe and America. But the society that they hoped for was not possible in a land where foreign trade was essential for survival. The growing demand for New England timber in overseas ports led to the continual expansion of the Massachusetts Bay Colony beyond the Merrimack and forced many of its political and economic—and even some religious— leaders to abandon many of their principles. In the struggle for survival during the 1640s and for power and wealth in succeeding decades the settlers of New England came to terms with their new environment and learned to exploit it, and in the process, both man and the land were transformed.

The scattered references to timber that tell the story of the settlers' reactions to the forest and efforts to exploit its resources are to be found in seventeenth-century documents in a number of great collections. I am deeply indebted to Thomas R. Adams and the staff of the John Carter Brown Library for their many kindnesses, and I wish also to thank the staffs of the Rockefeller Library of Brown University, the Essex Institute, the Massachusetts Historical Society, the Baker Library of the Harvard Business School, the American Antiquarian Society, the Boston Public Library, and the Massachusetts Archives. My research was supported in 1965–66 by a John Carter Brown Library fellowship. Publication of this book was assisted by the American Council of Learned Societies under a grant from the Andrew W. Mellon Foundation.

A number of friends and colleagues provided valuable assistance during the preparation of the manuscript. Professor A. Hunter Dupree read the entire work and provided valuable insight into the evolution of technology. Professor Richard Derry checked a number of points about the geography of his native Maine and provided several colorful bits of information that I had overlooked. John McCarthy read the entire manuscript in search of misplaced punctuation and grammatical inaccuracies. Professor Mary Blewett and Professor Peter Blewett read the entire work for consistency of the over-all theme. My wife, Pauline Cognac Carroll, a graduate student in history at Brown University, not only carefully scrutinized the text but also analyzed, evaluated, and collated scattered seventeenth-century economic data.

I would especially like to thank Professor Carl Bridenbaugh, who provided the initial suggestion that the relationship between the colonists and the forest was a fruitful topic for study. Professor Bridenbaugh has followed my research from its beginning and has read my drafts with great care. I will always remember his encouragement, his discerning advice and counsel, and his many acts of kindness.

 Chapter 1

SCOTLAND

NORTH SEA

Northumberland

Durham

Keswick

Westmorland

Yorkshire
●York

IRISH SEA

●Scrooby
PEAK DISTRICT
Lincolnshire
CANNOCK CHASE

THE WASH

MIDLANDS

Shropshire

ENGLAND

Norwich ●
Yarmouth ●

EAST ANGLIA

Herefordshire

Sudbury

Droitwich

WALES

Gloucestershire
Oxfordshire

Essex

THAMES RIVER

London Woolwich

WINDSOR PARK

FOREST OF DEAN

●Bristol

Deptford
Surrey
Chatham
Cranbrook Kent

ANDRED WEALD

BRISTOL CHANNEL

EXMOOR
●Barnstaple Somerset
WEST COUNTRY

Hampshire
Southampton●
Portsmouth

Sussex

Devonshire

NEW FOREST
Poole●

DARTMOOR
Exeter

Weymouth

Cornwall

●Dartmouth

ENGLISH CHANNEL

England and Wales

The Timber Shortage in England

In ancient times forests covered the greater part of the British Isles. The great oaks of Andred Weald shaded most of southeastern England, and the branches of towering firs hovered over the land from Scotland south to the Midlands. For thousands of years the men of Britain were forest dwellers, eking out a meager existence by hunting, fishing, and gathering roots and berries in the shade of giant trees. Constantly on the move, they traveled through the wilderness in primitive canoes. They felled trees with stone tools and fashioned the wooden agricultural and household tools that made life more bearable. They worshiped in sacred groves and lived in fear of wolves, bears, and other forest animals.[1]

Even in Roman times civilized men on the Continent looked upon Britain as an almost legendary land, "a new world of awesome isolation and uncharted risk." Caesar, who conducted two swift invasions of Britain in 55 and 54 B.C., found the region beyond the agricultural and trading settlements of the southern coast a wilderness in which his legions were in constant danger of surprise attack. The Romans slowly brought civilization to some parts of Britain, which meant the destruction of many timber trees. In 59 A.D. Roman armies defeated the Druids and systematically destroyed their sacred groves. Later the Romans cleared land for roads and towns, worked the valuable metal deposits, and destroyed the woodlands to get wood for the tin furnaces of Cornwall and the ironworks of the Forest of Dean. In the New Forest in Hampshire men made pottery to supply the Continent.[2]

Invasions by Angles, Saxons, and other tribes during the fifth century brought an end to Roman civilization in Britain, temporarily interrupting the destruction of the forests. But once the invasions had ended, forest clearing proceeded rapidly. After

3

the introduction of the heavy, wheeled plow, the heavier soils of such regions as the Midlands could be farmed. Peasants who had these plows often abandoned their old homes to found new villages amid oaken glades. Christian monks, seeking remote regions for peace and contemplation, cleared virgin forests with hatchets, billhooks, and fire. Their exemplary lives attracted many laymen to these outposts.[3]

The Clearing of the Forest

The clearing of the forest in Anglo-Saxon times slowly brought the peoples of Britain together and made them one. By the era of the Norman Conquest there were farming settlements in all parts of the island, some of which had taken on a gardenlike character. In all settled areas wild animals were uncommon, and everywhere there was extensive use of the woods and other non-arable land. Goats, swine, and oxen devoured seedlings and young shoots on the forest floor, which prevented the regeneration of the trees and prepared additional land for the plowman.[4]

Britain soon required additional plowland to feed a population that doubled between the eleventh and thirteenth centuries. Internal colonization proceeded rapidly, with husbandmen clearing heavier soils and opening new land farther and farther from the river valleys. Norman documents are full of references to enclosure and land clearing—indication that plowmen were destroying the forests. By the thirteenth century there was little accessible woodland left to conquer. Men had turned even village waste, rocky soil, chalky upland, and thin and barren heath into farmland. Herdsmen had converted great tracts of meadow and woodland into pasture, and thousands of sheep grazed on the upland of Lincolnshire, Shropshire, and Gloucestershire, and on the estates of the Cistercian abbeys in Yorkshire. Only the marshland, the combes and valleys of Devonshire, and the interior of Cornwall were still available for settlement. Britons constantly cut and lopped the remaining woodland for fuel, building materials, and hundreds of other needs. Many of the trees renewed themselves, but the fir, once common in middle England, remained only in Scotland and the counties on the northern border of England.[5]

A land once wild was tame. The bear, the elk, and the lynx were gone, the wild boar was becoming scarce, and wolves could be found only in the mountains of Wales and Westmorland and in the Peak District. The Saxon and Norman kings set aside "forests" as royal game preserves and staffed them with a host of officers—verderers, regarders, foresters, agistors, gavellers, woodwards, stewards, and lord wardens—who administered a strict and often cruel forest law. But the forest of an Angevin king was never completely wooded, and its bounds often embraced moorland, pasture, open wastes, and even populous villages.

When the growing population increased the demand for food and clothing in the High Middle Ages, many kings sold sections of their forests for plowland and pasture. They also sold licenses for hunting, charged fees for the gathering of timber and firewood, and granted assarts (the rights to grub up trees and bushes and create arable land). Forest law, which thus became a means of filling royal coffers rather than a means of preserving woodlands, was one of the chief symbols of arbitrary power. By the thirteenth century the attempts of kings to increase the size of the royal forests led to a series of constitutional crises and some disafforestation.[6]

Continued population increases might have resulted in destruction of the British woodlands by 1400, for in the thirteenth century the population was growing faster than the food supply. By destroying the forests and creating towns and great farming regions, man had upset the balance of nature. On marginal lands, farmers who did not have manure saw their crops grow thin, and some abandoned their fields. As the food supply decreased, malnutrition and disease increased. In the summer of 1348 black rats with fleas carrying bubonic plague entered England, and the Great Pestilence slowly spread across the land. Epidemics of bubonic plague, smallpox, measles, diphtheria, pertussis, influenza, dysentery, and typhus fever struck the people of Britain and the Continent again and again in the fourteenth and fifteenth centuries. The population of Britain decreased 50 per cent during those dark decades, and there was no sign of an increase until the early sixteenth century.[7]

As settlers abandoned their fields and returned to their old homes to die, large amounts of plowland reverted to woodland and waste; but without proper management, the quality of much of the returning timber must have been poor. Many species of wild forest animals did not return, but powerful men, taking advantage of lax enforcement of the royal forest law in a time of disease, chaos, and civil and foreign war, enclosed royal land and claimed that only they had the right to hunt the game that remained. In the late fourteenth century a statute of Richard II defined hunting as "the sport of the gentle" and deprived the lower classes of hunting dogs and ferrets as well as snares for deer, hare, and other game. Ordinary men were not allowed to harm game even when it endangered their crops. These game laws, strengthened in the following centuries, created a great deal of animosity between classes. One of the unfulfilled demands of the rebels of 1381 was that parks and woodlands should be common to all, "so that throughout the realm, in waters, ponds, fisheries, woods, and forests, poor as well as rich might take the venison and hunt the hare in the fields."[8]

The Great Revolt of 1381 was evidence that great economic and social change was taking place in the late fourteenth and early fifteenth centuries. The total wealth of the nation was less than it had been during the High Middle Ages, although those who survived wars and plagues gained from the redistribution of wealth and property. Many gentlemen augmented their estates, and a shortage of labor increased the wages and mobility of the lower classes. The decline in the demand for arable land and the shortage of labor encouraged many landowners to increase their herds of sheep, so that in many regions plowland became pasture; in a sense, sheep took the place of the lost population. By the late fifteenth century sheep were so numerous in England that some woodland was being converted to pasture, for sheep are grass-consuming animals and require extensive meadows or open country with scrub. Thus when the human population began to increase in the sixteenth century there was a struggle for land between sheepherders and farmers as both groups destroyed additional forested tracts.[9]

Although enclosure of some land for herding and farming created thousands of vagabonds, beggars, and homeless and broken men, the increase in population was a boon to the majority of Englishmen. The copyholder and yeoman classes, profiting greatly from high agricultural prices, and accumulating substantial savings, longed for a better life. They particularly wanted larger and more comfortable homes, and by the 1580s a building boom was under way. Many added parlors, halls, chambers, kitchens, and even additional stories to their houses, and others erected completely new dwellings. Carpenters built few houses wholly of wood, but in regions where large trees were available they used great numbers of framing timbers. Within their new or remodeled homes, many Englishmen installed wood-burning fireplaces. Wooden tables, chests, benches, cabinets, beds, trenchers, churns, and other furniture and household utensils were much in demand. Great amounts of wood were consumed in the manufacture of farm tools, wheelbarrows, carts, and wagons.[10]

Diminishing Resources in an Expanding Economy

The rising expectations of the common people and their increased demand for wood products reflect the changes that were taking place in Tudor and Stuart England. The discovery of the New World, great religious reform movements, and growing nationalism stimulated an already expanding economy. Merchants, aware of the importance of sea power, founded great companies for trade in far-off lands. Many introduced new industries from the Continent: cannon foundries, gunpowder and paper mills, sugar refineries, alum and copperas factories, and large saltpeter works. Italian glassmakers founded more than a dozen glasshouses in England by the end of the sixteenth century. The discovery of zinc in Somerset and success in copper mining led to the establishment of forges for hammering brass and copper ingots into plates. The production of lead, tin, and silver increased, and after the introduction of the blast furnace in 1540, iron production increased fourfold by 1625. By this date as many as 150 blast furnaces capable of producing from 100 to 500 tons of cast iron annually operated in England, Scotland, and Wales, and perhaps twice as many large forges hammered the cast iron into bars.[11]

The expansion of the British shipping industry was even more vigorous. By the late sixteenth century English ships were replacing Venetian, and some Dutch, vessels in the Mediterranean and Baltic trades. Some English merchantmen were searching the coasts of America for gold and for a northwest passage, while others were intruding on the Portuguese and Dutch trading stations in the Indian Ocean and along the African coast. In 1600 English merchants founded the British East India Company and built a 600-ton vessel for their first voyage. The East Indian trade was so successful that an 1,100-ton vessel was required for the sixth voyage.[12]

The English fishing fleet was expanding as fast as the merchant fleet and was beginning to challenge the Dutch monopoly of the English market by the late sixteenth century. Each year the catches of the east coast herring fleets grew larger, and Yarmouth, the outport of Norwich, prospered. Englishmen entered the Spitsbergen whaling industry and the Iceland fishery, and the men of Devon and Cornwall hauled in cod off the foggy coasts of Maine and Newfoundland. The English fishery in Newfoundland, which employed only 30 ships in 1574, employed over 200 by the early seventeenth century and from 300 to 500 by 1630.[13]

Merchantmen and fishermen were venturing into parts of the world their ancestors had never known, and though the benefits were many, the risks were great, for the English vessels might be attacked by pirate vessels or warships. To strengthen the navy, Henry VII built many large warships. Henry VIII continued to expand the Royal Navy, building not only men-of-war, but also dockyards at Woolwich and Deptford, and a naval base at Portsmouth. By the late sixteenth century, warships of more than 1,000 tons burden were built at these yards and at Chatham, and they were outfitted with cannon produced by new iron forges and furnaces.[14]

The extent of the demand for wood and wood products in that era of swiftly expanding population, industry, commerce, and naval power is difficult to imagine in this age of steel, plastics, and electricity. Carpenters required great numbers of construction timbers for mine shafts, factories, furnaces, sheds, and storage buildings. Millwrights needed great timbers for frames, giant water wheels, and sluices for the water- and wind-driven mills that ground grain, fulled cloth, made paper, broke lead, stamped tin, and drove the leather bellows of the great blast furnaces. Physicians depended upon the forest for many medicines, and sheepherders used tar distilled from wood for curing sheep scab. Hop growers destroyed thousands of young trees each year for hop poles. Coopers—extremely important craftsmen in an era when almost everything was made, stored, and transported in wooden barrels—required enormous numbers of staves and hoops and quantities of heading. Tanners and leather craftsmen—who made clothing, containers, straps, fasteners, whips, bellows, saddles, and many other necessary items—required great quantities of oak bark for tanning. And soapboilers, gunpowder manufacturers, and glassmakers needed potash (made from wood ash).[15]

Shipwrights, too, depended on the woodlands, for almost every part of a ship was fashioned from timber. Over 2,000 oak trees, many twenty inches in diameter and from 100 to 150 years old, went into the construction of a single large warship. Lesser ships required smaller amounts of timber, but no matter what the tonnage, only high quality oak would make a vessel safe and sturdy. Because many great oaks suffer from disease and decay, the choice of trees was always limited. The shipwright needed many naturally curved "compass" timbers, found only in hedgerows or other open areas. Coniferous trees (fir, spruce, and pine) were used for masts and spars and for the production of tar and pitch to seal the ship and make it seaworthy. Large amounts of timber were also required to keep older vessels in repair. Other craftsmen and seamen used wood to make ship's furniture and casks, or burned it as fuel for cooking and for drying clothes.[16]

The demand for wood for the construction of buildings was great, but the producers of essential goods needed even greater quantities for fuel. Coopers and shipbuilders used firewood to dry and bend timbers. Bakers and pastry cooks burned wood in their ovens. Maltsters, brickmakers, limeburners, glassmakers, pipemakers, and saltpeter and gunpowder manufacturers needed firewood to dry their products. And there were many others who burned wood in order to boil their products, among them soapmakers, clothmakers, hatters, bleachers, dyers, starchmakers, chandlers, saltmakers, brewers, distillers, sugar refiners, confectioners, vinegar makers, and alum and copperas makers. Some of these manufacturers used great amounts of wood in relation to the size and weight of the final product. It took one load of hardwood (about fifty cubic feet) to produce 2,000 bricks, and more than one load to produce two hundredweight of saltpeter. The requirement for wood in saltmaking depended upon the salinity of the seawater or brine; in the late sixteenth century, saltmakers at Droitwich used about four loads of wood to produce a single ton of salt. Limeburners needed about four loads of wood to produce one ton of lime. Glasshouses were great consumers of the forest, most burning 700 cords of wood a year. A glasshouse destroyed by fire in London in 1575 had 40,000 billets (200 wagonloads) of wood on hand, and this house alone used 400,000 billets of wood in one year.[17]

No industry, however, required as much wood fuel as iron manufacturing. In 1588 the blast furnace in Cannock Chase consumed 24.5 cords of wood—a pile 4 feet high, 4 feet wide, and 196 feet long—to produce 1.5 tons of cast iron, and at the forge 17.5 additional cords were required to hammer one ton of cast iron into wrought iron. One ironworks might use as much as 22,000 cords of wood a year. Many smiths, nailers, and other metal craftsmen also depended upon the forest for their fuel supplies.[18]

Because of sheepherding, farming, trade, and manufacturing, the woodland gradually disappeared. Some writers and some government reports of the late sixteenth and seventeenth centuries imply that there were great amounts of timber still standing in both Britain and Ireland. But Englishmen, accustomed to life on an island, had ideas of space and distance that were very different from those of the inhabitants of great continents. There may have been enough woodland in Elizabethan England for Robin Goodfellow and goblins and sprites to rove and wander in and to keep alive woodland superstitions among the English, but there were probably few forested tracts covering more than twenty square miles: in fact, in some regions there were no trees at all except in hedgerows.[19]

The Late Sixteenth-Century Crisis

In the late sixteenth century Englishmen were faced with a crisis: the woodlands were depleted just when the need for timber was increasing. The shortage of wood was beginning to cause great inconvenience, even suffering, in some regions, and the concentration of population in southern England aggravated the timber problem. In the seventeenth century the English were an agrarian people, but more than one-quarter of them lived in cities or towns, and about four-fifths of the population was south of a line running northeastward from the Bristol Channel to The Wash. By the end of the seventeenth century there were 1,000,000 people in or near the Thames valley. The population of London and its suburbs was even more compact. There may have been 200,000 persons in the environs of the capital in 1600 and as many as 300,000 by 1630; despite plagues and other disasters, immigration increased the number of inhabitants to over 400,000 by the end of the century.[20]

Some southern counties, particularly Sussex, Surrey, and Kent, had some of the largest timber supplies in Britain, but even there the woods had become thin, and some sections of Kent were described as the "garden of England" because of their extensive hop fields and orchards. Besides, much of the timber in these counties (as in the mountains of Wales and the Scottish Highlands) was inaccessible. Before the era of the canal and the railroad, it was difficult to transport timber once the forests near the ocean and the rivers had been cut. In a land where snowfall was light, and in an era when roads were unpaved, it was impossible to move wood and timbers a great distance over the ground. Heavy wagons drawn by several pairs of horses or oxen often sunk into the soft roads, and land carriage beyond twenty miles was generally too costly. In Kent and Sussex, which had some of the worst roads in England, the cost of transporting timber was one shilling a load for every mile.[21]

The decrease in available timber and increase in transportation charges drove up timber prices in the sixteenth and early seventeenth centuries. The price of firewood doubled between the 1540s and the 1570s and tripled again by the 1630s. This rapid increase in the cost of firewood was "almost without precedent in the history of Western civilization." The poor suffered the most from this—and there were many poor in Tudor and Stuart England. In London they were at the mercy of woodmongers, who virtually controlled all transportation in the capital. Despite regulation, there were many complaints that the woodmongers manipulated prices. Some of the poor, unable to afford firewood for heating or cooking, shivered through every winter, surviving on a diet of of bread and cheese.[22]

When unusually cold temperatures froze the rivers and prevented waterborne fuel from reaching the large cities, the suffering was more widespread. There were many crises in the sixteenth and seventeenth centuries. "Great and continual frosts and ice" often interrupted the fuel supplies of London. During the crisis of 1542–43, the mayor of London went to the wharves daily for wood, which he distributed to the poor at reasonable prices. In 1608 the Great Frost paralyzed much of England. Wood-boats could not reach London from points upstream or from the sea, and the whole city shivered. The city fathers provided some fuel for the poorest inhabitants, who lived on the outskirts of London: if they had not, "the unconscionable and unmerciful raising of the prices of fuel" by woodmongers—"who now meant to lay the poor on the rack—would have been the death of many a wretched creature through want of succour."[23]

During periods of intense cold, the poor in the countryside often suffered as much as the city dwellers, and the removal of the trees that formerly served as windbreaks in the hills and valleys aggravated their misery. Copyholders and others in the countryside had enjoyed the customary right to take wood to repair their houses or plows, as well as the right to top and lop the trees of the manors for firewood. But by the time of Elizabeth, many had lost such rights, for men of wealth and power consolidated and enclosed common land for sheepraising and farming. The overseers of the poor might provide landless families with a little fuel; but many—living in flimsy huts of clay and branches and suffering from the damp ocean winds—broke the law and cut trees and hedges, taking timber wherever they found it. In 1601 Parliament passed an "Act to avoid and prevent divers misdemeanours in idle and lewd Persons" and provided severe penalties for "illicit cutting and mischivous spoiling of woods, trees, or poles" on both public and private land. But such activity continued, and the poor were not the greatest offenders.[24]

Manufacturers, too, found it increasingly difficult to obtain enough timber. Coopers complained of a shortage of staves for liquid-tight casks, tanners of the poor quality and high cost of oak bark. Potash makers found suitable ash so scarce that they often sent horsemen around the countryside in search of small quantities. London clothdyers stood helpless during a fivefold rise in the price of English dyewood between 1550 and 1605. And during the reign of Charles I the clothmakers in the little town of Cranbrook in Kent complained that their trade was in danger because of the high prices the dyers were forced to pay for the firewood they burned beneath their vats. The production of the copper smelting works at Keswick was already in decline in the late sixteenth century because of a lack of trees fit for charcoal.

Glassmakers constantly moved to be close to the dwindling fuel supply. Though ironmaking techniques continually improved throughout the sixteenth century, the shortage of wood fuel checked the rapid growth of that industry by 1600 and brought expansion to a standstill before the Civil War. Some ironmasters had to close down, abandon valuable equipment, and seek sites closer to timber supplies.[25]

The timber crisis affected even the navy. Many still believed that God had planted the English forests with oaks of special "toughness and heart" to insure that the nation would be "mighty by Sea and navigation." But the ships of the Royal Navy, England's "wooden walls," were often in danger because of the timber shortage. Admiral Sir William Monson declared that lost trade might be recovered and lost seamen might be replaced, "but if our timber be consumed and spent it will require the age of three or four generations before it can grow again for use." But did Englishmen have the will or the means to preserve the woodlands and solve the timber problem?[26]

Conservation and Reforestation

The English at least attempted to save their dwindling forest resources. The most important conservation statute, the Act for the Preservation of Woods (1543), prohibited farmers from turning woodland more than two furlongs from their dwellings into pasture or tillage. This statute also ordered that cattle be kept out of young woods and that twelve standards (timber trees) an acre be left in all coppice woods of twenty-four years' growth or less. No one was to cut the standards until they reached a size suitable for building. Parliament passed additional conservation legislation during the Tudor and Stuart eras, but many of these laws were to protect such craftsmen as coopers, tanners, shipwrights, and ironmakers. And many citizens apparently exempted themselves from the law, for it seems that legislation did little to save the timber.[27]

There was little that one could call forest management in England during the sixteenth and seventeenth centuries. The fate of timber on private estates depended solely upon the whim of the owner. Some wealthy landed proprietors refused to cut any of their great trees, allowing them to grow old and useless. Other proprietors, especially those who had an immediate need for cash, slashed their young trees and sold them for firewood and small timbers. "For as the rate of Money now goweth," the merchant Josiah Child wrote, "no man can let his Timber stand, nor his wood grow to such years growth as is best for the Commonwealth." The administrators of the royal forests, still bearing their medieval titles, were notorious for their incompetence and dishonesty. They looked on as browsing cattle and deer chewed up the young trees, and they allowed many great oaks to pass their prime and become rotten. Wood wardens accepted bribes from trespassers who cut choice timber, and forest administrators often cut timber for their own profit. As a result of this mismanagement, the navy was able to procure only about 10 per cent of its timber from the royal forests.[28]

Reforestation was a possible solution to the timber crisis, but it took more than a lifetime for an oak to mature and become profitable, whereas a gentleman could obtain cash from the production of grain or wool in a relatively short time. As long as there was a growing market for agricultural products, there was little incentive for private citizens to plant trees. The first official attempt at reforestation was made in 1560, when Elizabeth's minister, Lord Burleigh, ordered thirteen acres of Cranbourne Walk in Windsor Park to be sown with acorns. But a second effort at reforestation was not made until these oaks were mature. In 1662 John Evelyn published *Sylva*, his famous report on the timber crisis to the Royal Society. Declaring that the waste and destruction of the woods in England had been so widespread that nothing but "a universal plantation of all sorts of trees" would be a remedy, Evelyn gave minute directions for planting a great variety of valuable ornamental and timber trees. In 1668 Parliament, aroused by Evelyn's propaganda, ordered 11,000 acres of waste land in the Forest of Dean planted in oak, and many landowners made similar plantings on their estates.[29]

Reforestation was a long-term solution for the timber crisis. The trees planted by Parliament in 1668 would not be of use to the Royal Navy until the time of the American Revolution. But it appears that reforestation attempts in later decades, despite Evelyn's efforts, were occasional and halfhearted. The administrators of the royal forests still thought tree planting was unprofitable, and by this era some gentlemen looked upon the production of timber in England as futile.[30]

Substitutes for Timber

Englishmen whose livelihood was severely impaired by the scarcity of wood could not wait for solutions to the timber problem. They actively searched for new materials and techniques to replace wood or at least limit its domestic and industrial use.

In the construction trades the scarcity of timber led to increased use of other building materials, among them flint, brick, stone, tile, lime, and plaster. In 1621 Parliament attempted to encourage this and ordered that new buildings in or near London and Westminster be of brick or stone. But using new materials did not completely solve the timber problem, for in many counties coppice timber was used in manufacturing brick, tile, plaster, and lime, and in every substantial dwelling timber was used for floors and frames. Substitutes for timber, such as building stones, were also scarce in some regions of England, especially the southeast. Other areas lacked lime for plaster and for mortar to bond brick and stone. In some areas lime was so scarce that limeburners sold it by the pound, and those who lived by the sea obtained limited quantities by burning seashells.[31]

Despite the intention of Parliament the demand for construction timber in cities continued to grow. After the Great Fire in London in 1666, when over 13,000 houses, numerous parish churches, and most commercial and public buildings were destroyed, a great effort was made to rebuild the city with brick and stone. Nevertheless, wood was still used in enormous quantities, and the price of boards and beams more than doubled.[32]

Skilled and experienced craftsmen, experimenting with ways to replace firewood in home and industry, were somewhat more successful than the builders had been. In the early sixteenth century some ironmasters in Devonshire were already trying to use peat from Dartmoor and Exmoor. By the seventeenth century the use of peat in iron manufacturing was common in many regions of

England. But because peat has a low caloric value, large amounts of charcoal had to be added, and the iron produced by the burning of peat was of poor quality and often required resmelting.[33]

Coal was much more important than peat. Some English dyers, smiths, and limeburners had been using coal since the High Middle Ages, but most Englishmen did not burn great quantities of it until the sixteenth century, when the price of firewood and timber more than doubled. Nearly 200,000 tons of coal were produced annually during the reign of Henry VIII, and production increased substantially during the reign of Elizabeth. By the 1630s nearly 1,500,000 tons of coal were produced, and by the end of the Civil War coal was a necessity in the homes of all but the wealthiest classes of London, the port towns, and the settlements in the river valleys. Coal also became the ordinary fuel used on ships. It is estimated that by 1690 almost 3,000,000 tons of coal were produced annually.[34]

The warming of rooms, the cooking of food, and other household activities created the greatest demand for coal during the sixteenth and early seventeenth centuries, but the industrial use of coal increased as well. By the 1630s the saltmakers near the mines at Durham and in Northumberland were burning 100,000 tons of coal annually, and many limeburners, smiths, brewers, brass casters, soap boilers, clothmakers, dyers, hatmakers, sugar refiners, and alum and gunpowder manufacturers, too, were using coal in place of firewood. Coal-fired furnaces were devised for converting iron into steel, extracting silver from lead, and making glass and brick. By the 1640s ironmasters were using coal for calcining iron ore before putting it into blast furnaces.[35]

Coal, more than any other resource, brought relief to Englishmen during this timber shortage. However, because of the difficulty of land transportation, coal was not available everywhere in England in the seventeenth century. In rural Herefordshire and northern Oxfordshire, for instance, the poor suffered through a long period in the seventeenth and eighteenth centuries without coal or firewood, burning only furze, dried grass, weeds, and dung when such lowly fuel was at hand.[36]

Even where coal was available it was often expensive. The shipment of coal overland by packhorse or wagon was always very costly, and even where water transportation was available, shipping costs increased throughout the seventeenth century. Furthermore, coal delivery was as undependable as timber transport because of uneven supply at the source, dangerous ocean transport, and ice-blocked rivers and harbors. Coal selling for twenty shillings a chaldron in London during a mild winter might cost fifty or even eighty shillings a chaldron in times of scarcity. Complaints about profiteering among coal dealers were similar to those made about the woodmongers, and the poor suffered during cold weather despite the increase in the coal supply. During the cold wave of January 1684, John Evelyn wrote, "All sorts of fuell [were] so dear that there were great contributions to preserve the poore alive."[37]

Far from solving the timber problem, the widespread use of coal tended to aggravate it. For as the demand for coal grew seven- or eightfold in the century after 1530 and doubled again by the end of the seventeenth century, colliers sunk shafts to greater and greater depths. Shafts of 200 or even 300 feet, requiring large amounts of timber for shoring, ventilation shafts, and drainage equipment, were not uncommon. Colliers also required many heavy wooden carts to move the coal from the shafts to the rivers or the sea, where great wooden ships waited at large wooden docks to transport the coal to cities. Much of the fivefold increase in ships of over 100 tons burden in the English merchant fleet between 1560 and 1629 can be attributed to the coal trade. Moreover, many of the 95 vessels of more than 100 tons burden launched in England between 1629 and 1633 were built to transport coal. By this era there were from 300 to 400 colliers of over 100 tons burden transporting coal from northern England alone. By 1660 the tonnage of the coal fleet exceeded the total merchant tonnage of 1582, and by 1700 the fleet numbered 1,600 vessels. To build so large a fleet must have required many great timber trees.[38]

The use of coal for domestic heating also increased the demand for iron, for thousands of iron firebacks, baskets, grates, and pokers were needed to keep coal fires burning. Similarly, the great increase in saltmaking near the coalpits was followed by a greater demand for large iron pans and rectangular iron basins, often three feet high and twenty to thirty feet wide. Coal miners used iron picks, shovels, and other tools, and the shipwrights who built the coal ships needed nails, bolts, clamps, anchors, chains, and cannons. The forges in Sussex and other regions began to produce more and more of this and other hardware. And despite costly experiments conducted at many ironworks in the seventeenth century, no method was found whereby coal could be introduced into the blast furnace. Thus the growing demand for iron, stimulated by the expanding coal industry, increased the demand for wood charcoal and aggravated the timber problem.[39]

Timber from Northern Europe

In the sixteenth and seventeenth centuries Englishmen could obtain many of the timber products for home and industry only in heavily forested regions beyond their shores. They had been importing small quantities of timber products from northern Europe since the High Middle Ages, especially potash from the Russian ports on the White Sea and fir and spruce masts, spars, turpentine, rosin, pitch, and tar from the Norwegian and Baltic ports. These imports greatly increased as the supply of British forest products diminished. By the early seventeenth century, Russian potash was the most valuable forest import, with an estimated value of 39,000 Danish rix-dollars in 1625 and 80,000 rix-dollars a decade later. But the quantity of imported naval stores was increasing, too: the value of imported pitch and tar, for example, exceeded 12,000 rix-dollars by 1635.[40]

English merchants also imported large quantities of fir boards from northern Europe and, by the middle of the seventeenth century, large amounts of oak timber as well. Much of this timber was used for buildings, with Baltic oak particularly in demand after the Great Fire. But English shipwrights, too, depended more and more on imported oak despite the common belief that English oak was the best in the world. Shipbuilding and repairs by the Royal Navy in 1677–79 and 1686–87 depended heavily on imported oak timbers as well as fir deals, masts, tar, pitch, sailcloth, and cordage. In 1689 shipbuilders in the outports and in the River Thames used five loads of foreign timber for every load obtained in England.[41]

The importation of potash, naval stores, and timber from northern Europe allowed the English cloth industry to expand, the navy and merchant marine to increase, and the construction and woodworking industries to survive. But the trade gave rise to many problems and, like the coal trade, aggravated some phases of the timber crisis.

Great wooden ships were needed to carry foreign timber to English ports. Every hundred deals (120 boards) required four tons of shipping, a small mast required five tons, and medium and large masts twelve and sixteen tons, respectively. And though distances between England and the timber ports of the Continent were relatively short, bad weather further intensified the need for wooden timber carriers by severely limiting the number of voyages a single vessel could make each year. The shipping tonnage required by the growing timber trade in the seventeenth century seems to have been very large.[42]

English shipwrights certainly could not supply the great number of vessels needed to move timber. Although the English tonnage employed in the northern trades increased during the first four decades of the seventeenth century, English merchants still relied heavily on the large, slow-moving, flat-bottomed vessels called flyboats that were built and operated by the Dutch specifically for the timber trade. England was finally saved from the humiliation of continued reliance on Dutch carriage, first by the Dutch involvement in the Thirty Years' War, which forced up the Netherlands shipping charges by 50 per cent between 1625 and 1647, and then by the English Navigation Acts of 1651 and 1660, which prohibited the import of most products in foreign vessels other than those of the country of shipment. Moreover, English victories in the Dutch Wars led to the seizure of large numbers of Dutch flyboats. But in spite of these changing conditions, the demands of the northern trade still forced English merchants to purchase ships from foreign nations, especially flyboats from the Dutch. In 1660 it was claimed that four ships were bought abroad for every one built at home.[43]

In 1662 Parliament limited the use of foreign-built ships other than prizes, which led to an increase in English tonnage. But there was such demand for timber after the Great Fire that the government sanctioned the purchase of sixty Dutch flyboats. Even this did not free England from dependence on others, for the merchant fleets of Norway and Sweden were on the rise, carrying large amounts of their own timber to English ports. Northern Europe had a great advantage in this trade because shipbuilding costs were low there: a 300-ton flyboat could be built in Scandinavia for £1,300, but the same ship might cost as much as £2,200 to build in England.[44]

No matter what nation carried timber to England, transportation costs, including insurance, continued to be high. The price paid for timber at the stump in Norway or Pomerania was insignificant compared to that finally paid in England. Deal boards selling for nine or twelve pence at the port of entry were not cheap when even a skilled craftsman could purchase only about a half-dozen with his entire weekly pay. Heavier timber and the special timber used in shipbuilding were obviously much more expensive. Was it not deplorable, John Evelyn asked, "that we, who have such perpetual use and convenience for ship-timber, should be driven to procure of foreign stores so many thousand loads at intolerable prices?"[45]

The lack of bulky products that could be sold in the northern countries meant even higher timber prices, for the majority of timber ships were forced to make their return voyages from England in ballast. Although the great number of empty vessels heading for Oslo Fjord, the Baltic, and the White Sea made export rates to those regions very low (indeed, English goods were often carried outward free when a return cargo was guaranteed), there was a very unfavorable balance of trade from the English point of view. In "the Norway Trade at present," one merchant wrote, "we are having occasion for such vast quantities of Timber, [that it] swallows up abundance of our Money for want of more proper things for exportation."[46]

But the greatest problems in the northern trade were not economic but political. In the seventeenth century a great portion of the English economy and the whole of the Royal Navy depended on the steady flow of potash, timber, and naval stores from regions over which the English had no direct political control. The rulers in these regions were keenly aware that England depended on their timber products, and as English trade in timber increased, duties, taxes, and other commercial fees did also. Denmark, which controlled the Sound (the strait between Denmark and Sweden at the entrance to the Baltic), collected tolls and interfered with the operation of the Eastland and Muscovy companies. And despite protests by members of Parliament, the political problems of the northern trade worsened after 1640. In 1649 Czar Alexis of Russia, enraged by the execution of Charles I, broke diplomatic relations with England and forbade the shipment of potash to English ports. A crisis on the English cloth market ensued, in the course of which the price of potash leaped from fourteen to forty shillings a hundredweight.[47]

In 1651, while England was still in the midst of civil strife, another crisis occurred when Denmark granted the Dutch the rights to collect the Sound toll in exchange for £35,000 a year and to close the Sound to the English in time of war. When the first of the Anglo-Dutch wars broke out in 1652, timber ships flying English and neutral flags were seized in the Sound, and the British navy found itself dangerously short of masts and other essential timber. Consequently Cromwell sought a treaty with Sweden so that the freedom of the Sound would not depend upon the king of Denmark or the Netherlands, but gained only a commercial treaty. Even when England acquired most-favored-nation status on the Sound at the end of the first Dutch War, the problems of the northern timber trade did not end. England and the Netherlands were continually embroiled in the petty quarrels of the northern nations, and there were serious crises in the Baltic throughout the seventeenth century. Essential timber shipments often proceeded under convoy, and the Royal Navy often moved into the Baltic to keep the timber routes open. The precariousness of the northern timber trade and the need for a dependable source of timber was emphasized when, on several occasions, a substantial portion of the navy was unable to act because its supplies of timber products (especially masts) for maintaining the fleet had been cut off.[48]

Chapter 2

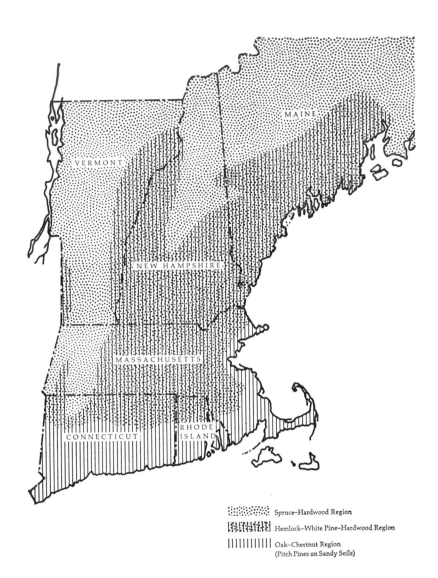

::::::::: Spruce–Hardwood Region

▓▓▓▓▓▓▓ Hemlock–White Pine–Hardwood Region

|||||||||||| Oak–Chestnut Region
(Pitch Pines on Sandy Soils)

The Presettlement Forest Regions of New England

SOURCES: David M. Smith, "The Forests of the United States," in John W. Barrett, ed., *Regional Silviculture of the United States* (New York, 1962), pp. 3–29; John W. Barrett, "The Northeastern Region," in John W. Barrett, ed., *Regional Silviculture of the United States*, pp. 30–84; Stanley W. Bromley, "The Original Forest Types of Southern New England," *Ecological Monographs* 5 (1935):61–89; Betty Flanders Thomson, *The Changing Face of New England* (New York, 1958).

The Presettlement Forests
of New England

The intrepid seamen who approached the New England coast in the sixteenth century were searching for precious metals, a passage through the continent to the fabled riches of the East, or off-shore waters teeming with fish. But one of their most important discoveries was the primeval forest, which, as their frail wooden vessels plowed toward the shore, appeared to be rising from the sea. The adventurers were heading for an unfamiliar forest world, a world with many plants and animals that they could not adequately describe. Most written descriptions of the New World were hampered by inadequate vocabulary, constant references to allegory and classical mythology, and pastoral and biblical imagery. Most pictures drawn or painted by the early explorers lack detail and perspective, and are conventional and stylized.

By the time concrete, scientific accounts of natural phenomena were written and landscape painting became more realistic, the original forest world had been destroyed. For the woodlands—which had emerged victorious from their long struggle against the invasions of the sea, the movements of the earth's crust, the advance and retreat of glaciers, lightning, the browsing of the wild animals, and the fires of the Indians—succumbed in little more than a century to the axes and sawmills of the European settlers. Devastation of flora and fauna proceeded at such a rapid pace that as early as the eighteenth century, much of eastern Massachusetts, with its gently rolling hills, looked like the tame and treeless English countryside. By the first half of the nineteenth century, Thoreau found only second-growth trees surrounding Walden Pond. And he found that in the part of Maine settled by the seventeenth-century immigrants, most of the original trees were gone, too. Contemplating the destruction of the virgin forests, he wrote that New England timber was disappearing at such a great rate that "we shall all be obliged to let our beards grow at least, if only to hide the nakedness of the land and make a sylvan appearance."[1]

By 1880 only 40 per cent of Massachusetts, 27 per cent of Connecticut, and 34 per cent of Rhode Island were forested. Even in sparsely populated New Hampshire, only half of the land was covered with trees, and in Maine 74 per cent of the land was still classifiable as woodland. By this date, however, almost all of the diminishing New England forest was made up of second- or third-growth timber.[2]

Man's Influence on the Forest

Man had either destroyed or tamed the New England forest by direct assault before 1880; he influenced its size and composition in the next two decades merely by retreating from the conquered land. For wood was quickly giving way to steel: the iron horse was roaring across the plains of the West, men stringing wire fences were destroying the cattle kingdom, and farmers were breaking the tough western sod with heavy steel plows. Agricultural products for the growing national and international markets could be produced more cheaply in the West, and the New England farmer was forced to sell his cattle and abandon his rocky and unproductive fields for the mill town or great city. The victory of the trees that drifted back over the abandoned fields was short-lived, however, for as soon as the new trees grew tall, the men of the twentieth century, armed with portable steam and gasoline saws, cut them to the ground—along with the few remaining trees of the presettlement forest community, which had previously been inaccessible.[3]

The trees have returned again, and there is now as much forest land in New England as there was in the late eighteenth century. Recently the United States Forest Service classified 85 per cent of Maine and New Hampshire, and a little less than 66 per cent of Massachusetts, Rhode Island, Connecticut, and Vermont as woodland. But the spindly trees in this extensive stand, decadent descendants of a once-majestic presettlement community, testify to man's ignorance of the ecological principles of land management.[4]

These trees are quite young: very few in the New England stand are over seventy-five years old, and a tree over a hundred years old is rare. But even if the trees in the present New England forest are allowed to grow old, the character and appearance of the primeval forest will not return. For when trees are destroyed en masse—the term used by foresters is "clear-cutting"—the severe and sudden change affects all living things in the forest. Shade-loving plants die, food chains are interrupted, birds and animals migrate, and new microbes and insects invade. The relation of sun, land, vegetation, and fauna is drastically changed, and in the struggle for existence only those things that can adapt to the new environment will survive.[5]

By clear-cutting, the New England farmers and lumbermen of past centuries created an environment in which the size of the returning trees would be greatly diminished. Furthermore, many cutover lands were invaded by new species, so that the New England forest today has not only a poorer crop of timber, but also different plants and animals living in entirely new communities that European men wittingly—and unwittingly—created. The Indians are gone. Passenger pigeons no longer eclipse the sun. Wolves no longer howl against the moon. Stubby pines and birches dot lands where great oaks flourished. In the nineteenth century the vigorous chestnut moved into many cutover oak regions in southern New England, but a blight virtually destroyed that species in the early twentieth century. Today, the black walnut survives only on protected estates. And because the roots of the fragrant white cedars do not sprout after their trunks are severed, vast tracts of this valuable timber tree have disappeared. Now disease is destroying even the elms that line the streets of the oldest New England towns. Today New England trees are of such poor quality that even with soaring timber prices nobody wants them.

Too little of the original forest remains to give more than a dim idea of what the whole area looked like—and the reports of the early visitors and settlers are not very helpful, for the English pioneers of the sixteenth and seventeenth centuries called coniferous trees "pines" and hickories "walnuts" and used other confusing designations. However, although the members of some forest communities died centuries ago, their pollen, often preserved in peat bogs, can be identified by microscopic examination; radiochemical dating and fossil analysis also provide valuable information.[6]

Such studies reveal that the major species in the present New England forest have been there for at least 5,000 years. In this period, climatic changes have shifted many botanical communities, but the climate has brought about no change in the basic composition of the forest since the first explorations. The New England forest today would be almost identical to that of 1600 if men had not moved against it.[7]

Pollen studies also indicate that the presettlement woodlands covered almost all of New England—perhaps as much as 95 per cent. In some regions the forest reached to the edge of the sea and extended back mile upon mile into the interior, where many creatures never felt the full intensity of the sun. There were probably three-quarters of a million trees three inches or more in diameter within every ten square miles of heavily timbered land, slightly more than that number of seedlings, and almost four times as many shrubs. And within this same small area there were between one-quarter and one-half billion herbaceous plants on the forest floor—all nipped, perforated, and deformed by a host of voracious insects.[8]

Even the islands along the New England coast that are now completely denuded of trees nurtured valuable timber. Giovanni da Verrazzano saw "five small islands, very fertile and beautiful, full of tall spreading trees" in Narragansett Bay. Samuel de Champlain remarked that the islands north of Mount Desert Island were "covered with pines, firs, and other inferior woods." On Mount Desert Island there were only birches, pines, and firs, but Champlain found that farther south the islands off Cape Ann were covered with trees of many species. Aquidneck Island in Rhode Island and almost all of the islands in Boston Harbor had valuable trees for fuel and for construction timbers.[9]

Although a major part of the mainland and the islands of New England was forested, there were natural clearings—some quite extensive—where only wild flowers, native grass, and thorny bushes grew. Champlain saw two meadows, each a league in length and half a league in breadth, near the present town of Wells, Maine. And farther south, even in the timber-rich Piscataqua River valley, there were miles of open grassland along the

main channel and branches of the Piscataqua. Along the Merrimack there were extensive treeless tracts, and farther south, in
Massachusetts, there were great broad meadows. Near the Rhode
Island border there was the treeless Seekonk plain, and, to the
west, a woodless tract in the region surrounding Plainfield, Connecticut. Beyond lay the open land along the Connecticut River
and the nearly barren, dry, and forbidding soil along the Quinni-
piac River north of New Haven. These were just a few of the
river meadows and sand plains of New England—regions with
soils too moist or too dry to nurture the seeds of timber trees that
wind and creature vainly planted season after season.[10]

New England also had many coastal marshlands into whose
soggy and saline bottoms no tree could set down its roots and
survive. These salt marshes are still found along sections of the
New England coast, and they often stretch for some distance into
the interior. North of Boston they are extensive, stretching into
New Hampshire.

In addition to the natural clearings of salt marsh, river meadow,
and sand plain, there were man-made clearings, where the Indians
planted beans, corn, squash, and pumpkin. The Indian clearings
were much more numerous in southern than in northern New
England. In Rhode Island the Narragansetts cleared many miles
of timberland, especially along the western shore of Narragansett
Bay southward through Kingston, and they may have extended
these clearings inland almost as far as the Connecticut border.
The Indians on Cape Cod also cultivated large fields, and when
two men from Plymouth Colony, Edward Winslow and Stephen
Hopkins, visited the Indian tribes along the Tauton River in
1621, they noted that the ground was "very good on both sides,
it being for the most part cleared." Farther north, near Wollaston
(Quincy), were the "Massachusetts Fields," tilled by the Neponset Indians, and nearby, the "Indian Field" in Unquity stretched
from the top of Milton Hill northward to the falls of the Neponset River. Champlain saw the Indians constantly at work in
northern New England, felling trees, burning branches, and planting corn, pumpkins, tobacco, and squash. The sight of Indian
fields stretching for three miles along the northern New England
coast made one explorer homesick for the treeless English countryside, and another was delighted that sections of coastal land in
Maine near the Piscataqua were cleared and ready for the plow.

There were Indian cornfields—varying in size from a few acres to several hundred acres—at Berwick, Wells, at the mouth of the Saco, and along the Androscoggin, the Kennebec, and the Penobscot.[11]

Before the time of the first large English settlements, most New England Indians, infected with European diseases, had died. Winslow and Hopkins, believing that thousands of men had lived along the Taunton River, thought it was a pity to see "so many goodly fields, and so well seated, without men to dress and manure the same." Although overgrown with weeds and small bushes, the Indian fields were a boon to the first settlers. Indeed, they may have saved the lives of the Pilgrims, who stood helpless and dismayed before the forest world.[12]

The Three Vegetation Regions

Beyond the lands settled by the first European adventurers lay the spruce-hardwood forest of Vermont, central and northern New Hampshire, and the hill country of western Massachusetts. This forest extended over most of Maine, but it reached the seacoast only between Mount Desert Island and Eastport. There were many dense and extensive stands of spruce and balsam fir in this vegetation region, but the monotony of those stands was occasionally broken by white pines, junipers, and tamaracks, and often by aspens, beeches, yellow birches, sugar maples, and other northern hardwoods.[13]

To the south and east of the spruce-hardwood forest lay a complex hemlock–white pine–hardwood stand, a forest region extending from the Maine seacoast below Mount Desert Island into the interior and covering all of southwestern Maine, southern New Hampshire, portions of Vermont, and most of Massachusetts except the Berkshires, Cape Cod, Plymouth Colony, and a narrow strip extending along the coast of the Bay Colony. This forest also included the extreme northern sections of Connecticut and Rhode Island.[14]

The amount of hemlock in this forest region at the time of colonization is uncertain, for the hemlock is sensitive to fire, and large numbers may not have survived in areas burned by the Indians. The early explorers and settlers do not mention the hemlock, which was unknown in England, but they might have confused it with the more familiar white pine.[15]

The white pine, too, is sensitive to fire, and, in some areas within this New England forest region, burning may have limited its growth to water-soaked soils. Early settlers may have been so impressed by the height of the white pines that they exaggerated their number. However, there were many extensive white pine tracts that were readily accessible for commercial lumbering in the area between the Merrimack and the Piscataqua, and in the coastal region between the Saco and the Kennebec. There was an extensive pine belt stretching north along the Connecticut River from the extreme northern border of Connecticut, through Massachusetts, and extending for about twenty miles into New Hampshire and Vermont.[16]

The predominant hardwoods in the original hemlock–white pine–hardwood region now are the red oak, the American beech, the sugar maple, the red maple, the black birch, and the white ash. But these trees are almost always found in the company of other species. North of Cape Ann and in the high elevations farther south and to the west, the white birch is common, and sometimes such hardy northern species as the aspen and the spruce penetrate what is often a supple climatic barrier.[17]

In the seventeenth century the composition of the hemlock–white pine–hardwood region was much the same as today, although white and black oaks may have been much more common. Champlain noted that oaks were growing as if they "had been planted designedly" as far north as the Kenduskeag Stream, which enters the Penobscot at Bangor. A century later royal commissioners reported that the best white oaks for ship timber grew beyond the Kennebec, and one visitor saw "stately Oaks, excellent Ship timber, not inferiour to our English," along the banks of the Merrimack.[18]

White and black oaks, however, are not now predominant species in the hemlock–white pine–hardwood region. Today, as in the seventeenth century, they are predominant trees in the region that embraces the coast of Massachusetts Bay, southeastern Massachusetts (including Plymouth Colony), and all but extreme northern Rhode Island and Connecticut. In the seventeenth century they mingled frequently with the other predominant species, the chestnut. This was the oak-chestnut region, although hickories, red oaks, yellow poplars, ashes, black and yellow birches, red maples, beeches, and sugar maples were also very common. Within this oak-chestnut region, in southeastern Massachusetts, the scarlet oak, the most valuable fuel tree in the New England forest, probably outnumbered the other oak species. The holly, seldom found north of Boston, also thrived on certain soils in the oak-chestnut region, but such valuable northern species as the white birch and the spruce do not grow readily in the more temperate climate of southern New England. Contemporary accounts, the slow development of sawmills, and the predominance of oak boards in surviving colonial buildings all indicate that at the time of settlement there were few white pines in southern Connecticut and Rhode Island, and in Massachusetts south of a line drawn between Plymouth and Fall River.[19]

The three vegetation regions of New England—the spruce-hardwood region, the hemlock–white pine–hardwood region, and the oak-chestnut region—contained many subdivisions where unique local conditions greatly influenced the formation of the forest community. Within the oak-chestnut region, Cape Cod—with large amounts of dry, shifting, sandy soil subjected to continual battering of wind and sea—had certain unique forest features. Oaks predominated on the more fertile land, but many dry Cape soils could not have supported them. On dry soils, solid tracts of pitch pine often extended for miles; sometimes the pitch pine and the dwarf oak were mingled. The hemlock probably did not grow on Cape Cod, for the soil is too dry and the winds are too strong.[20]

Many regions in New England where the ground was unusually moist and spongy were heavily timbered. Even where Indians burned the forest, the timber standing on these wet tracts must have survived. The English explorers and settlers, unfamiliar with moist timberland (the valuable timber trees on the moist soils of England had been destroyed long before the era of discovery), used the word *swamp* to describe these timbered bogs.[21]

Many New England swamps have disappeared, but early travelers indicate that many were extensive—"ten, some twenty, some thirty miles" in compass, according to one writer. The composition of the timber in the swamps varied from one vegetation region to the next. In northern New England there were swamps composed solely of spruce extending for several miles;

in the hemlock–white pine–hardwood region pine and hemlock swamps are common. In the oak-chestnut region many moist lands supported the red maple, the American elm, the black gum, and the swamp white oak. The pin oak, too, was common in the swamps in southern New England, its upper branches visible above the tops of the other trees. Of all the swamp trees of New England, the white cedar was the most striking and valuable. White cedar swamps were very common in Massachusetts, Connecticut, and Rhode Island, and even in northern New England there were a number of these fragrant and shady wetlands. Today the white cedar is rare, for when it is clear-cut, it never returns; red maples, yellow birches, white pines, and hemlocks quickly move in. Because of the disappearance of white cedars, the present New England forest can never convey the atmosphere of the seventeenth-century forest world.[22]

Dense and Open Woodlands

In New England at the time of the first English settlements there were vast junglelike thickets interrupted only infrequently by narrow, meandering Indian paths or an occasional cornfield, river meadow, or sand plain. John Winthrop, the governor of the Massachusetts Bay Company, wrote of almost impenetrable tangles of trees and underbrush growing close to the seashore north and south of Boston, and the Pilgrims found similar thickets even on outer Cape Cod. One visitor to northern New England said that even many swamps were "infinitely thick set with Trees and Bushes of all sorts," and in 1694 the commanders of a British expedition against Canada described the vegetation on both sides of Lake Champlain as "a mere morase cumbered with underwood where men cannot go upright, but must creep through bushes for whole days' marches, and impossible for horse to go at any time of the year." During the summer, many sections of the New England woodlands were often obstructed by a snarl of such woody vines as climbing ferns, ivy, and ampelopsis.[23]

Even after the leaves had fallen and portions of the undergrowth had withered and died, many New England woodland tracts remained almost impassable. In the nineteenth century, Thoreau noted that in the virgin forests of Maine the ground was everywhere spongy and saturated with moisture; in the early twentieth century, a layer of humus almost a foot deep was found in the primeval forest in Litchfield County, Connecticut. The older trees, rotting within, continually creaked, even when the air was calm. With little warning, massive trunks snapped and tons of timber crashed onto the forest floor. Many travelers in the North American forest mentioned the countless fallen and decaying trees that blocked their paths. When the great trees fell, their roots, together with the soil that had nourished them, shot forth from the ground, leaving large holes. Mosses soon gathered on the fallen and decaying trunks and limbs, and insects began their work beneath the pale green halo. Before long the mightiest forest giant was transformed into a pile of humus that nourished its successors.[24]

Although there were dense and impassable woodlands in many sections of New England, a number of the early explorers and settlers emphasized the open, parklike quality of the countryside. Verrazzano, entering the woodlands near Newport Harbor, observed that they were so free of underbrush that they "could be penetrated even by a large army." Champlain noted that the forests in the interior of the Saco region were open, and another observer mentioned swamps farther north in Maine composed of spruce trees, "under the shades whereof you may freely walk two or three mile together."[25]

Although it is probable that where large trees were common their shade alone prevented the growth of underbrush and vines, Thomas Morton believed that the Indians had kept the forest open: "The savages are accustomed, to set fire of the country in all places where they come; and to burn it, twice a year, viz., at the spring and the fall of the leafe." The Indians' purpose in burning the woods is not entirely clear. Morton says that they did it to make the forest passable, Roger Williams that they did it to destroy vermin and keep down weeds and thickets.[26]

At least in southern New England, the Indians significantly altered parts of the primeval forest long before the arrival of the European settlers. But the burned-over areas probably were not very extensive; forest dwellers would surely realize that a great woodland fire could easily rage out of control. A fire set by Indians to drive out one of the early English exploration parties was limited to a one-mile area, and during the first years of Plymouth

Colony, two Pilgrims were surprised to discover a burned-over region five miles in length.[27]

Nature may have had a greater influence than the Indians on the development of dense and open forest tracts in New England. Fires can be started by lightning and internal combusion as well as by men. The rise and fall of the water table, snow and ice storms, and winds, hurricanes, and tornadoes exert a strong influence over all botanical communities. Mighty trees can withstand fire and weather for centuries and then succumb to disease. The destruction of the underbrush and the lower branches of the trees by deer and other browsing animals can significantly alter the relation of trees, plants, and animals. And insects can disturb what appears to be a peaceful, verdant world, as in 1668, when John Winthrop, Jr., reported that caterpillars had destroyed great numbers of oaks and other species in the forests of southern New England. When trees were stripped of leaves by insects, plants that had been shaded for many years by the larger trees might regain their vigor, compete for dominance, and eventually alter the composition of the forest.[28]

Sylvan Giants

The several vegetation regions of New England contained trees that varied greatly in age and size. Where the trees were young, the forest may have been quite dense. Along the Kenduskeag Stream near Bangor, Champlain saw thick woods that extended far into the interior. John Winthrop, Jr., observed that in many parts of New England, especially in the south, there were stands containing only a "few large old timber trees of oak."[29]

Sometimes the young trees mingled with ancient ones, but where soil, moisture, and wind provided optimum conditions for the growth of a particular species, large trees prevailed. These were the sylvan giants before which the first explorers and settlers stood in awe, the trees that produced an environment much different from the vapid woodlands of the present day.[30]

The white pine was by far the tallest of the New England forest giants, dominating the landscape wherever it was numerous. The bark of a huge white pine was as rough as that of an oak or elm, and the lower portion of the tree was often bare of limbs up to 100 feet from the ground. Today the scrawny, youthful descendants of this once-majestic species, with smooth bark and branches almost touching the ground, give only an inkling of the dark and mysterious forest created by their ancestors.

There are many tales of gigantic white pines, but there is no evidence to support the claim that some rose 300 feet before stretching forth their first branches. Even the redwoods of coastal California and the Australian eucalyptuses do not always reach such a fantastic height. But Timothy Dwight's report of a white pine 250 feet tall with a trunk 6 feet in diameter at the base is probably reliable. And Thoreau tells of two men lost in the Maine woods who, searching for the smoke from houses in the clearings, "climbed the loftiest pine they could find, some six feet in diameter at the ground." But pines of this size must have been exceedingly rare. Most full-grown pines were probably between 150 and 200 feet high, and trunks measuring from 3 to 4 feet in diameter were common, although those of many larger trees were rotten at the core.[31]

The New England oak was not as tall as the white pine, but in 1826 the famous Charter Oak at Hartford was 36 feet in circumference. Although trees of this size were probably rare, white oaks 100 feet tall with trunks 20 feet in circumference were common, and the horizontal spread of these mighty oaks was often over 150 feet.[32]

Many other species of New England timber trees were much larger than they are today. In the early eighteenth century, some white ashes rose 80 feet from the forest floor before extending their first branches. Sugar maples stretched to great heights, with trunks 15 feet in circumference not uncommon. Thoreau found a canoe birch in the Maine woods 14.5 feet in circumference. In southern New England, chestnut stumps can still be found that measure 4 feet or more in diameter. When the remote virgin forest in Litchfield County, Connecticut, was studied in 1913, the most impressive feature in that stand of hemlock, sugar maple, black birch, red oak, and other species was the magnitude of the mature trees. Many were over 100 feet high and over 3 feet in diameter at breast height. Almost all were free of branches for a distance of 30 to 50 feet from the ground, which accentuated their size.[33]

Many of the larger trees in the New England forest were not very ancient. (The oldest trees in the Litchfield County virgin tract

were hemlocks, from 275 to 350 years old in 1913; but the majority of these ancient trees were rotten at the heart.) It was the
number rather than the size of the trees that most impressed the
early English explorers. Sailing from a land where timber and
wood fuel were in short supply, they discovered a vast primeval
forest with trees that could be used for construction, shipbuilding, cooperage, tanning, and many other crafts. There appeared
to be an unlimited amount of wood fuel for the metal industries,
and for limeburning, brickmaking, and saltmaking. Some adven-
turous Englishmen believed that if they could obtain sufficient
capital, they could quickly exploit the forest riches of the newly
discovered land and solve the national timber crisis. But few investors were willing to risk the enormous amount of capital required for the exploitation of a virgin wilderness, and few Englishmen were prepared to settle among the towering trees.[34]

Chapter 3

Early Settlements in New England

Modern boundaries are shown.

English Exploration
and Settlement, 1602-1628

The early explorers of North America found forests instead of gold, silver, or a gateway to the riches of the East, but
the belief that America was an earthly paradise did not soon
fade away. Even educated men of the sixteenth and seventeenth
centuries believed that the Garden of Eden, the Fountain of Youth,
and the Cities of Gold might lie somewhere beyond the shores of
America. And even if such romantic notions proved to be dreams,
men could still search for precious metals and collect and experiment with familiar and unfamiliar plants and animals. There
were many hazards, but those who dared to enter the sylvan wild
could make great profits.[1]

Most Englishmen had little interest in America for nearly a
century after Columbus landed. The voyages of John Cabot, Sir
Francis Drake, Sir Martin Frobisher, and Sir Humphrey Gilbert
stirred the hearts of a few patriots but failed to release the purse
strings of those who could support sustained exploration and
colonization. England was not yet a great sea power, her navy and
merchant marine were still young, her foreign commerce was not
fully controlled by native citizens, and the new merchant class
was not ready for risky New World ventures.

But late in the sixteenth century, the English attitude toward
America was changing. Richard Hakluyt, who had collected original narratives written by the early explorers of the New World,
became the leading English geographer and advocate of overseas
expansion. If Englishmen, "through the special assistance and
blessing of God," had discovered and explored vast sections of
North America, was it not God's will, Hakluyt asked, that they
exploit the newly discovered land? His *Discourse on Western
Planting* (1584) set forth the first comprehensive plan for English
colonization of America. Men from the treeless English countryside would settle in the forests, set up sawmills, and produce

boards for English craftsmen. Sales would be enough "to defraye all the chardges of all the begynnynge of the enterprize." Hakluyt and a number of merchants believed that once permanent English settlements were established, craftsmen would settle in America to make pipe staves, bows, "targets of Elme and tough wood, for use against the darts and arrowes of Salvages," and "spades like those of Devonshire, and of other sorts, and shovels from time to time for common use." Coopers would make casks that could be filled with forest-fed pork and shipped to England to be used again in the herring fishery. And there would be an abundance of bark for tanning, potash for soap, oak for ship frames, and conifers for masts, planking, and ship's stores.[2]

The Great Sassafras Hunts

Hakluyt and his associates had read accounts of miraculous drugs discovered by the earliest explorers, and in 1577 John Frampton's *Joyfull Newes out of the new founde world* described the sassafras, which grew all along the North American coast. Its bark, wood, buds, and roots were used by the Indians for medicine; concoctions made from those parts were said to cure swellings, fevers, colds, headaches, toothaches, the "grief of the Stone," the "griefes of the stomach," and the "evils of the Poxe." Sassafras was said to cure lameness, the gout, "foul and diseased hands," and barrenness in women, and was thought to prevent illness, too. In 1580 Hakluyt published translations of the voyages of Jacques Cartier, whose account of the miraculous tree excited Englishmen who lived in an age of plagues and innumerable chronic diseases. Soon they were preparing to risk life and fortune in search of the sassafras tree.[3]

The first English sassafras hunts were directed toward the southern part of North America, where Sir Walter Raleigh and other West Country gentlemen, encouraged by Hakluyt's propaganda, were determined to plant the first English colony in America. Ships that returned from Raleigh's colony in 1586 probably brought back some sassafras; those that returned in 1587 certainly did; and in 1602 Raleigh sent an expedition to gather sassafras and to learn what had become of his colony. Raleigh's monopoly over the importation and sale of sassafras was soon challenged by the earl of Southampton and others. In 1602 they sent two ships under Bartholomew Gosnold and Bartholomew Gilbert to the New England coast, where, ignoring Raleigh's claim to that region as well as Virginia, they sought gold, trade with the Indians, and, first of all, sassafras.[4]

Having sighted land "full of faire trees" off the coast of Maine, Gosnold and Gilbert sailed southwest and entered Nantucket Sound, finally landing at Cuttyhunk Island off the coast of Massachusetts. The small band soon found the sassafras in "great plentie all the Island over," and while some felled trees for a fort, others gathered the most valuable parts of the magic tree. The "easie laborers" volunteered for the sassafras hunt, but harvesting sassafras was hard work, for to obtain the roots of the tree (which supposedly had the greatest curative power) took a good deal of digging, cutting, and pulling. One of the gatherers soon had an opportunity to test the power of New England sassafras, for having devoured so many dogfish bellies that his own belly ached, he was restored to health by a concoction of sassafras within twelve hours.[5]

Curious Indians soon came for a closer look at the strange men with pale complexions who were uprooting their trees. The first meeting was friendly, and some Indians aided the sassafras gatherers. But when other Indians attacked a party of explorers that had separated from the main body, no one wanted to remain in the wilderness among hostile Indians despite the abundance of sassafras. In June the whole band departed with many bundles of sassafras, a load of cedar wood, and a few skins and furs.[6]

The fantastically high price of sassafras began to fall as soon as the Gosnold expedition returned to England, but it fell even more when another ton of sassafras arrived from America. Raleigh, who had enjoyed profits of a thousand per cent, demanded compensation for his loss, but in vain, for the backers of Gosnold's expedition were men of great influence. This squabble, however, by publicizing the huge profits to be made from sassafras, must have made it easier for Hakluyt to persuade Englishmen to invest in American enterprises. In any case, in 1603 he was able to persuade a group of Bristol merchants to support an expedition to New England.[7]

The Bristol expedition, consisting of two ships under the command of Martin Pring, sailed late in the spring of 1603. Pring and his men searched many islands and mainland regions along the coast of Maine, observing "goodly groves and woods replenished with tall oaks, beeches, pine-trees, hazels, wich-hazels and maples." Finding no sassafras, the expedition headed south, crossed Massachusetts Bay, and finally dropped anchor in Provincetown Harbor. Here they found a quantity of sassafras, and by the end of July they had cut and dug enough to fill their smaller bark, the twenty-six-ton *Discoverer*, which they sent home before beginning to fill their larger vessel. But they found it impossible to work in the New England heat except in the morning and late afternoon, and hostile Indians soon forced them to leave by setting fire to the woods. Pring's expedition to the New England coast is the last recorded English voyage undertaken exclusively to procure sassafras. But accounts of the Gosnold and Pring voyages impressed an increasing number of Englishmen with the potentiality of the tree covered New England landscape.[8]

Early Settlements

Most colonization between 1600 and 1625 was in Virginia, but adventurers, explorers, and colonists came to New England to fish, trade with the Indians for furs, hunt for sassafras, or escape religious and political persecution. All became inhabitants of a woodland world and made use of its vast timber resources.

In 1605 the young earl of Southampton and Lord Arundell of Wardour sent George Weymouth to New England to find sites for profitable plantations. Arriving off Nantucket in May of 1605, Weymouth turned north and began a month-long journey alone the coast of Maine. Like Champlain, who was exploring the same region for France during these years, Weymouth discovered many wooded islands and, on the mainland, great white pines that could provide "masts for ships of 400 tun" and huge oaks "of an excellent graine." Here was a land where ships could be built, naval stores manufactured, and valuable medicines discovered. Weymouth and his men cut yards and other timber for their ship, and their carpenter and cooper built a shallop. At Monhegan, an island "woody growen with Firre, Birch, Oke, and Beech," they picked up a boatload of firewood. In June they sailed for home with samples of white pine and new information about New England resources.[9]

James Rosier wrote an account of Weymouth's voyage that influenced two groups of merchants from London, Plymouth, and other ports, who, in 1606, successfully petitioned the crown for the right to settle and exploit a large section of North America. The London Company planted the first permanent English settlement in North America at Jamestown in the spring of 1607. A few months later the Plymouth Company—with large financial contributions from Chief Justice Sir John Popham—had gathered over a hundred people to settle on New England shores.[10]

The Popham colonists sighted land off Cape Elizabeth in July 1607 and saw immediately how rich the Maine forest was. The trees were much larger than those at home, although there were tracts of open woodland along the shore that resembled the parks of England. They landed at Sagadahoc (near Phippsburg) at the mouth of the Kennebec and cut trees for a fort and a storehouse. Most of these men were unaccustomed to such work, and their hands blistered and their muscles stiffened and became sore. They cut and hewed timber for a trading vessel, the pinnace *Virginia*, the first ship of any size built of New England timber.[11]

The Popham colonists were eager to exploit the fishery and the forest in Maine. There was fish "in great plenty" in season, as well as mast trees and "goodly oaks and cedars" for the English market. But the blasts of winter cooled their enthusiasm, and by December 1607 forty-five colonists had departed. The remainder, undernourished and inadequately clothed, shivered through the Maine winter in ill-built cottages, unable to exploit the greatest supply of fuel they had ever seen. Only two settlers died during the long winter, and in the spring, many decided to remain and clear the land for farming. But in October, after a meager harvest, most abandoned the settlement, boarded the supply ship, and returned to England.[12]

Some of the Popham colonists may have moved to one of the semipermanent fishing stations like Pemaquid or Damariscove, which the English had established. There they would have found sections of the virgin forest already damaged, for fishermen had been felling trees for shanties, storehouses, and barricades, as well as for stages (spindly fish wharves) and flakes (wooden frames), on which they split, cleaned, salted, and dried their catches. Fishermen had been cutting timber for kenches (salting boxes) and for tubs, vats, and presses used to make and store fish oil. They cleaved thousands of staves, destroyed a multitude of saplings for casks, and felled timber to build or repair small boats. The fishermen also used large quantities of wood fuel for processing their catch, drying wet clothing, cooking food, and heating their shanties.[13]

Plymouth Colony

Few Englishmen settled permanently in New England in the decade following the abandonment of the Popham colony, and many of those who attempted to do so during the 1620s were ill-equipped to survive in a forest world. The Pilgrims, who settled at Plymouth Colony, were more successful. Their story is well known: those emigrating from England were fleeing persecution, and those who left Leiden feared that the liberal atmosphere and religious customs of the Netherlands would corrupt their children. But the majority of those who sailed on the *Mayflower*, the Pilgrims' servants, were not separatists; they were apparently motivated by economics rather than religion. The Pilgrims seem to have been heading for the Hudson River, where they hoped to engage in fishing and fur trading; but they were forced to seek shelter in Cape Cod Bay, where, on 11 November, the 101 passengers who had survived the dangerous passage looked out on the forest world.[14]

The outer Cape is now barren save for the beach grass and dwarf trees that have been planted there to arrest the shifting sand. But the settlers from the streets of Leiden, the unwooded English countryside, and the crowded tenements of the Aldgate ward of London saw "a hideous and desolate wilderness full of wild beasts and wild men." The land, said William Bradford, had a "weather-beaten face, and the whole country, full of woods and thickets, represented a wild and savage hue." At Provincetown Harbor were woods containing oak, pine, sassafras, juniper, birch, holly, ash, walnut, and vines—not a mere cluster of stunted trees or a scraggly thicket, but a "wood for the most part open and without under-wood, fit either to goe or ride in." When the Pilgrims finally encountered Indians at Truro, they chased the braves "through boughs and bushes, and under hills and valleys, which tore [their] very armor in pieces."[15]

Thoreau was puzzled by the Pilgrims' account of open woodland and excellent black earth. "Now what strikes the voyager," he said, "is the barrenness and desolation of the land." He could find too little black earth in Provincetown "to fill a flowerpot" and "scarcely anything high enough to be called a tree, except a little low wood at the east end of the town, and the few ornamental trees in the yards." There were a few small trees on the sand hills, and some "thick shrubbery, without any large wood above it," but all this was "very unfit either to go or ride in." At East Harbor Creek, where, the Pilgrims claimed, the boughs and bushes had torn at their armor, Thoreau saw "neither bough nor bush, not so much as a shrub to tear our clothes against if we would." Indeed, he remarked, a sheep would lose none of its fleece in that land, "even if it found herbage enough to make fleece grow there. We saw rather beach and poverty-grass, and merely sorrel enough to color the surface."[16]

Thoreau knew that the settlers and their descendants had altered the land by using the timber for fuel and building and by clearing the woods for orchards, pastures, and cornfields. In many areas, the wind had blown the topsoil into the sea, and elsewhere forest land had become "an extensive waste of undulating sand," which had to be "anchored to the heavens, as it were, by a myriad of little cables of beachgrass." But Thoreau thought that the Pilgrims, overwhelmed by the strangeness of the woods, had exaggerated the extent of the original forest and the size of the trees. For Captain John Smith had described Cape Cod as "a headland of high hills and sand, overgrown with shrubby pines, hurts [whorts], and such trash," and Champlain had written of dunes and a large open area along the shore. Thoreau decided that the Pilgrims had been so glad to get to land that "everything appeared to them of the color of the rose, and had the scent of juniper and sassafras." He concluded that the trees had never been large and the soil never very deep.[17]

Though fearful of the new land, the Pilgrims began to use the forest at once. Some gathered firewood, and while the ship's carpenter reassembled a shallop that had been cut in two for stowage, others helved tools, felled trees, and sawed timber for a new shallop. Most of the men caught cold from wading through the icy waters between ship and shore, and some died. The landing parties discovered the juniper, a tree "which smelled very sweet and strong," and burned great numbers not only for heat, but so that the aromatic vapors would drive away illness.[18]

The benefits of the woodland were offset by dangers. The men who chased the Indians through the thickets at East Harbor Creek had received only scratches from the undergrowth, but those who constructed a temporary fortress with logs, stakes, and thick pine boughs were nearly killed. Unaccustomed to woodland defense, they left the fortress open on one side "to defend them from any sudden assaults of the savages, if they should surround them." But the Indians merely hid behind the trees and fired their arrows through the open side of the fort at their human targets, who were conveniently silhouetted against a great fire.[19]

Pilgrim landing parties encountered other dangers, too. One party, led by Stephen Hopkins—who may have considered himself a woodsman because of a previous journey to Virginia— came upon a young tree with its upper portion bent to the ground. A cluster of acorns lay beneath its spindly trunk. Then, Hopkins relates, "as we were looking at it, William Bradford being in the rear, when he came looked also upon it, and as he went about, it gave a sudden jerk up, and he was immediately caught by the leg." Hopkins was certain that this was a trap set by Indians to catch deer, and after they had disentangled the future governor of Plymouth Colony, all marveled at the ingenuity of the Indians and agreed that this was "a very pretty device."[20]

Woodland experiences such as these substantially delayed the choice of a permanent settlement. Because the forest was full of surprises and dangers, the Pilgrims—despite ill health, overcrowding on the *Mayflower*, and the lateness of the season— preferred an unwooded location. Plymouth Harbor was selected as the site for permanent settlement on 15 December, and the *Mayflower* dropped anchor there the following day—thirty-five days after her entrance into Cape Cod Bay.[21]

At Plymouth there was plenty of fresh water, good fishing, and a hill for a fort to protect the settlement from attack by land or sea. But the cleared land—the overgrown cornfields of the Patuxet Indians decimated by the plague of 1617—was its best feature. (A site three miles up the Jones River, in the present town of Kingston, was rejected because it was "so encompassed with woods, that we should bee in much danger of the Salvages; and our number being so little, and so much ground to cleare.") The open land at Plymouth Harbor appeared a naked and barren place to some, but for the majority it was a welcome buffer between the tiny settlement and the frightening forest. In this tiny tract, which must have reminded them of the treeless English countryside, men from Leiden, Scrooby, and the narrow and winding lanes of London began their plantation, trapped between the unfamiliar surroundings of the forest and the sea.[22]

The cleared land at Plymouth Harbor may have been psychologically comforting, but during the early months of 1621 and for a number of years thereafter, this site increased the Pilgrims' physical hardship. For, although game was abundant, these inexperienced settlers found it very difficult to kill or capture even a few pigeons and turkeys. (It is probable that, because of the game laws in England, few had ever fired a gun.) But their greatest labor was spent in getting wood, which was "half a quarter of an English mile" from the settlement. Firewood might be expensive in England, Edward Winslow remarked, but those who came to Plymouth Colony to obtain cheap fuel might "plunge themselves into a deeper sea of misery."[23]

The absence of snow, combined with periods of warm weather, is often cited as a blessing enjoyed by the settlers of Plymouth Colony during their first winter. But the lack of snow made it difficult to move firewood and heavy building timbers over the plain between the forest and the plantation. This problem was aggravated by the lack of horses, cattle, or wheeled vehicles. And the great fluctuation of the winter temperature increased the colonists' susceptibility to illness. The third week in January was as fair and warm "as if it had beene Aprill," one Pilgrim wrote, "and our people so many as were in health, wrought cheerfully." They felled trees, carried timbers, rived clapboards, sawed planks, or hewed boards and beams. But the temperature fell suddenly, and there were days of icy rain. Only half of the settlers who had arrived in November survived the cold, damp winter, and for them, work in the woodland was harsh and trying. Like the men of the ill-fated Popham colony at Sagadahoc, the Pilgrims were unfamiliar with woodland labor; few could wield the heavy felling ax or the broadax. Soon a poor diet and backbreaking labor took their toll even among healthy settlers. This was "so tedious a time," Bradford later wrote, that "many of our arms and legs can tell us to this day, we were not negligent."[24]

The forest remained mysterious and dangerous. Axes and other tools left unattended in the woodland sometimes disappeared, and many a novice woodsman believed that he performed his tasks before the eyes of thousands of skulking Indians and dangerous wild animals. Tales of encounters with wild animals—tales that were undoubtedly embellished as they circulated through the plantation—must have intensified the settlers' fears.[25]

Fear of the woodlands, illness and exhaustion, the demands of farming, and the lack of craftsmen, vehicles, and draft animals kept the men of Plymouth Colony from building more than seven small cottages, three storage houses, and a meetinghouse by December 1621. Even these buildings were extremely crude. They were almost certainly framed with hewn beams, but the beams were probably small, for without draft animals, it would have been too great an effort to move heavy hardwood timbers from the forest to the settlement. The roofs of all the buildings were thatched, and the spaces in the walls between the studs were usually filled with wattle and daub—a mixture of clay, straw, twigs, and leaves. The fact that much of this wattle and daub washed away during heavy storms in February 1621 suggests that the walls of the cottages may not have been clapboarded. However, in the following summer and fall the Pilgrims loaded a ship with timber products, among them clapboards and wainscots, worth several hundred pounds. If the Pilgrims rived clapboards and sawed wainscots for their backers, they probably did so for themselves. After the harvest of 1621 they began "to fit up their houses and dwellings against the winter"—an indication that the outsides of the houses were being boarded. Some may even have installed interior walls of wainscoting, but there was no glass available for windows. "Bring paper and linseed oil for your windows," Edward Winslow advised prospective settlers in December 1621.[26]

During the winter and spring of 1621–22, the colonists prepared timber for many new structures, sometimes neglecting spring planting to cut, hew, and carry the planks, summer beams, and girts. They felled thousands of small trees for an 8-foot-high palisade that extended 2,700 feet around the settlement. Outside the palisade they constructed "four bulwarks or jetties" and within, on the hill that overlooked the settlement, a flat-roofed fort. Without draft animals, moving the heavy timbers across the plain and onto the hill "was a great work for them to doe in their weakness, and times of want; but the danger of the time required it."[27]

When Emmanuel Altham, an English merchant, visited the colony in the summer of 1623, the fort was complete, and he judged it strong "both by nature and art." Unlike most forts built in the seventeenth century, however, it did not have walls of squared logs but of "thick sawn planks stayed with oak beams." There were about twenty houses on Leyden Street by this time, some betraying their builders' inexperience, but four or five "very fair and pleasant." Altham observed that "those that live here need never want for wood, for here is great store." In 1623 he sent samples worth £300 back to England aboard a ship that the Pilgrims had loaded with clapboard. But the colonists probably did not ship many forest products from Plymouth Colony after this ship departed. They were inexperienced foresters, and their settlement was poorly situated for lumbering. In 1626 the leaders of the colony, fearing that inconveniences might "befall the plantation by the want of timber," forbade the export of even small shipments of timber products.[28]

The financial backers in England were more interested in developing a fishing industry than a lumber trade, and they continually urged the Pilgrims to take to the sea. But the settlers were not experienced in fishing, and few craftsmen were available to transform timber into sturdy fishing vessels. An English-built pinnace, *Little James*, "a fine, new vessel" that had reached Plymouth in the summer of 1623, broke up in a violent storm off the coast of Maine the following April, but by then a ship carpenter had finally arrived. According to Bradford, he "quickly built them two very good and strong shallops, which after did them great service, and a great and strong lighter." He also hewed timber for two ketches, but died before they could be built, and the Pilgrims put to sea in open shallops even in winter. In the fall of 1625 one shallop, fitted with a deck to keep the cargo dry, made a voyage to the Kennebec River with surplus corn. But the Pilgrims were afraid to sail this vessel in bad weather without a shelter, and in 1626 an ingenious house carpenter, after sawing one of the biggest shallops in the middle and lengthening it, built a deck and a deckhouse. This comfortable vessel remained in service for many years.[29]

A few additional craftsmen came into the settlement during the first decade. By the late 1620s the colony had several house carpenters, a number of coopers, sawyers, and possibly a wheelwright. There were enough dwellings and storehouses for all, and there had been substantial improvements in construction. One improvement was the substitution of shingles or boards for thatch on roofs, thatch having been outlawed as a fire hazard in 1626.[30]

Forestry husbandry—the raising of pigs, goats, and chickens in the woodlands—was already under way by 1623. The first cattle arrived in 1624, and the settlers probably sent them off to browse in the forest, since there were few meadows. Sheep, so characteristic of the open countryside of England, were not to be seen in the Pilgrim settlement.[31]

The colonists' marksmanship seems to have improved, too, for in September 1623 Altham reported that "one man at six shoots hath killed 400" fowls. The leaders of the colony, seeking to make money by trading in furs, built trading posts in northern and southern New England. In 1627 they erected the Aptucxet trading post on the Manomet River (in the present town of Bourne, Massachusetts), where the servants who were stationed there permanently planted corn and raised pigs in the adjacent woodland. Traveling through the forest was no longer a frightening experience, and in 1628 a Dutch observer reported that "from Aptucxet the English can come in six hours, through the woods, passing several little rivulets of fresh water, to New Plymouth." By this time the Plymouth traders had built a second post (at Cushnoc, on the Kennebec), and in 1633 they erected a third post on the Connecticut at Windsor.[32]

Other Settlements

Many settlers who arrived in New England in the 1620s fared worse than the Pilgrims. Thomas Weston's colony at Wessagusset (Weymouth), at the mouth of the Weymouth Fore River, was a complete failure. It was settled by sixty-seven men, mostly "rude fellows" from the alleys and narrow streets of London who did not know how to survive in a forest. The colony was ill-supplied, and the Indians soon recognized its weakness, taking settlers' boats and blankets in unequal exchange for corn and forcing the young men to chop wood and carry water. During the winter of 1622–23 the settlers learned that the Indians planned to annihilate them and sent a messenger through the snow-covered forest to get help from the Pilgrims at Plymouth Colony. But Miles Standish and his small militia from Plymouth, still unaccustomed to woodland warfare, were unable to save the colony at Wessagusset. Refusing to settle at Plymouth, one contingent of Wessagusset men sailed for the fishing settlement at Monhegan Island. The other men, in groups of from six to ten, "scattered up and down in the Woods by the Waterside, where they could finde Ground-nuts and Clams" and where, scorned by the Indians, they learned the ways of the woodland through trial and error.[33]

The settlement established by Robert Gorges at Wessagusset in September 1623 fared no better than Weston's. Gorges's settlers were unskilled, and skilled workers from Plymouth Colony were forbidden to work for outsiders. By the summer of 1624 Gorges had returned to England, leaving behind only William Blaxton (Blackstone), Samuel Maverick, Thomas Walford, William Morrell, and a few others. Blaxton soon moved to Shawmut (Boston); Maverick and Walford set up their own forts near Boston Harbor; and Morrell soon sailed back to England.[34]

In spite of his enthusiasm about the timber resources of Maine, where he dreamed of founding a city named after his native York, the efforts of "His Majesties Woodward of Somersetshire," Christopher Levett, also ended in failure. He found an abundance of "excellent timber for joiners and coopers" and for "masts and yards of all sizes," trees "whereof pitch and tar is made," and timber for building ships; for the latter purpose, he claimed, "The World cannot afford better." But after spending the winter of 1623–24 on an island in Casco Bay, he and most of his party returned to England.[35]

In 1628 most of the colonists in the tiny settlements at Nantasket (Hull), Naumkeag (Salem), Cape Ann, the Piscataqua River, Richmond Island, Damariscove, Sheepscot, and Monhegan Island looked primarily to the sea, rather than to the forest, for their livelihood. In 1623, however, in the only recorded attempt at commercial lumbering in northern New England during this decade, Sir Ferdinando Gorges hired men to make clapboards, build houses, and erect sawmills at his plantation at Agamenticus (later York) on the York River. There is no evidence that a saw-mill was built, and a few years later, the men who came over to make pipe staves on Gorges's plantation "either for want of skill or industry, did not good."[36]

Mount Wollaston (Quincy) was settled in 1625 by Thomas Morton and his boisterous companions. Led by Morton, who, according to Bradford, "became the Lord of Misrule, and main-tained (as it were) a School of Atheism," these men spent the profit they made in the Indian trade "quaffing and drinking, both wine and strong waters in great excess (and, some reported) £10 worth in a morning." In the spring of 1627 Morton's men scandalized the Pilgrims by setting up a pine tree eighty feet tall as a Maypole. More alarming, Morton was selling guns to the Indians. Finally, the men at Plymouth and other settlements saw Morton as a threat to their control over their indentured servants, for he "would entertain any, how vile soever, and all the scum of the country or any discontents would flock to him from all places." And so, in June 1628, Miles Standish and a small band representing most New England settlers took Morton by force and sent him back to England, whence he soon returned to find the Maypole still standing. Only after "that worthy gentleman Mr. John Endecott" arrived in New England was Morton permanently banished and the Maypole cut down.[37]

The clash between the Pilgrims and Morton's drunken band was a struggle between the two groups that had most successfully adapted themselves to the New England forest before 1630. The sassafras hunters had quickly gathered the medicinal wood and reurned to the safety of England. Most of the young men from the streets of London whom wealthy English investors had sent to Sagadahoc, Wessagusset, and Casco Bay did not have the will or motivation to become woodsmen. Only the Pilgrims, with their strong faith in eternal salvation and their desire to form a Christian commonwealth, and the carefree men of Mount Wollaston, living for the moment and in virtual anarchy, were able to survive in the harsh and bitter land.

Chapter 4

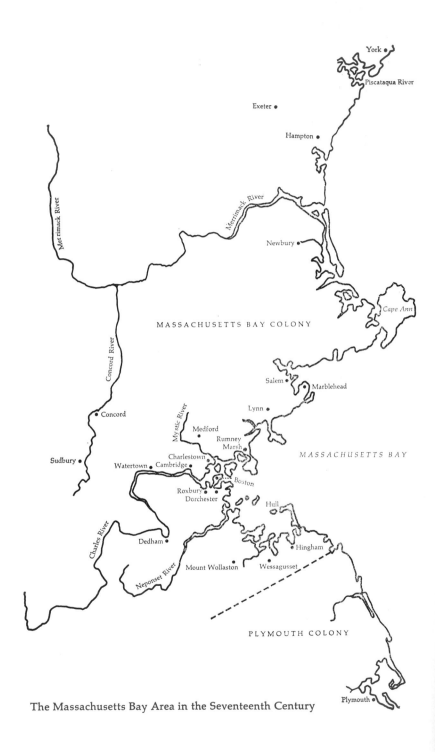

York •

Piscataqua River

Exeter •

Hampton •

Merrimack River

Newbury •

MASSACHUSETTS BAY COLONY

Cape Ann

Concord River

Salem •

Marblehead •

Lynn •

Concord •

Mystic River

Medford •

Rumney Marsh

MASSACHUSETTS BAY

Sudbury •

Watertown • Cambridge •

Charlestown

Boston

Roxbury •
Dorchester •

Hull •

Charles River

Dedham •

• Hingham

Neponset River

Mount Wollaston •

Wessagusset •

PLYMOUTH COLONY

Plymouth •

The Massachusetts Bay Area in the Seventeenth Century

The Great Migration, 1630-1640

Religion was the prime motive for the Great Migration, for the dissolution of Parliament in March 1629 convinced many Puritans that their last great hope for religious reform in England had died. They believed that England was entering "evill and declininge tymes" and that they had to embrace a "wilderness condition" for the sake of their immortal souls. They came neither for Spanish gold nor silver, but for "the Propagation of Piety and Religion to Posterity."[1]

Not everyone who came to New England during the 1630s was prompted solely by piety, however; most of those who settled north of the Merrimack were Anglicans, whose motivation was primarily economic. And even the most devout Puritans wanted to escape rising prices, unemployment, and unhealthful conditions in England. Many were concerned about the timber crisis, which drove the poor to destroy young trees, hedges, stiles, paling, posts, rails, and even gates and bridges to get fuel. In the borough of Sudbury (a town in Suffolk from which many immigrants came to New England) there had been constant trouble over firewood and fuel prices during the 1620s.[2]

The reports of Martin Pring, Bartholomew Gosnold, Christopher Levett, and John Smith must have made New England seem inviting, for they made much of the abundance of wood for fuel there and the opportunities for starting forest industries to make such products as pitch, tar, potash, and masts. In any case, glowing reports of a rich and verdant land blessed by the "prosperous good hand of Providence" were well received in England, and plans to exploit the woodlands were easily squared with religious ideals: Joshua, arousing the children of Joseph to subdue the land of Canaan, had said, "If thou bee muche people, get thee up to the wood, and cut trees for thyselfe there in the land of the Perizzites, and of the gyants, if mount Ephraim be too narrow for

57

thee." New England was to be the Puritans' new forested Canaan, and the great task of exploiting the woodlands would be an obstacle for them to overcome to prove their faith.[3]

The New Forested Canaan

In 1628 the Council for New England granted the New England Company a patent for the land between the Merrimack and Charles rivers. That same year John White, a promoter of religious enterprises who had been instrumental in obtaining the grant, sent John Endecott with about fifty colonists to a settlement at Naumkeag (later Salem) that had already been started by Roger Conant and a few men from a short-lived fishing enterprise on Cape Ann. The principal objective of some members of the New England Company was to establish a religious refuge; but such wealthy London merchants as Matthew Cradock, Sir Richard Saltonstall, Theophilus Eaton, William Pynchon, and Richard Bellingham expected financial returns. These merchants instructed the settlers to fill the returning ships with fish, beaver skins, and timber products; among the latter, they were particularly eager to get "shoomacke" (for tanning and dyeing), sassafras, and sarsaparilla. With these instructions in mind, Matthew Cradock, the governor of the company, hired two coopers and cleavers and ordered John Endecott to recruit men to help make staves and other timber products. Soon cargoes of New England timber were arriving in England, and the directors of the company (renamed the Massachusetts Bay Company in 1629 under a new royal charter) were discussing the sale of clapboards and other forest products.[4]

About 300 colonists settled at Salem and at Charlestown near Boston in 1629, but they represented only the ripples of an oncoming tide. During the fall and winter of 1629–30, hundreds of Englishmen left their homes and farms, gathered provisions, and prepared for a long and dangerous voyage to the wilderness. Fewer than 500 had come to New England during the 1620s, but during the following decade there were 20,000 immigrants. John Winthrop, the new governor of the Massachusetts Bay Company, and hundreds of colonists sailed in 1630, and after this initial wave, the tide of immigration did not ebb until the end of the decade.[5]

Governor Winthrop hoped to establish a compact settlement when he and the first colonists reached New England in June 1630; but with Salem and Charlestown already settled and new-comers landing all the time, the settlement gradually spread along the coast and into the interior. Medford, Watertown, Roxbury, Dorchester, Lynn, and Boston were soon founded, and by 1640 there were new towns in eastern Massachusetts, the Connecticut River valley, Rhode Island, and along the Connecticut coast. Some Puritans settled north of the Merrimack, founding Hampton and Exeter in what is now New Hampshire; others settled among the Anglican colonists along the Piscataqua River, where their arrival marked the beginning of bitter religious contention.[6]

Although the settlers of 1630 found a lush, green forest instead of the bleak November landscape that the Pilgrims had encountered ten years before, they, too, wanted to avoid settling in the forest. They sought salt marshes, meadowland along rivers, and land that had been burned or cleared by the Indians; natural clearings attracted them to lands along the Charles, Mystic, Concord, and Connecticut rivers.[7]

There was not enough unforested land for everyone, however, and many who came to Massachusetts Bay during the 1630s were forced to leave the shore and the open regions to live in the woods. The forest, they thought, was mysterious and frightening, and the Indians were men "transformed into beasts" or "bond-slaves of Sathan." Most of the Puritans were glad that the Lord had sent his destroying angel with the plague to sweep away large numbers of the Indians—and indeed, it was fortunate that there was no immediate conflict with the Indians, for these men from the villages of East Anglia and the West Country had much to learn about life in the forest.[8]

In summer, when the direct rays of the sun did not penetrate the branches of the great trees, the forest floor was suffused with an eerie light. There were many temptingly beautiful poisonous plants like poison sumac, ivy, and oak, and even the scent of some plants could be overwhelming. Although the forest was open in some areas, the undergrowth was extremely dense in others, and Indian paths were hard to find. Those who moved inland to the meadows along the Concord River complained of having to clamber over "crossed Trees," wade through deep water, and pass through underbrush that tore at their clothing and flesh so much that blood trickled down with every step.[9]

Much of the forest was silent by day. In the deep woods few birds sang, and only the occasional sounds of the Indians, the chatter of squirrels, the cries of jays and hawks, the rustle of leaves or crackle of twigs interrupted the silence. But at night the heavily wooded regions came alive with the noises of frogs, toads (some with voices "as big but not altogether as loud as a great bull"), and crickets, whose chirping made "such a dinn in an Evening."[10]

Englishmen were superstitious about woodlands and readily believed tales of great monsters that roamed the forest, reflecting that it was not the least of God's blessings that England was "void of noisome beasts." They feared snakes more than any other animal, and the rattlesnake most of all. Although taught to fear the "ravening wolves of heresy" and the "wild boars of tyranny," the settlers were more frightened by the tangible beasts of the New England forest. In an area of ten square miles, there were perhaps five black bears and two or three pumas, feared but rarely seen by the colonists. Gray wolves were no more numerous than pumas, but, hunting in packs, they made "no more bones to runne away with a Pigge, than a Dogge to runne away with a Marrow bone." Their number may have increased when they began to feed on the settlers' sheep, hogs, and cattle.[11]

The wild animals made life difficult enough, but the settlers complained most about insects. Seventeen-year locusts "ate the green things, and made such a constant yelling noise as made all the woods ring of them, and ready to deaf the hearers," and many colonists thought that the locusts caused serious illness. In the spring and early summer, the buffalo gnats, whose bite caused "an itching upon the hands or face, which provoketh scratching which is troublesome to some," were so thick that they sometimes made it hard to breathe. Large biting and bloodsucking flies were troublesome especially where there were cattle, and ticks would "cleave to a mans garments and creep into his breeches eating themselves in a short time into the very flesh." And many a colonist, coming for the first time upon something that looked like a "pine Apple plated with scales," must have been stung by wasps.[12]

The gnats and mosquitoes that hovered in clouds beneath the

forest cover were the worst plague of all, and the colonists often moved through wooded areas with their bodies completely covered even on the warmest days. Many who were unprepared for this bug-ridden world were stung so much that their faces were "swell'd and scabby" as if from smallpox. Some, noticing that mosquitoes avoided smoke, lighted fires even on the hottest days. But the real danger from the mosquito was yet to come, for by destroying the forest and making still water holes, ponds, and pools, the settlers increased the breeding places of the anopheles mosquito. When malaria protozoa were introduced later in the century, the ague, "the chills," and "the fever" became a regular part of frontier life.[13]

The first goal of every new settler was mere survival in the wilderness. In the 1630s most brought provisions for a year or more, but some were too poor to purchase much food, and others lost their stores at sea. Although there were probably from 10,000 to 20,000 gray squirrels, 400 white-tailed deer, and 200 turkeys in ten square miles of forest, most of the settlers were no better at shooting them than the Pilgrims had been. It seemed to be "hardur to get a shoot then it is in ould England," and the poor had to obtain food from charitable neighbors or gather groundnuts and acorns in the forest and shellfish along the shore.[14]

For those with enough food, shelter was the immediate problem. Some had brought tents, but raw cloth or canvas could not keep out the cold or repel water for long, and tents were used only temporarily except by the poor. Some colonists built their own versions of Indian wigwams with a few poles and some canvas. (A few adventurers may have lived in empty casks, but none seem to have lived in the rotten cores of trees, as some men in the Carolinas did.) For their first shelters, many simply dug a ditch six or seven feet deep, covered it with the trunks of small trees, and sealed it with canvas and mounds of dirt and turf. Such a shelter, even if it had a plank floor, wooden walls, and a board ceiling, was miserably damp (particularly after a heavy rain), and it is no wonder that immigrants who saw how men lived in the New England forest often took the next ship for home.[15]

Most of the settlers who came during the Great Migration had to clear their own land. Instead of killing the trees by girdling them, as settlers in Virginia did, most New England colonists felled them by ax. Most of the trees destroyed for plowland in the early period were probably oaks, for it was commonly believed that the lands on which oak stood were best for farming. But the oak is much more difficult to fell than many hardwoods and all conifers: ax handles blistered inexperienced woodsmen's hands and serious accidents were common; a number of men were killed by falling trees. After the trees had been destroyed for cropland, the settlers put the valuable timber aside and burned the rest. Unlike the Indians, who would plant around the stumps, the settlers often left fertile soil unplanted until the stumps had been removed and the land was ready for the plow.[16]

Forest Husbandry and Wooden Fences

In England the sheep was the dominant domestic animal. Hogs were raised in large numbers only in orchard regions where fruit was superabundant, in wooded regions like Hampshire where there was still a supply of nuts, and wherever the waste products of dairies, malthouses, distilleries, and starchworks were available. In the Midlands, from which hundreds emigrated to New England, hogs had to be fattened on grain, peas, and beans grown for that purpose.[17]

Whereas in deforested England the hog population did not significantly increase until the eighteenth century when potato cultivation became widespread, in New England hogs multiplied rapidly after they were introduced. Indeed, these animals, forest dwellers before their domestication, were so easy to feed in the wilderness that pork production could be doubled every eighteen months. (On one plantation, the number of hogs rose from 70 to 300 between 1634 and 1636.) Soon hogs were considered "cattell for proffeit," and Englishmen were practicing forest husbandry more than they had since Anglo-Saxon times.[18]

Although hogs provided urgently needed food, allowing them to roam endangered cornfields. In southern England, where most of the colonists came from, timber had been too scarce to be used for fences; ditches, hedges, or hays (high, woven barriers) were used instead. But in New England, fencing the common fields with posts and rails to keep out wolves and restrain roaming animals soon became an essential community activity, and in most towns fence viewers were appointed to see that fences were properly built and maintained.[19]

But hogs continued to break through the fences, and in 1636 the Massachusetts General Court decreed that loose hogs were wild hogs, that it was "lawfull for any man to take them, either alive or dead, as he may," and that all towns appoint a hogreeve to impound wild hogs. This decree was very unpopular, and most towns worked out their own hog codes. (Dorchester, for instance, required that hogs be kept two miles from any cornfield.) Almost everywhere hogs had to be ringed and yoked, and some towns required that they be tended by a hog keeper. Nothing is more conspicuous in the early town records than the hog and fence regulations—and their violation. The pigs were pests, and many a farmer in this land of grunts and squeals must have longed for the pastoral English countryside.[20]

Wood-framed Dwellings and Barns

Carpenters, joiners, and other skilled workers were needed if substantial wooden houses were to be built, and, although some of these craftsmen were persuaded to come to New England, the demand for them during the early years was always greater than the supply. They would accept no less than three shillings a day, which raised the prices of goods in general and caused so many complaints that the Massachusetts General Court limited the pay of carpenters, joiners, sawyers, clapboard rivers, and other craftsmen to two shillings a day and that of common laborers to eighteen pence a day. The prices of food and English manufactures were extremely high at this time, and although the court had promised the craftsmen to control prices, it failed to do so, eventually leaving wage and price control to the towns. But local control was not effective, and prices remained so high that many craftsmen abandoned their trades, at least temporarily, to clear land and become farmers.[21]

The craftsmen who continued in their trades found it difficult to train apprentices in New England. An apprentice was customarily bound to serve a master craftsman seven years, during which he learned the craft and was given bed, board, and clothing. But in New England, where the demand for skilled workers was so great that people were willing to hire a man who had learned only the rudiments of a trade, apprentices often broke their contracts, ran away, and found work before they had mastered their crafts. Some master carpenters, who desperately needed men to fell trees, saw, rive, and do other backbreaking work, tried to force their apprentices to follow their written agreements to the letter. But the rules of apprenticeship could not be enforced, and this contributed to the shortage of carpenters and other skilled workers during the 1630s. As at Plymouth Colony a decade before, men who wanted houses had to build them themselves.[22]

The settlers of the 1630s built their houses as Englishmen had done for centuries, framing them with hewn oak beams. Cellars were not common, and the groundsels of most dwellings were often placed directly on the earth. As in England the roofs were usually thatched; but the outer walls were covered with clapboards, whereas in southern England, especially since the beginning of the timber crisis, houses often had outer walls of sand and lime (with hair, dung, or ashes for a binder) applied to wicker or hazel lathing. Many New Englanders would have preferred outer walls of plaster—or of brick or slate, which were also common in England—but few deposits of lime were available for plaster or mortar. The spaces between the studs were filled with soft bricks or wattle and daub, and the filling was covered on the exterior with riven clapboards. Because it was extremely difficult and time-consuming to saw boards by hand, boards were more commonly used for floors than interior walls. Thomas Dudley, a deputy governor of the colony, aroused criticism when he nailed clapboards to the interior walls of his house "in the form of wainscot."[23]

Most of the dwellings built during the 1630s were very small: usually they had only one room on the ground floor, and not all had an upper story. The doorways were small, and some houses had a few small glass windows, although glass was still scarce and expensive. These dwellings were dark, cold, and drafty, and many settlers suffered during the harsh New England winters. For, although there was an abundance of wood to build houses and make fires, it was not so easy to obtain wood as many had imagined. Boston, for instance, was on a treeless peninsula, and the timber set aside at Dorchester Neck and Muddy River was not sufficient. There was enough timber on the harbor islands, but it was difficult to transport even when boats were available and the harbor was not icebound. In Boston, where the poor suffered from the lack of fuel as much as their counterparts in England, the settlers were "almost ready to break up for want of wood" in the winter of 1637–38.[24]

Even where there was no shortage of timber, it was difficult to build large fires indoors, since there was not enough lime for mortar to bond bricks for fireplaces. The settlers sought new ways to make mortar, but such dubious mixtures as "2 loade of wast soapashes, one loade of lyme, one loade of loame, and one loade of Woolwich sand, tempered together" probably could not have withstood the great heat in a large chimney. The lower parts of the chimneys were often built of brick or stone (using mortar made with lime from sea shells) and the upper parts of wood with a heavy, fire-resistant clay covering. A chimney like this, if regularly inspected and repaired, was reasonably safe if the wooden frame was strong enough to bear the weight of a large load of clay. But the builders were often careless, and the use of wood in chimneys near thatched roofs led to many serious fires. After two houses in Boston burned down in 1631 when one caught fire from a poorly constructed chimney, wooden chimneys and thatched roofs were prohibited; but they continued to be built, and more fires occurred.[25]

Because the chimneys had wide flues, much of the heat generated by a fire was drawn off, and people would be singed or seriously burned trying to get as close to the fire as possible. Sometimes a wooden lug pole from which pots hung over the fire would burn and break, spilling boiling mixtures over the unwary. And many fires were started by small children who carried embers from near-by houses to rekindle fires. Some fires were even caused by the igniting of gunpowder, which often seems to have been placed near the fireplace to dry.[26]

By the middle of the fourth decade, thousands of poorly built houses stood in the forest clearings of New England. Clapboards rived and lapped by unskilled workers did not keep out the cold. Because of the shortage of nails, many boards became loose and fell off. Roofs leaked, and floors and groundsels rotted. The large, unseasoned framing timbers cracked and buckled, and some dwellings were in danger of falling down.[27]

Many men, however, found time to improve and enlarge their

houses or to build new ones. In 1637 John Winthrop, who had criticized Thomas Dudley's clapboard wainscoting, was reluctant to make his new house too fine, but his carpenter persuaded him to build a house of "Commodious neatness," fit for the governor of a settled commonwealth.[28]

Commodious neatness also characterized the house built by Deputy Governor Samuel Symonds in 1639. Thirty feet long and over sixteen feet wide, it was built over a full cellar and was "stronge in timber, though plaine and well braced." There were two entrances opposite each other in the middle of the house; the doorways were high, although there were only a few small windows. Two large fireplaces extending the width of the house were placed at each end, with chimney frames of heavy timbers protected by clay. The ground floor may have been unpartitioned, but there were two rooms on the second floor, reached by stairs near the front door. The garret was unpartitioned and had a single window. The exterior walls were filled with clay and protected by clapboards, and the roof was probably thatched.[29]

By the late 1630s there were enough frame dwellings in many New England towns "to intertain such as come over, with house-room and other refreshings, while they build and made Provision upon their owne lotts." The colonists did a thriving business in real estate, meeting new settlers at the boat to offer houses or building timbers in exchange for English goods. Even Governor Winthrop was willing to sell his house at Boston to anyone who offered the right price. Typical of many new house buyers was Thomas Hale, who brought ironware, window glass, clothing, and other English goods to sell in New England when he migrated in 1637, so that he could buy "a cottage to dwell in and a milshe cow for his children's sustenance."[30]

In England cattle were commonly left outdoors all year, and barns were usually built only for the wealthy; but in New England, where there were wolves and long, severe winters, barns were needed to protect the cattle and hold large quantities of fodder. Because timber was so abundant, the barns that were built were probably larger than those built in England; with the exception of Harvard College, they were the largest structures built during the Great Migration. In 1640 a barn seventy-two feet long, twenty-six feet wide, and ten feet high at the sides was built for a wealthy Massachusetts merchant at Rumney Marsh (Revere).

This barn, which cost almost £100 to build, was covered with clapboards and had a plank floor, two porches (each twelve by thirteen feet), and eight doors.[31]

Carts and Canoes

During the early years, it was very difficult to travel between settlements, and sometimes—because of the fallen trees, stumps, hewn timber, and piles of construction debris—difficult or dangerous to travel through the towns themselves. In the 1630s efforts were made to remove obstacles from paths inside the towns and at the waterside, and many communities passed regulations to "keepe the street cleane from wood and all other things."[32]

By 1639 paths through the towns around Massachusetts Bay had been cleared of many hazards, and the more difficult task of breaking roads through the woodlands was begun. But the new roads could not remain open without continuous clearing, for decayed and fallen trees and luxuriant summer undergrowth continued to make travel between some towns almost impossible. During the winter, deep snow sometimes isolated settlements for long periods. Nevertheless, there was soon a continuous highway along the coast between Newbury (near the Merrimack) and Hingham (about twelve miles southeast of Boston).[33]

With the opening of roads during the 1630s, New Englanders turned to the forest for raw materials to make carts. Wheelwrights were needed, for to make wheeled vehicles required knowledge of different kinds of wood and the ability to put felloes, spokes, hubs, and axles together correctly. In 1629 the Massachusetts Bay Company had sent a wheelwright to Salem, who instructed others in the trade; many more wheelwrights came during the 1630s, when they were still so much in demand that one town was willing to grant a wheelwright several acres of woodland "for imployment in his trade." The wheelwrights made hundreds of wheels for carts and wheelbarrows, and some probably made plows. But they could not keep up with the demand, and their labor was so costly that many farmers fashioned makeshift vehicles themselves, perhaps attaching a log axle and wheels made from cross-sections of a big log to a boxlike body.

Besides these rough carts, sledges were also widely used; where paths had been cleared of rocks and stumps, draft animals could pull heavily loaded sledges over the soft, moist forest floor; slightly modified, they served as sleds in the winter, when the heaviest loads were moved. Many an early road through the New England forest was broken as a sledgeway, or "drawen way."[34]

To travel by sledge or cart even over frequently used ways must have been extremely uncomfortable and dangerous. Four-wheeled wagons and coaches were not used for many years, and until then people walked beside their vehicles. But the early settlers found that the canoe, which the New England Indians had been using for centuries, was the best means of carrying passengers through the forest. Colonists introduced to the canoe at a ferry must have been as apprehensive as one woman was even as late as 1704, when she crossed a river in a canoe so unstable that even a "wry thought" would have upset it.[35]
Some settlers refused to ride in canoes, but most welcomed a vessel that was so easy to build. Great numbers of canoes were built in the 1630s—usually by hollowing out the trunk of a tree with an adz—and used on the inland waterways to carry passengers and such goods as firewood, clay, thatch, and furs. In Massachusetts canoes were in use at almost all ferries, and in communities like Dedham (on the Charles) and Salem (with its inland waterways), canoe travel increased rapidly. The men of Salem crossed the rivers in small canoes "made of whole pine trees, being about two foot & a half over, and 20 foote long," in which they also went "sometimes two leagues to sea." However, the use of the canoe by the inexperienced led to many drownings.[36]

Shipbuilding and Lumbering

The original promoters of the migration to New England had hoped that the settlers would be able to exploit the wilderness by setting up forest industries. But during the early years of colonization, most of these efforts failed. Although the forest abounded in fur-bearing animals, the settlers who arrived after 1630 had neither the time nor the experience to collect pelts themselves, and Plymouth traders dominated the fur trade with the Indians. In any case, there were substantially fewer fur-bearing animals in the coastal regions by 1640, and trade in furs was never a major part of the economy in most settlements.[37]

It was unpractical—often impossible—to undertake complicated manufacturing in the initial stages of colonization. Skilled workers were seldom available, and costs were prohibitively high. While immigration continued, the colonists obtained clothing, nails, iron tools, gunpowder, vinegar, candles, and other manufactures from the latest settlers in exchange for cattle, foodstuffs, and timber products. Apparently some effort was made to manufacture naval stores, but pitch and tar were still imported in the 1630s. Although there had once been some interest in setting up a potash works, New Englanders imported soap made from Baltic potash for many years. There were several attempts at salt manufacturing—an industry appropriate for a forest community because large quantities of firewood were needed to boil off the liquid—but projects at Plymouth Colony in 1624 and in the Piscataqua region in 1631 were failures. The Bay Company investors had hoped that an ironworks could be established; but in New England, not enough charcoal was produced for black-smiths to use, let alone for an ironworks. Of all the forest industries that were attempted during the 1630s, only shipbuilding and lumbering were successful.[38]

Shipbuilding started in the spring of 1629, when the New England Company sent six or seven shipwrights to Salem, where the settlers had often had to release fish from their nets "for want of boats and men." Several fishing shallops were built at Salem before Governor Winthrop arrived the following year. Many more shipwrights arrived during the 1630s, only to find that such supplies as nails, cordage, and sailcloth were scarce and capital was often unavailable even for the construction of small vessels.[39]

The number of small fishing vessels increased slowly. Several shallops were built by 1632, and a number of small craft—shallops, pinnaces, and the like—were operating at fishing stations and settlements in northern New England. Several large trading vessels, however, were built during the 1630s. A thirty-ton bark, the first large vessel built in the Bay Colony, was built for John Winthrop at his plantation on the Mystic in 1631. By 1633 a ship of 100 tons was being built at Matthew Cradock's plantation at Medford, and a vessel twice that size was planned. A 60-ton vessel was launched at Medford in 1633, and by the summer of 1635 there were "6 sayle of shipps at least if not more belonginge to the plantations" in New England. A vessel of 120 tons, built in 1636 at Marblehead, made voyages to the West Indies and England.[40] During the later 1630s Salem was beginning to look like a shipbuilding center. At least three shipwrights had received grants of land along the waterside, and efforts were made to reserve large white oaks for shipbuilding. Although large ships were not built at Boston or Charlestown during these years, a few substantial vessels were built north of the Bay Colony. At the Trelawny plantation on Richmond Island off the coast of Maine, a thirty-ton bark was launched in 1637, and a double-decked vessel of about a hundred tons was started in 1638 but not launched until 1641, its construction delayed by the departure of the original shipwright, who found supplies too hard to obtain and laborers too little "insighted in the Carriege of the worke." These difficulties and delays were typical of the frustrations of life in the forest wilderness. Nevertheless, at a time when most other forest industries failed, shipbuilding was relatively successful, and vessels built at Medford, Salem, Richmond Island, and other primitive shipbuilding centers returned from England, southern Europe, Bermuda, Barbados, and Virginia with essential products.[41]

During the 1630s lumbering was already an important industry in Maine and New Hampshire, and even in some southern New England towns, where many farmers worked at lumbering as part of their land-clearing operations. The masters of Dutch and English ships that brought immigrants and tons of supplies to Boston and Salem wanted return cargoes, and some sought timber to sell in England, the Azores, Madeira, the Canaries, and southern Europe. Masts from northern New England could be sold at a considerable profit in English ports, and white pine boards also made profitable return cargoes. At Captain John Mason's plantation on the Piscataqua, men were sawing boards by hand for the English market as early as 1630.[42]

A water-powered sawmill was built in 1634 by English and Danish carpenters on Mason's plantation near the present town of South Berwick, Maine. Another mill was built in the same year at Sir Ferdinando Gorges's settlement at Agamenticus (York), Maine, in an attempt—probably the first in North America—to use tidal power. These mills were not successful for long, however. Mason's mill produced boards for several years, but was abandoned in 1638 after the death of the proprietor. High wages and a lack of skilled workers and transportation limited the profits from Gorges's mill; but although its foundations were repeatedly washed away by the tide and saws and other metal parts that were costly and difficult to repair continually broke, the sawmill continued to operate during the late 1630s. In 1638, perhaps with the help of craftsmen from the Mason and Gorges plantations, John Wheelwright built another mill in northern New England, at Exeter, the town he had founded in New Hampshire.[43]

Few boards were produced at these early sawmills. Many settlers in Maine and New Hampshire continued to saw boards by hand, and the fishing stations in northern New England were still importing boards from England during the 1630s. But many red and white oak clapboards for barrel staves were produced for sale in the wine islands, southern Europe, England, and the West Indies. Captain John Mason's men rived these thin, narrow pieces of wood at the mouth of the Piscataqua, and in the mid-1630s Edward Trelawny began to make thousands of staves at his fishing station on Richmond Island. In 1636 he contracted with an English merchant to prepare a shipload of staves for the wine islands, Spain, and England. Unable to produce enough on his own plantation to fill large vessels, Trelawny collected 250 tons of staves from other settlers in northern New England. Trelawny and others undoubtedly continued to supply staves in the following years, for staves could be sold for as much as £28 a thousand, which made up for poor profits from fishing.[44]

By the end of the fourth decade, the settlers had made their initial adjustment to life in the New England forest, and signs of their new society were everywhere: wooden fences, sawmills, clapboard houses, large barns, blazing oak and hickory fires, canoes, sailing ships, piles of raw oak staves at the waterside, and even the ubiquitous hogs—all were evidence that a thriving economy was emerging in the New England wilderness.

Chapter 5

GREAT BRITAIN

London

EUROPE

NORTH AMERICA

Newfoundland

ATLANTIC OCEAN

Bilbao

Boston

Oporto

Alicante

Azores

Cádiz

Málaga

Madeira

Bermuda

Canaries

Gulf of Mexico

Bahamas

Gulf of
Campeche

AFRICA

WEST INDIES

Jamaica

Dominica

Caribbean Sea

Barbados

Curaçao

Tobago

Trinidad

SURINAM

BRAZIL

SOUTH AMERICA

PACIFIC OCEAN

ATLANTIC OCEAN

Trading Regions

The Timber Trade, 1640-1688

During the 1630s most economic activity in New England was based on the demands created by a steady stream of new settlers. The ships that carried thousands of religious refugees to New England were laden with English textiles, leather goods, ironware, and other manufactures. Many of these goods belonged to the new immigrants, who exchanged them for cattle, corn, houses, building timber, and various New England products. In this period shipbuilding and the export of fish and timber, although they brought wealth to some, were of little importance south of the Merrimack.

But the economy of New England, after growing steadily and flourishing for a decade, was suddenly and dramatically shattered in 1640. In that year, John Winthrop sadly relates, "there came over a great store of provisions, both out of England and Ireland, and but few passengers," so that prices for timber, cattle, and foodstuffs in New England went down as demand decreased. By the fall of 1640 almost all of the specie in New England had been spent to obtain English manufactures, and the Massachusetts General Court, because of the "great stop in trade and commerce for want of money," required creditors to accept New England products at fixed values. By then, however, many debtors had lost their houses, lands, and other possessions.[1]

The Great Migration ended because many of the Puritans, who might in earlier years have sought religious liberty by migrating to America, now hoped to find that liberty in England. For the famous Long Parliament of 1640 defied the king, executed Strafford, his hated minister, imprisoned many bishops and judges, and began civil and religious reforms. This revolution and the resulting economic depression in New England had a profound effect on the colonists. Some thought of returning to England to fight the king and his army. Others prepared to move farther south, "supposing they should find better means of subsistence there." Several groups moved to New Netherland (New York), and hundreds of settlers went to the West Indies.

Nevertheless, most colonists were determined to endure the rigors of the New England wilderness. But they desperately needed clothing, leather goods, gunpowder, glass, salt, shot, and ironware (pots, pans, nails, weapons, tools, and cutlery). Their leaders hoped to encourage local production of raw materials for these goods, as well as production of the finished goods themselves. Families in Connecticut were required to plant hemp and flax, and in Massachusetts sheep raising was encouraged, along with the manufacture of garments, gunpowder, and glass. Tanners, who had turned to farming during the Great Migration, returned to their trade, and laws were enacted to discourage the wasting of hides. Salt manufacturing was begun at Plymouth Colony, a fulling mill was built at Rowley, and, after great difficulty, ironworks were completed at Braintree in 1645 and at Saugus in 1650.

These efforts did not begin to satisfy the immediate need for finished goods. There were few trained clothworkers, and the wooded regions were not suitable for raising sheep. Although some saltpeter was collected, little gunpowder was produced, if any. The saltworks could not even meet household needs, and the Salem glassworks produced only bottles, not the essential window glass. In spite of legislation, there were not always enough hides available for tanning.

The only solution to the economic crisis, therefore, was to export surplus products in exchange for essential manufactured goods—but there was little to export. Grain surpluses in New England, because of the sour and rocky soil and the short growing season, could not be depended on, although they were available temporarily. Furs, although easily transported and highly profitable, could be obtained only from those who dealt with the Indians in the interior, since trappers had killed almost all the beavers in the coastal areas by the mid-1630s. Most New Englanders still knew nothing about salt-water fishing or boatbuilding, though some probably began to fish with the small groups of experienced fishermen on the Maine coast or in the fishing communities of Marblehead and Hull. Others may have built boats and put to sea with their families or neighbors. But large numbers of fishermen could not be trained in one or two fishing seasons, nor could large surpluses of fish be accumulated for export. Thus it was clear that the settlers would have to turn to the forest now more than ever for products that could be sold to procure essential English goods.[2]

The Wine Ports

After 1640 the merchants of Boston began to develop important timber markets in Spain, Portugal, the Canaries, Madeira, and the Azores. For the export of wine from such Continental ports as Bilbao, Oporto, Cádiz, Málaga, and Alicante was increasing, while the supply of ship timber and timber for wine casks was rapidly diminishing. The merchants at Bilbao had been unable to obtain enough timber from the interior and, since the late sixteenth century, had been importing large quantities of forest products from the Baltic in Dutch, Flemish, and Hanseatic vessels. The Spanish settlers of the Canaries, having planted the islands with vines by the early seventeenth century, were importing large amounts of staves and heading for the huge pipes used in storing and shipping wine. Madeira—the name means "timber"—had been cleared of woodlands by fire and was covered with vineyards. The Azores had been heavily timbered—the name of one island, Faial, means "beech forest"—but these islands, too, had been cleared and were planted in vines.[3]

Without wooden containers that would enhance the flavor of the wine, the economy of the wine regions, especially Madeira and the Azores, would fail. New Englanders had been supplying some wine growers with white oak for wet casks—casks impermeable to wine but porous enough for air to filter through to influence the oxygenation of the wine—since the 1630s. Before the end of 1640 a merchant-adventurer exported 8,500 pipe staves from Boston aboard an English vessel. And in 1641 Samuel Maverick sent a shipment of staves to an English agent in Málaga, who sold the cargo and forwarded Spanish money and fruit to a Bristol merchant. The latter gave Maverick credit for English manufactures destined for New England.[4]

During 1642 at least seven vessels sailed from Boston for the wine islands and Mediterranean ports. Some carried fish, wheat, corn, peas, and other provisions, but cargoes probably consisted mainly of white oak pipe staves. In 1642 New Haven merchants sent out a 180-ton vessel with a cargo of staves for the Canaries. In 1643 the 300-ton *Mary Ann* of Dartmouth (England) took on pipe staves in the Piscataqua for Madeira and Málaga. The deputy governor at Agamenticus had at least 2,000 pipe staves loaded on this ship to pay for his passage to England.[5]

The Puritans had misgivings about trading in popish regions; but trade with the wine ports was extremely profitable, and it was the major factor in the growth of the New England shipbuilding industry. Because of this trade, ships were built for the first time at Boston and Charlestown. In 1643 at least five New England–built vessels sailed for the wine islands and Mediterranean markets, and in 1644 four visited the Canaries. The 400-ton *Seafort*, built at Boston in 1644, was lost off Cádiz, but a Cambridge-built vessel laden with pipe staves, fish, and other commodities arrived safely at Málaga in 1645. This vessel was to proceed to London with a cargo of wine, but broke up in a violent storm along with five other vessels off the coast of Spain.[6]

By the late 1640s, in spite of the loss of a number of New England–built vessels, the wine islands and southern Europe were becoming valuable markets for New England fish as well as timber. The size of the New England catch increased as the fishermen gained experience, and when the English West Country fishing industry, a prime supplier of Spanish and Portuguese markets, was disrupted in the 1640s by the Civil War and in the 1650s by hostile Dutch and Spanish vessels, the New Englanders sent more and more mixed cargoes of timber and the better grades of fish, especially cod, to Continental markets. In 1650, for instance, a Charlestown merchant shipped 10,326 pipe staves, 800 hogshead staves, and 165 quintals of dried fish to Madeira.[7]

In the late 1640s and early 1650s, fish was still not the chief export from New England to the wine ports in terms of shipping tonnage. Even in the form of white oak staves, timber took up more space than fish. Nor is it certain that the fish caught and exported by the permanent settlers of New England had a greater value than timber exports in this early period. But after 1645 fishing was extremely profitable, and in 1647 the catch at Marblehead alone was worth £4,000.[8]

Nevertheless, very large cargoes of staves were shipped from New England in this period. In 1648 one Bristol ship took aboard 60,000 white oak staves. If these staves sold for £20 per thousand in the wine regions, the total value of this cargo was £1,200. The following exchange took place between Boston and Madeira in 1653:

OUTWARD TO MADEIRA

16,735 pipe staves at £16 a thousand	£265.16.00
533 clapboard bolts at £5 a hundred	26.07.06
	£292.03.06

INWARD TO BOSTON

40 pipes of wine at 7s. 1od. a pipe	£300.00.00
1 pipe "Vendridy wine"	4.15.00
Oil and Linen cloth	3.00.00
Money	20.12.00
	£328.07.00

Mixed cargoes of staves and provisions were also sent to the wine regions. In 1647 a Charlestown merchant sent a ship to Madeira with 15,300 "good sound and merchantable white oak pipestaves," "sixteen tunnes of shaken cask, to say, in thirty two peices strongly hooped and nailed," and 200 bushels of "good and merchantable rye corn."[9]

Trade with the wine regions revived the depressed economy of the new forest society. But neither the forest nor the ocean resources of New England could have been fully exploited by this trade alone. For merchants in the wine islands and southern Europe bought only premium grades of fish and white oak staves. Red oak staves were too porous for wet casks, and other species of timber gave an unacceptable flavor to the wine. It was not profitable to ship other timber products, such as shingles and white pine boards, across the Atlantic.

New England merchants who traded with the wine regions also had difficulty obtaining suitable return cargoes. Fish and timber were sometimes traded for such products as fruit, salt, or iron, but wine was the chief item of exchange. Although many New England merchants preferred to receive bills of exchange as credit toward English goods, many did bring back large quantities of wine to New England—so much that in 1645 the Massachusetts General Court imposed a duty of ten shillings on every butt entering Boston, the proceeds to be used for harbor defense. In the following year, when 800 butts of wine were landed, the

Boston merchants bitterly complained about the duty; some refused to pay, and their wine was seized. Finance and harbor defense were probably not the only reasons for the Puritan magistrates' action, since some believed that the abundance of wine
would increase drunkenness and "bring some stroake of Gods
heavy hand" upon the colony. But before the divine stroke fell,
a new market for surplus Spanish and Portuguese wine as well
as for New England timber and fish was opened in the West
Indies.[10]

The West Indies

Englishmen had been settling on the Caribbean islands
for many years, and by the 1620s permanent English settlements—peopled by young indentured servants from Britain
and Ireland—had grown up on Saint Kitts, Nevis, and Barbados.
Many other Englishmen and Irishmen immigrated to the Caribbean during the 1620s and 1630s, and when the Great Migration
ended, hundreds of New Englanders went to Barbados and other
islands.[11]

Barbados was by far the most important colony in the British
West Indies in the seventeenth century. By the early 1640s there
were more settlers in its 166 square miles than in all the New
England colonies. The leading products in the 1630s and early
1640s were tobacco, corn, indigo, and tropical fruits and nuts,
although cotton was thought to be potentially more important.
During the 1630s small amounts of cotton had been shipped to
New England. But after 1640, when they were cut off from
direct commercial contact with England and unable to raise
enough wool or flax themselves, New Englanders found cotton essential for winter and summer clothing. And to obtain cotton they
relied primarily on the export of woodland products.[12]

In Connecticut, where there were few merchants, the General
Court organized the trade with the West Indies. In 1640 the
court ordered a vessel sent to the regions where cotton was available, "the pay for the said Cotton wool to be made in English
Corn or pipe-staves as the country shall afford." Each town was
to supply part of the cargo and buy part of the cotton. To insure
"that the country may have provisions of pipe staves for the

furthering the said trade of cotton wool," no timber was to be felled on public lands without permission, and no pipe staves were to be sold on the Connecticut River or "transported into foreign parts," without being inspected "both for the goodness of the timber, and due proportion and size thereof." In 1641 the felling of trees on public land was no longer restricted, although individuals could export this timber only to discharge debts or obtain necessary provisions. To collect even small amounts of pipe staves in rural Connecticut required a great deal of time and effort, but enough was collected to buy £400 worth of cotton for the spinners of the colony.[13]

The settlers of Portsmouth, Rhode Island, also sent a shipload of planks, clapboards, and pipe staves to the West Indies in 1640, but most trade between New England and the Caribbean was carried on from Boston and Salem. For the merchants of Massachuetts, by developing an extensive trade with the wine regions and England, had a distinct advantage over the merchants in other colonies. In 1641 Massachusetts sent ships to the West Indies, and two ships returned in 1642 with "a good supply" of cotton, but apparently too little to satisfy the needs of the settlers. Moreover, clothing made from cotton was little protection against the New England cold and was highly flammable as well. Cotton garments easily caught fire near the huge open hearths, and children were "scorched by fire, yea, divers burnt to death."[14]

The cotton trade was significant only because it enabled New England merchants, especially Boston merchants, to establish trade with the West Indian islands. And as more and more settlers left New England for Barbados and hundreds of Barbadians migrated to New England, commercial contacts were established that would later prove valuable to both regions. For by the middle of the fifth decade, changes in the West Indies suddenly and completely transformed the economy and society of Barbados, invigorating and balancing the economy of New England as well.

By 1640 a number of Barbadian planters had realized that cotton and tropical fruits and nuts would not bring large and sustained profits, and the tobacco grown on the island was too poor to compete with that of Maryland and Virginia in the English and Continental markets. Accordingly, a few planters began to import sugar canes from the Dutch colony of Brazil. A number of years passed before they learned how to raise and process the canes and manufacture a salable product. The first products, the coarse brown sugars called muscovados, turned out "so moist, and full of molasses, and so ill cur'd, as they were hardly worth the bringing home for England." But after skilled sugar workers and processing equipment had been brought from Brazil, sugar cultivation was successful, and plantations spread along the leeward shore and inland on the rich, black soil of the hills and valleys. By 1650 sugar was already a major part of the total export of Barbados. The total value of Barbadian crops in a twenty-month period beginning in 1650 was £3,097,800, and by 1660 about 80 per cent of Barbados was covered with sugar canes.[15]

Large-scale sugar production transformed not only the economy of Barbados but the composition of its population. Although cotton, ginger, and other tropical crops were grown, sugar quickly became the most valuable export. And because sugar requires intense cultivation, it was more profitable to import large numbers of African slaves than to use white indentured servants or day laborers. As a result, the more ambitious men drove poor independent farmers and tenant farmers off the best land. Consolidating the small farms, these planters—and many small planters as well—bought more and more African slaves, increasing their fortunes and political power. In 1640, before the development of the sugar plantations, the population of Barbados was 10,000, the majority of it Irish. In 1660, when the sugar plantations had been well established, the population had risen to 40,000—half of it African slaves. The Irish and English population declined because thousands died of tropical diseases, or in wars, or migrated to other parts of the New World, and the slave population increased. By 1680 Barbados had twice as many Africans as Europeans. By then 175 planters controlled more than 50 per cent of the property on the island. Controlling both the assembly and the militia, they oppressed the small white planters, whom they forced onto marginal lands. Buying Africans "as men b[u]y horses in a Fayre," they transformed a small and seemingly insignificant island into "one large sugar factory," the most fully developed, populous, and profitable colony in English America.[16]

The transformation of Barbados gave New Englanders a market for timber products. Before sugar was introduced, there had been some demand for red oak staves and heading for tobacco casks, but little demand for other timber products. Barbados was still heavily timbered then, and Barbadians themselves sent valuable mahogany and brazilwood to English furniture makers and dyers. After sugar was introduced, some woodland was set aside for fuel and building timbers, and some land was reserved for food crops and cattle. But sugar was very profitable, and when the fertility of the soil decreased, additional arable land was urgently needed. All accessible forests were soon leveled, the hillsides were terraced, and even pastures were turned into cane fields. As early as 1652 it was said that Barbados could not last "in a height of trade three years longer, the wood being almost already spent." By the 1660s most of the arable land on the island was under cultivation, and hordes of slaves were used to produce ever-increasing amounts of sugar, "hoeing, dunging and planting the canes" during the rainy season and "cutting the canes, grinding them at the mills, boyling up the liquor, and making thereof Muscovado Sugar" in the dry season.[17]

The destruction of the forests and use of almost every acre of arable land for sugar production made Barbados totally dependent on the outside world for most of its basic needs. Wood fuel for sugar manufacturing could be imported from nearby islands, and some timber products used in making and shipping sugar were obtained from Brazil, Tobago, Saint Lucia, and later from Saint Vincent and Dominica. But much of the timber came from North America.[18]

The new Barbadian market allowed the New England merchants to develop the timber trade fully. Barbadian planters eventually used large quantities of white oak staves in the rum industry, but during the early years of the sugar plantations, the demand was for red oak staves. These, valueless in the wine trade because of their porosity, made excellent hogsheads, barrels, and tierces for sugar and molasses. A plantation of 100 acres required over eighty 1,000-pound hogsheads annually for shipping sugar and another twenty hogsheads for molasses. In addition, almost every planter with fifty acres—and many who had less—built a large wooden mill to drive the great rollers that crushed the cane. Boiling houses, still houses, curing houses, drying houses, barns, storage houses, and packing houses were essential for sugar production. Almost all of the operating equipment was of wood, and the planters were constantly seeking large numbers of building timbers, shingles, and boards to construct new buildings and replace those destroyed by fire, hurricane, or tropical rot. New Englanders now had an outlet for red oak staves, red-, white-, and black-oak building timbers, barrel hoops, cedar shingles, and white pine boards. And, since some machinery required more power than slaves could provide, there was a market for horses from the woods and fields of Rhode Island and Massachusetts.[19]

As the number of sugar plantations grew, their prosperous owners bought more of the wine that New England merchants brought from Madeira, the Canaries, the Azores, and southern Europe. New Englanders also shipped quantities of forest-fed pork, salt beef, butter, cheese, flour, peas, biscuits, and corn to Barbados. Although they could not supply all the food needed by the white planters, overseers, and servants (provisions had to be imported from Ireland, England, and Virginia, too), they could supply the plantations with cheap, low-grade fish. The New England economy was finally balanced when the poorest grades of cod and mackerel, which could not be sold in the wine regions and hitherto had been used by New Englanders only as fertilizer, were sold in Barbados to feed the slaves.[20]

Newfoundland

During the 1640s and early 1650s the New England fishing industry supplied only a small part of the demand for fish in the wine regions and the West Indies, for the English merchants of Plymouth, Dartmouth, Exeter, Southampton, Bristol, Barnstaple, Weymouth, and Poole still dominated British fishing in North America. However, New Englanders went to Newfoundland to purchase the excess of the catch and made large profits by selling it in the wine regions. And Newfoundland itself was a market not only for wine, tobacco, sugar, molasses, and other provisions but also for New England timber and timber products.

Like Barbados, Newfoundland had been heavily forested when it was discovered in the late fifteenth century. As late as 1610, some Englishmen, hoping to develop a lumber industry there, spent the winter cutting timber and making charcoal from birch, pine, and spruce for the English market. A few fishermen also tried to profit during the off-season from "a shipps lading of masts, sparres, and deal boards." And during the second decade of the seventeenth century a sawmill was set up. By the 1620s, however, 20,000 fishermen were visiting Newfoundland every season. Arriving each year about a month before the beginning of the fishing season, they cut shoreline timber for casks, oil vats, firewood, boats, flakes, shanties, cookrooms, and storage sheds. They also cut thousands of trees merely to obtain bark for roofing and for covering fishing stages. Labor and timber would have been saved had they built permanent structures, but this was impossible in a restless, unorganized, and ungovernable society. The boards used by one group of fishermen for flakes, stages, and storage sheds during one season were often taken by those who arrived early the following season for their own buildings or even for firewood. Even when stages and buildings escaped such damage, there was a great danger that they would be destroyed by accidental fires. Forest fires were frequent, and drunken fishermen often burned down their own or their neighbors' shacks.[21]

Inevitably coastal timber on Newfoundland was used up and New England timber was in demand. In 1645 a group of Boston and Charlestown merchants sent a fishing expedition to Bay Bulls, and it is probable that other New England fishing vessels and trading ships had begun to visit Newfoundland in this period. By the early 1650s commercial relations between the two regions were well established, and the fishermen of Newfoundland were beginning to rely on New England for at least part of their timber.[22]

England

Although the demand for New England oak staves, barrel hoops, cedar shingles, and white pine boards continually increased in the wine regions, the West Indies, and Newfoundland, neither New England nor any other region of America ever supplied a major portion of the timber used in England. Some New England timber was sent to London by the Pilgrims in the 1620s, and some white pine boards were probably shipped from New Hampshire during the early 1630s. In 1641 Edward Hopkins, the governor of Connecticut, organized the preparation of 70,000 staves that he hoped to exchange in London for desperately needed manufactures. But in spite of early attempts to develop trade with England in staves, shingles, boards, and perhaps building timbers, regular trade in these items was not possible. The cost of shipping bulky timber products almost 3,000 miles across the Atlantic put American timber merchants at too great a disadvantage in the English market. Although the timber purchased by Englishmen in the Baltic was relatively expensive, the freight rate of from nine to twelve shillings per ship-ton between England and the Baltic was much lower than the Atlantic rate of from eight to ten pounds per ship-ton.[23]

Like oak staves and deal boards, timber and timber products for the British navy could be bought at much lower prices in northern Europe than in North America. But the possibility that an enemy nation could blockade the Sound and cut off the timber supply made it desirable to procure at least some of these naval stores in New England. The white pines of New England cost a good deal more than the Riga firs, and they were softer and less durable. But a large supply was always available, and because of their size—sometimes over three feet in diameter—a single tree could serve as a mainmast in the largest ships of the line, whereas the Riga firs had to be spliced.[24]

The first supply of New England masts reached England in 1634, and by 1641 it was claimed that the new settlement could supply the kingdom with "cordage, cables, sailes, canvas, pitch, tar, masts for the tallest ships on the coasts, and timber fit for navigation which is almost altogether decayed in this kingdome."[25]

Apparently New Englanders began to send shipments of naval stores to England with some regularity after 1645. In October of that year, Adam Winthrop and a Boston shipwright assured four English merchants that they would prepare a hundred white pine or spruce masts, each between sixteen and thirty-six inches in diameter, at Kennebunk, Maine. The same men sent cargoes of masts and several hundred thousand tree nails to England in 1647 and 1648. Masts were sent again in 1649 and 1651, and in 1653 two mast ships set out from New England. From this time on, New Englanders shipped masts to England almost every year. In some years the New England merchants also sent huge oak ship timbers and tar to the royal dockyards, but because of the prejudice of the English shipwrights against American naval stores, it was many years before these products were in great demand.[26]

Trading Patterns

Because of the markets for timber, fish, and provisions that had been established in Madeira, the Canaries, the Azores, southern Europe, the West Indies, Newfoundland, and England, the New England economy emerged from the depression of 1640 viable and strong. And during the next quarter of a century continued demand for timber, fish, and provisions throughout the Western world enabled New Englanders to increase their exploitation of the forest and the sea to obtain essential manufactured goods that they were unable to produce at home.

The ports of the wine islands and southern Europe that received the largest part of the Boston export tonnage in the 1640s probably continued to do so during the 1650s, 1660s, and perhaps even the 1670s. The Navigation Act of 1660 seemed initially to threaten this trade, although it was intended to apply only to tobacco and other enumerated West Indian products, whose shipment from the colonies to foreign ports was forbidden. The careless wording of the act led English customs officials to attempt to apply it to all commodities laden in the colonies, including New England fish and timber. But in 1661 the New England merchants were granted permission to ship their products directly to the Continent and, as well, to enter English ports with wine and other goods that they received in return.[27]

Of the total tonnage departing from Boston for overseas ports in a six-month period in 1661 and 1662, 790 tons (40 per cent) went to the wine regions, 580 tons (29.5 per cent) to the West Indies, 360 tons (18 per cent) to London, 176 tons (9 per cent) to ports in continental North America, and 60 tons (3 per cent) were sent to Newfoundland (see table 1). In terms of shipping tonnage, England was a more important market for New England exports than these figures suggest; for masts, the bulkiest and in some ways the most valuable New England exports, were not shipped from Boston but direct from the Piscataqua region, and their departure was not officially recorded. A large mast required from 16 to 30 tons of shipping, a medium-sized mast 12 tons, and a small mast 5 tons. Mast ships were specially built and were much larger than the vessels that transported other New England products. Most of them were rated at 400 tons or more, and two or three of these giant ships departing from the Piscataqua region for the royal dockyards each year represented a significant part of the total New England export tonnage in the 1660s. White pine and spruce masts were bulky and difficult to transport and thus extremely expensive. In England the largest white pine mast, a yard in diameter, was worth almost £150, and even a relatively small mast was worth £50. Three mast ships carrying approximately ninety masts, with an average value of £75, had a combined value of over £6,000.[28]

In the 1660s there was obviously little demand for New England trading goods in Newfoundland or the ports on the continent of North America. In Newfoundland there were few permanent settlers, the fishermen still brought their own provisions, timber supplies were not yet depleted, and the rum trade was just beginning. The permanent population in the North American colonies south of New England was still so small that there could not have been much demand for goods there. The West Indies received less than a third of the New England export tonnage, for the only significant trade was with Barbados. Jamaica, captured from Spain in 1655, was the largest British possession in the Caribbean, but most of its 4,400 square miles was undeveloped. In the British Leeward Islands, colonists on Antigua and Montserrat were beginning to grow sugar, but they lacked capital and credit, and land clearing was difficult. Furthermore, when the French invaded Antigua and Montserrat during the Anglo-French War (1666–67), they burned the sugarworks and made off with a thousand slaves. Nevis, the most highly developed of the Leeward Islands and the chief commercial and shipping center for both Montserrat and Antigua, was dotted with sugar plantations, but agriculture was diversified there. Saint Kitts was devastated during the Anglo-French War, and its economy was slow to recover.[29]

Thus the wine regions must still have been the primary market for New England exports in the 1660s, and even in the 1670s the most significant part of the New England shipping tonnage may have been absorbed by the Canaries, the Azores, Madeira, and southern Europe. At least 170 tons of shipping entered Boston from France and over 200 tons from the Canaries between 10 and 17 June 1676. During the previous month, a Boston vessel of 150 tons had arrived from the Canaries with 70 pipes of wine, and "about the same time, another Bostoner [of] 160 tuns" arrived from Málaga with wines, oil, and other goods. In April 1679 several New England vessels that had waited at Cádiz for cargo had been "forced to goe home halfe freighted" because of the danger of the Turks.[30]

The demand for New England products in the Caribbean was continually growing, however, because sugar production in the West Indies was expanding rapidly. Between 1669 and 1700 the yearly sugar exports to England from the British West Indies increased from 11,700 to 24,000 tons. By 1673 the population of Barbados had reached 50,000 or 60,000, including from 30,000 to 40,000 African slaves. A decade later there were over 70,000 persons in Barbados, more than 46,000 of them slaves. By 1678 the Leeward Islands had over 10,000 white inhabitants and over 8,000 slaves. Although agriculture on Nevis was still diversified, the planters there were shipping 1,500 tons of sugar annually to England by the late 1670s, and sugar production on the other Leeward Islands was also increasing. After 1674 the number of sugar plantations on Antigua grew rapidly. By 1672 the population of Jamaica had reached 17,000 persons, about half of whom were slaves. The seventy sugar works on Jamaica producing over a million pounds of sugar annually were clear evidence of the great potential of that island.[31]

The rapid development of Jamaica and the British Leeward Islands, as well as the increased sugar production of Barbados, led to a significant shift in the direction of New England trade. At some point between 1660 and 1685, New England merchants began to send a greater proportion of their total shipping tonnage to the West Indies than to the wine regions. Between 1686 and 1688, from 57 to 66 per cent of the total export tonnage of the port of Boston went to the West Indies. By then trade in this area was no longer exclusively with Barbados, for between 18 and 34 per cent of the export tonnage of Boston was sent to the other West Indian islands. In contrast, only from 9 to 16 per cent of this tonnage was sent to the wine regions, and by the early eighteenth century, southern Europe and the wine islands accounted for an even smaller part of the total New England export tonnage. (See tables 2–6.)[32]

Even in the 1680s the number of vessels departing from Boston for Great Britain was small. The average tonnage of the vessels in this trade, however, was still much larger than that of vessels trading with other regions. Moreover, the departure of the mast ships was not recorded, although ten of these vessels, each rated at 400 tons, left Piscataqua for England almost every year. If these ships are included, Great Britain probably received about a fifth of the New England export shipping tonnage.[33]

Trade between Boston and Newfoundland remained quite small, and it is unlikely that many vessels from other New England ports visited the tiny harbors of Newfoundland. In 1676 only eight vessels from all New England regions brought cargo to the island. The slow growth of this trade between Boston and Newfoundland was a result of a decline in the Newfoundland fishery. In 1679 there were only 1,700 permanent settlers on the island, and this number had risen only to 2,159 by 1701. And in some years few fishermen visited the island. Only 150 fishing vessels carrying about 7,000 men arrived in 1675, and in other years as few as 30 vessels might arrive.[34]

In contrast to the Newfoundland trade, trade between Boston and the English colonies in North America grew very rapidly between the 1660s and the 1680s. The great increase was a result of new settlement in Pennsylvania and the Carolinas and a large natural increase in population. By the 1680s New Englanders were not only carrying tobacco from Virginia and Maryland but perhaps also monopolizing the tobacco trade of North Carolina. The coastal trade was much larger than the figures in tables 2–6 indicate, for few trading vessels under ten tons were recorded by the customs agents. Indeed, in 1676 several hundred vessels rated from six to ten tons carried goods between Boston and surrounding towns, and many of these probably visited the colonies to the south. In any case, the tonnage of the coastal trade certainly exceeded that departing for the wine regions by the 1680s.[35]

Timber always required a larger amount of shipping tonnage than any other New England product. Even the 60,000 quintals (about 3,000 tons) of fish exported from New England in 1675 took up only from 20 to 25 per cent of the total tonnage. The demand for timber, however, did not develop at the same rate in every region where New England merchants traded. Just as there was a shift in the distribution of the total New England shipping tonnage among certain ports in the wine regions and in the West Indies, there was a shift in the relative importance of fish, timber, and provisions in these ports in terms of tonnage and value. Soon after 1650 the value of premium grade fish shipped to Continental ports almost certainly exceeded that of provisions or white oak staves. And despite the steady increase in catches by New England fishermen, prices for fish in such ports as Cádiz, Nantes, and especially Bilbao remained steady throughout the second half of the seventeenth century. In 1676 it was reported that "the great quantities of cod, mackrel, and herring taken upon this [New England] coast are exported to Spain, France, and other Parts and bring in above £50,000 yearly to the Markets." And in the 1680s the cargoes of all vessels departing from Boston for Bilbao, Cádiz, Alicante, and Portugal consisted of fish.[36]

New Englanders shipped quantities of fish to the Canaries, Madeira, and the Azores, but in these islands the market for New England timber continued to be significant. Between 18 May and 29 September 1686, two vessels departed from Boston for Madeira, one carrying only timber and the other timber and train oil. Between 25 March and 29 September 1687, seven vessels departed for Madeira, of which one, rated at 40 tons, carried only timber, and the others mixed cargoes of timber, fish, and oil. Of the four vessels that departed for Madeira in the same period in 1688, three carried timber and provisions, and the fourth was fully laden with 18,000 white oak pipe staves. The vessels departing for the Azores and the Canaries in the late 1680s carried mixed cargoes of staves and provisions.[37]

Although New England timber and other products were welcome in the wine ports, the wine industry was not completely dependent on them. But by the 1670s the survival, let alone development, of the British West Indian sugar islands depended upon trade with New England, and in terms of shipping tonnage, timber was the most important cargo. Without a trade "for Boards, timber, pipestaves, horses and fish," a group of Barbadian planters explained to Parliament in 1673, "they could not maintain their buildings, nor send home their Sugars, nor make above half that quantity with out a supply of those things from New England."[38]

The increased demand for New England timber in the West Indies was directly related to the development of Jamaica and the Leeward Islands, increased sugar production on Barbados, the increased cost of timber procurement and processing in the Caribbean, and the depletion of timber on Tobago, Saint Lucia, Saint Vincent and Dominica. West Indian planters, who had needed barrel staves, heads, and hoops for the equivalent of 20,000 thousand-pound hogsheads for their sugar and molasses in 1655, needed materials for the equivalent of 28,000 in 1669 and 66,000 in 1700.

As rum production increased, the larger planters also needed white oak staves for wet casks. The planters believed that shaken casks of red or white oak prepared by New England coopers were cheaper than those that West Indian laborers could provide. Even in Jamaica, where planters still had access to standing timber, the demand for sugar hogsheads rose from 1,000 in 1671 to 10,000 in 1684, and most of the casks were bought from New England traders after 1680. Increased production of indigo and cacao in the British West Indies created additional demand for cask materials, and the planters on all the English islands needed more and more cedar shingles, white pine boards, and heavy oak building timbers for new mills, distilleries, buildings, and machinery and for the repair of the older sugar manufacturing plants. Of the fifty-four vessels that departed from Boston for the West Indies between 18 May and 29 September 1686, all but one carried some timber, and seven were completely laden with it. Between 25 March and 29 September 1687, sixty-six of eighty vessels bound for the same region carried timber, and nine others were fully laden with timber products. During the same period in the following year, all but one of the seventy-two vessels that departed for the West Indies had timber on board.[39]

Fish certainly was not as important as timber in the West Indies trade in terms of shipping tonnage. For between 18 May and 29 September 1686 only nine of fifty-four recorded departures from Boston had fish as part of their cargoes; however, thirty-seven of the vessels carried provisions. Between 25 March and 29 September 1687, fish was part of the cargo of thirty-four out of eighty vessels, and provisions were carried on fifty-one. Of the seventy-two recorded shipments to the West Indies during the same period of 1688, all but one consisted of lumber and provisions, and fish was mentioned only once.[40]

Other products shipped from New England to the West Indies in the 1680s were horses, train oil, tar, tobacco, wine, beer, and English manufactures. Because of infertile soil, crop diseases, and early frosts, grain shipments were relatively small by the late seventeenth century, for there was little surplus wheat to export, except in the Connecticut valley, and this region could not supply enough to satisfy the growing population of the sugar islands. By the 1680s the rich agricultural regions of Virginia and the newly opened lands in South Carolina and the Middle Colonies supplied Barbados, Jamaica, and the Leeward

Islands with most of the grain they needed, and by the 1690s Virginia was supplying New England itself with corn, wheat, rye, barley, oats, and peas.[41]

The shipment of fish, provisions, tobacco, wine, and almost every other product in the trade between Boston and the Caribbean increased the use of the New England forest, for in the seventeenth century, trade depended on wooden containers and ships, just as it now depends on the products of mines and mills. Moreover, many of the wooden casks that were rolled into the holds of wooden ships at the Boston wharves contained forest-fed pork and beef. Many of the horses sent to turn West Indian sugar machinery were raised in the woodlands. By the 1680s trade in horses was quite large, and to ship them required a good deal of valuable space. At least 300 horses were shipped from the port of Boston every year, and their value was probably from £4,000 to £5,000.[42]

Timber and timber products were not important in the trade with Newfoundland, for even in the 1670s and 1680s, settlers and transient fishermen there were still able to find enough timber for firewood, casks, dunnage, and at least some parts of their buildings. Most fishermen and settlers, however, were still destroying the sections of seaside forest that remained. Indeed, it has been estimated that the fishermen alone destroyed as many as 50,000 large trees and 250,000 young trees every year. With such wanton destruction of the forests, timber was growing scarce in certain coastal regions of Newfoundland. At Saint John's, for instance, fishermen either had to go several miles to collect their timber or purchase New England staves and white pine boards at the waterside.[43]

Of twelve vessels departing from Boston for Newfoundland in 1686 and 1687, half carried some timber, and one vessel was fully laden with it. Although tar was in great demand in the Newfoundland seaside communities, even in the 1680s the amount of tar brought into the island by Massachusetts vessels was still small. To the dismay of the English authorities, the rum trade was so vigorous that the fishermen were becoming more debauched than ever. But Boston merchants shipped sugar, molasses, tobacco, and other provisions to Newfoundland, and more of their ships carried timber and timber products than kill-devil, wine, or beer.[44]

Late in the seventeenth century there was a market for New

England white pine boards, construction timbers, and oak staves even in such heavily wooded regions as Bermuda and the colonies of continental North America. Between 25 March and 29 September 1687, half the vessels departing from Boston for such ports carried timber or timber products as part of their cargoes. At least eight of fifteen vessels departing for Virginia carried timber; others carried wooden pails or tar. One craft, rated at only eight tons, carried 7,000 feet of white pine boards to Maryland, and another, rated at eighteen tons, carried 2,500 feet of boards, 2,000 pipe staves, and wine, brandy, flour, and beer to Bermuda.[45]

Ironically, there was still no regular trade in staves, boards, and shingles with England, where hope for a steady flow of American timber had all but vanished. Of fourteen recorded cargoes of ships departing Boston for London in 1686 and 1687, about half contained no timber at all, and each of the others had only a few thousand staves. However, some of the most valuable cargoes sent by New Englanders to Great Britain consisted of logwood and brazilwood, the dyewoods of the West Indies and Central America. Hundreds of tons of dyewood were loaded aboard London-bound vessels at Boston, together with sugar, molasses, tobacco, cacao, oiled horn, whalebone, lime juice, fish, cranberries, hops, and deer, moose, and beaver skins. But sometimes the ships departing for London could not be filled. One vessel, rated at ninety tons, departed in June 1687 carrying a mixed cargo that had been collected from many lands, yet "12 great guns" had to be stowed aboard for ballast. (For a discussion of the size of trading vessels built in New England after 1640, see Appendix A, "Shipping Tonnage and the Timber Trade.")[46]

In the seventeenth century, trading patterns in the Atlantic changed remarkably from decade to decade, and a change in one trading center greatly affected the economic development of the others. The emergence of sugar plantations in Brazil and the West Indies forced the settlers in the Canaries and Madeira to concentrate more and more on viticulture and wine making. The enormous sugar production of the West Indian islands eventually ruined much of the Brazilian sugar trade and seriously affected the economy of Portugal. But West Indian sugar production bolstered the economy of New England and was directly related to the exploitation of the great timber regions of New Hampshire and Maine. The lack of food supplies in Madeira stimulated the development of great grain fields in the Azores. The inability of the Mediterranean nations to produce sufficient food supplies led to the expansion of the Newfoundland fishery. And the expansion of the population in New England and in the West Indies stimulated the development of the rich, arable lands on the continental plantations south of Connecticut. Thus a series of apparently unrelated developments in many regions of the Western world greatly affected the lives of men on many islands and three continents and made them part of an interrelated economy.

In terms of shipping tonnage, timber was the most important element that New England contributed to this commercial network, for probably well over half the annual export tonnage from that region was timber and timber products. Yet few Englishmen of that age recognized, and still fewer historians of our own day have fully understood, the nature or the consequences of New England trade in forest products.

One consequence of this trade in timber was that, although a vessel had to be filled to capacity during every stage of a voyage to earn maximum profits, it was difficult for New England timber vessels to return fully loaded. Bulky cargoes of timber could not be exchanged for similar quantities of wine, fruit, or sugar, for relatively small quantities of the latter products had the same value as a whole shipload of timber. Moreover, since barter was not the only means of exchange, cargoes were sometimes exchanged for coins or bills of exchange, and many New England vessels were forced to return home empty or nearly so. From September 1677 until the following September, only 362 tons of West Indian products were shipped from Barbados, Jamaica, Nevis, and Saint Kitts to New England, and in the 1680s many ships returned home to Boston from the West Indies with only small amounts of molasses, sugar, or cotton. To find bulky return cargoes, New England timber carriers went to such places as Tortuga, where they might pick up a cargo of salt, or the Gulf of Campeche, where they could pick up logwood. The latter was the most important return cargo and became a major item of export from Boston in the last quarter of the seventeenth century. By the 1670s New Englanders gathered over 1,000 tons of logwood in the Gulf of Campeche each year, and in 1676 at least seventeen New England vessels made their way to Campeche.[47]

But even the large quantities of salt and logwood that were returned to New England did not match the enormous tonnage of outgoing timber. Consequently, masters of New England vessels trading with the Mediterranean ports took on fruit, wine, cork, and salt not only for English ports but for Dutch, German, and other northern European trading centers. And there must have been a very strong temptation to return to New England with manufactured goods from Continental ports (in violation of the Navigation Act of 1663) or to take on sugar in the West Indies and sail with it to the Continent (in violation of the Navigation Act of 1660). Some New England vessels also carried cargoes of tobacco from Virginia and Maryland to France, Portugal, and Spain. However, such illegal trade was probably never extensive, and most violations of the Navigation Acts were minor or merely technical. The nations of continental Europe could not supply New England with manufactures as well as England could, British West Indian sugar was excluded from Spain and Portugal, and French duties on foreign sugar were extremely high. Although New England ships picked up wines in France and Spain in violation of the Navigation Act of 1663, most wines stowed aboard New England vessels were obtained in the wine islands in conformity with the law.[48]

Nevertheless, merchants in England and Virginia induced the government to tighten trade restrictions, and the Navigation Act of 1673 laid export duties on sugar, tobacco, cotton, indigo, dyewood, and cacao beans transported from one British colony to another. During the 1670s over 200 English vessels with a combined rating of 20,000 tons entered West Indian ports each year, and the majority of them departed for England fully laden with sugar and other tropical products. If the owners of these carriers had taken out a bond in England or Wales, they were not required to pay duties imposed by Parliament until they reached England —and they received a rebate if they reshipped enumerated goods to the Continent. On the other hand, the owners of New England timber carriers returning home nearly empty with only a few enumerated products were required by the Navigation Act of 1673 to pay a duty in the West Indies—and the New England merchants claimed that when they transshipped these products to England, a second duty was imposed. Moreover, English merchants whose sugar carriers arrived partly empty in the West Indies continually pressed the government to forbid the sale of

New England provisions in the sugar islands on the grounds that beef, pork, and corn from Rhode Island, New Hampshire, and Connecticut competed with English and Irish foodstuffs. Many English merchants would have been happy to limit New England trade in the West Indies to timber.[49]

Far from the seat of power and lacking easily transportable trading goods, the merchants of Boston, Salem, and Ipswich may have had to compete unequally with their British counterparts. But if these New England merchants were at a disadvantage in the markets of the British West Indies, their entry into these markets increased their political power in their newly adopted land and gave them great influence in the shaping of its physical boundaries.

Chapter 6

Settlements North of the Merrimack

Timber Imperialism, 1632-1692

Its coastal areas settled and with limited access to the interior, southern New England could not have met the growing demand for forest products in the North Atlantic, Caribbean, and Mediterranean markets. But to the north and northeast of Cape Ann, there was a vast forest region in which the tallest white pines mingled with the yellow birch, beech, sugar maple, and red and white oak. Both the climate and the geography of this region lent themselves to lumbering: an abundance of snow made it possible for animals to draw bulky logs across rugged terrain, and the region was drained by a system of rivers and streams that made millions of acres of timber accessible and provided power for cumbersome wooden sawmills. Thus it is not surprising that some Englishmen attempted to exploit the timber north of Cape Ann soon after their arrival in the sixteenth century. The early fishermen of Maine used large amounts of timber in processing their catch, and, even before the Great Migration ended, the settlers in northern New England had built a number of sawmills and had shipped masts, white oak pipe staves, and perhaps even white pine boards to distant ports. When the merchants of Massachusetts Bay increased their trade with the wine islands, southern Europe, and the West Indies during the early 1640s, a great part of the timber they exported was drawn from the region north of Cape Ann. As a result, the settlers of this region, most of whom were not Puritans, found themselves drawn into an economy controlled by Massachusetts Bay.[1]

Even before 1640, the Puritans had wished to control the region north of the Merrimack, fearing that the godlessness of the fishermen on the coast might spread to their society and destroy the great religious experiment. They also feared that the growth of the Mason, Gorges, and Hilton plantations in the north would greatly increase the Anglican population, threaten the autonomy of the Bay Colony, and lead to the revocation of the Massachusetts Charter.

In 1632 fear of an Anglican conspiracy at Dover (New Hampshire) caused the leaders of the Bay Colony to have their Puritan friends in England purchase the Hilton plantation at Dover Point. But Governor Winthrop refused to claim political jurisdiction in New Hampshire or to try men for crimes committed there until 1638, when John Wheelwright and his followers founded Exeter. Fearing that protests by Anglicans and Wheelwright's Antinomian faction might lead to the loss of the Bay Colony Charter, the Massachusetts General Court began to press for full control of New Hampshire. Even before new surveys of the Merrimack River were completed, the court claimed that Exeter was inside the northern boundary of Massachusetts. The court also warned the settlers at Dover that they had no right to harbor religious exiles from the Bay Colony. To assert its authority over New Hampshire, the court laid out a township at Wenicunnett (Hampton), not far from Exeter.[2]

Religious differences and suspicion continued to sour relations between Massachusetts and the northern New England colonies during the following decades and even in the eighteenth century. But after the opening of overseas timber markets, the drive to control the northern timberland complicated the basic religious antagonism, creating a highly unstable society along the northern frontier.[3]

Expansion into New Hampshire, 1641-1644

During the early 1640s, when fish and timber products had become essential for the survival of the new Puritan society, the Bay Colony increased its efforts to bring the region north of the Merrimack within its jurisdiction. Now some of the Puritan political leaders, once opposed to commercial relations with the outside world, conceded that foreign trade was essential for survival. And the merchants of Boston, Charlestown, Salem, and Ipswich, whose political power was increasing, wanted a stable government and efficient courts north of the Merrimack. Without them, they could not make capital investments or collect debts.

There were controversies over land patents and land ownership in the north, for the opening of the timber trade suddenly made unimproved land extremely valuable. The original grants—those of Mason, Gorges, Rigby, and others—had been made without adequate surveys, so that often several settlers claimed legal title to the same piece of land or a single settler possessed several titles to the same tract. Hundreds of thousands of oak staves cut on timberland north of the Merrimack therefore became subjects of bitter legal battles, in the course of which timber shipments from the north would be held up for months while northern judges, whose authority was often dubious, attempted to determine the ownership of the land on which the timber had been cut. These conflicts convinced some influential men in the north that government by the Bay Colony would bring stability to the commercial life of the region. And those among them who were not Puritans hoped that the moderate and less fanatical Puritan merchants in the Bay Colony would guarantee freedom of worship and prevent harassment by the more zealous Puritan leaders and congregations.[4]

In 1641, after another bitter religious dispute in Dover had disrupted the government there, the Massachusetts General Court sent three commissioners—Timothy Dalton, Hugh Peter, and Simon Bradstreet—to settle the dispute and bring the town under the jurisdiction of Massachusetts. Although religious conformity was the prime motive for this action, two of the commissioners had a financial interest in the development of the northern frontier: Peter had encouraged wealthy Englishmen to invest in New England timberland; and Bradstreet, the husband of the poetess Anne Bradstreet and an influential merchant in northern Massachusetts, was involved in the timber trade. In any case, the commissioners succeeded both in cooling religious passions at Dover and in bringing that town and Strawberry Bank (Portsmouth) within the jurisdiction of the Bay Colony. Under the court system established by Massachusetts, six local magistrates were to have authority similar to that of the magistrates of the Salem and Ipswich quarter courts, and two deputies from the "whole river" were given seats in the Massachusetts General Court. In 1643 Exeter also became part of Massachusetts Bay.[5]

That a number of Puritans had moved north in the 1630s and early 1640s to engage in lumbering and cattle raising must have made it easier for the Massachusetts government to extend its authority into New Hampshire. And many of the common people in New Hampshire towns favored union because Massachusetts land policy discouraged speculation. A number of influential gentlemen of Strawberry Bank who had supported the claims of Mason and Gorges also approved of annexation by Massachusetts. These were the "lords and gentlemen" of Piscataqua, who, John Winthrop said, "finding no means to govern the people there, nor to restrain them from spoiling their timber etc., agreed to assign their interest to us." Most of these men were Anglicans and Royalists, but the Puritan commissioners allowed them to retain the extensive tracts of land that they had received (or confiscated) from Mason and Gorges as well as the timber rights that they had enjoyed.[6]

The economic motivation of the Massachusetts negotiators is evident in their waiving in New Hampshire of the strict religious test of Congregational Church membership for voters and officeholders that prevailed in Massachusetts: to insure the survival of the Puritan experiment, the General Court seems to have yielded at least one point of religious principle to economic expediency. The annexation of the land between the Merrimack and the Piscataqua did not immediately bring about stable government and efficient courts in that region. But the courts were soon in session, the trials—despite some complaints—seem to have been fair, and the economy seems to have operated much more smoothly under the new system.[7]

Expansion into Maine, 1645-1658

The demand for oak staves in the wine islands and southern Europe had led Massachusetts merchants to press for expansion into New Hampshire in the early 1640s. In the 1650s, demand for masts in England and Massachusetts as well as for white pine boards and staves in the Caribbean led the same merchants to press for expansion into Maine. Many influential settlers in Maine preferred to remain independent of the Bay Colony, but they were unable to resist the political and economic forces that made them dependent on their creditors in Boston and other Massachusetts ports.[8]

During the 1640s Massachusetts merchants began their incursion into Maine by buying land from the Indians, and as early as

1645 a group of Bay Colony merchants, including several members of the Winthrop family, had agreed to supply English merchants with masts of white pine or spruce from the forests near Kennebunk; thereafter masts—some probably cut north of the Piscataqua—were shipped to England on a fairly regular basis. In the early 1650s the effort to extend the jurisdiction of Massachusetts into Maine was encouraged by events not directly related to the economic changes of the period—the deaths in 1647, 1649, and 1650 of the three most influential English supporters of the Maine settlers who desired to remain independent of Massachusetts: Sir Ferdinando Gorges, Charles I, and Alexander Rigby, the holder of the Lygonia Patent between the Kennebunk River and Cape Elizabeth.[9]

An independent union of towns known as the "Province of Maine" was formed in July 1649, two years after Gorges's death, by his agent, Edward Godfrey, in the region between the Piscataqua and the Kennebunk; but it proved to be weak and ineffective. Although a number of influential men in Kittery and Agamenticus (York) favored the union, a majority in Wells refused to take part in it. And beyond the Kennebunk the settlers at Cape Porpoise (Kennebunkport), Saco (Biddeford), Black Point (Prouts Neck), Winter Harbor (Biddeford Pool), Richmond Island, around Casco Bay, and at fishing stations like Pemaquid, Sheepscot, Saint George, and Sagadahoc (near modern Phippsburg) remained independent of the union.[10]

In October 1651 the Massachusetts General Court took advantage of this situation to declare that "by the extent of the line of our patent, it doth appeare that the toune of Kittery, and many miles northward thereof, is comprehended within our graunt." This judgment, as well as the alleged desire of the majority of the inhabitants of Kittery for union with Massachusetts, "the comodiousness of the River Piscataque," and the fear that the whole region might be taken over by those "as are no friends to us," prompted the court to send three commissioners north bearing a "loving and friendly letter" empowering them to bring the inhabitants of Kittery under the Massachusetts government on terms of mutual consent. The three commissioners, leading politicians and merchants of Essex County in Massachusetts, were involved in exploiting furs, fish, and timber north of Cape Ann. William Hawthorne, who had recently been granted over 400 acres on the Piscataqua, was granted additional acreage at the time of his appointment; Daniel Dennison received 600 acres adjoining the western boundary of Rowley. The third commissioner was Simon Bradstreet, who, with a business associate, received 1,000 acres on the Maine side of the Newichawannock River (now the Salmon Falls River) "together with such privilege of timber as might be useful of the imployment of theire sawmill."[11]

The commission did not begin to function immediately, and during the delay some of the most influential supporters of an independent union of Maine towns attempted to oppose annexation by Massachusetts. On 5 December 1651, Edward Godfrey, Nicholas Shapleigh, and Richard Leader—all unsympathetic toward Massachusetts religious, economic, and political practices—drafted a petition to the Council of State asking Parliament to establish an independent colony in Maine. Leader, who at this time was building a huge mill at Assabumbedock Falls on the Little Newichawannock River (now the Great Works River), where Captain John Mason had built the first sawmill in New England, carried the petition to England. The former manager of the Saugus ironworks, he knew many influential men in England and hoped to return with a charter for Maine and a large amount of capital to develop its timber resources. But Leader's influence on the Council of State was outweighed by that of the Massachusetts agent, Edward Winslow, who convinced the Puritan faction that an independent colony in northern New England was a Royalist scheme. And although Leader had previously won some financial backing for his Maine ventures, he apparently obtained no additional capital.[12]

In the summer of 1652, the Massachusetts General Court, having declared that the northern boundary of the Bay Colony was three miles north of "the northermost part of the river Merimacke" and ran from that point "upon a straight line east and west, to each sea," sent four surveyors to find the source of the river. Meanwhile, the three commissioners finally arrived in Kittery, where Edward Godfrey and other leaders refused to give up their control of the government until they received orders to do so from England.[13]

In October 1652 the Massachusetts General Court received the report of their surveyors, who had followed the Merrimack as far as the present site of Franklin, New Hampshire, and from that point had followed the Winnipesaukee River to Lake Winnipesaukee. At the point where the river entered the lake, they had taken measurements and set the northern boundary of Massachusetts three miles beyond, at 43°43'12" N. From this it was clear that Kittery, the Isles of Shoals, and Agamenticus (York) were within the borders of the Bay Colony, and the General Court again appointed commissioners to proclaim the "just right" of Massachusetts.[14]

Bradstreet, Hawthorne, and Dennison were reappointed, and three new members were added—Bryan Pendleton of Great Island (New Castle), New Hampshire; Thomas Wiggin of Dover, New Hampshire; Samuel Symonds of Ipswich, Massachusetts. The new members were Puritan merchants who had actively traded fur, fish, and timber in northern New England. Pendleton was a recent settler in New Hampshire, but he had lived in Watertown, Massachusetts, since the 1630s, and it is likely that he had been involved in commercial projects in northern New England for many years. Wiggin had long been a settler in the Piscataqua region and favored the expansion of Massachusetts; he was Bradstreet's partner in a sawmill on the Maine side of the Newichawannock. Symonds, too, was interested in lumbering, and the Massachusetts General Court had granted him 300 acres of timberland beyond the Merrimack on the condition that he set up a sawmill within seven years.[15]

In November 1652 the commission persuaded Nicholas Shapleigh and other inhabitants of Kittery to submit to the authority of Massachusetts; later, at Agamenticus (which was renamed York at this time), Edward Godfrey and other leaders also agreed to submit. In return, all inhabitants, whatever their religion, were to be freemen; they were to have representatives in the Massachusetts General Court; and local courts were to be established within a new county, York, to settle conflicting land patents. The commissioners even agreed that the militia would not be called for duty outside the county.[16]

The surveyors did not establish the northern border of Massachusetts on the coast until the fall of 1653, when they located 43°43'12" N on the shore of Casco Bay opposite the northernmost point of "the upper Clapboard Iland." But the General Court had already sent a commission in the summer of that year to Wells, Saco, and Cape Porpoise (Kennebunkport), which soon agreed to submit. The inhabitants, regardless of religion, were to become freemen, and land titles were confirmed. Although these settlements were not immediately represented in the General

Court, their inhabitants were allowed to vote for the executive officers of Massachusetts and were exempted from public rates.[17]

The residents of Kittery, York, Wells, Saco, and Cape Porpoise were now citizens of Massachusetts Bay. But the settlers between Saco and the northern end of "upper Clapboard Iland" remained outside the jurisdiction of the Bay Colony until 1658, when another commission persuaded the inhabitants of Spurwink, Black Point, Blue Point, Casco Bay, and the islands to join Massachusetts. Out of these tiny, scattered, wilderness settlements, two towns were formed—Scarborough and Falmouth (Portland). The commission granted these towns the same privileges they had promised at Wells, Saco, and Cape Porpoise and agreed that an instruction from England might nullify the union at any time and that the civil privileges granted would not be forfeited in the future because of "differences in matters of religion."[18]

There is little doubt that the presence of many recent immigrants from Massachusetts Bay in some of the settlements in Maine made it easier for the commission to annex the towns. But, as in New Hampshire a decade before, it seems that the liberal attitude of the merchant-commissioners induced many settlers who were not Puritans to accept Bay Colony jurisdiction. Apparently many colonists who were hostile to the Puritan way of life nevertheless favored union with Massachusetts as long as the leaders of the Bay Colony respected their religion (or lack of it) and allowed them some political power. Like those of New Hampshire, the settlers of Maine had never had fair and efficient courts. Proprietorship naturally encouraged appeals to England and tended to undermine local justice. That Massachusetts law denied the right of appeal to England but allowed appeal to higher courts within the colony must have encouraged many to accept union in the hope that they would at last be able to collect debts and resolve conflicting land patents.[19]

Undoubtedly, many in Maine also believed that the gathering of the scattered settlements under the jurisdiction of a new county would allow local officials to coordinate plans for roads, bridges, and other internal improvements. For at this time there were no highways connecting the settlements in Maine, and almost all communication was by water. And many of the common people also welcomed the democratic land policy of Massachusetts. For in spite of the growing value of farm and timberland in northern New England (especially along rivers and streams) and the steady increase in land speculation (particularly among Bay Colony merchants), a majority in the General Court still believed that within the boundaries of a town, at least, a man should own no more land than he himself could use.

Furthermore, the steady growth of the Maine settlements during the 1640s had brought on increasing danger of attack by the Indians and French, and the merchant-commissioners never failed to point out that Massachusetts had the financial resources and manpower to construct and maintain forts to defend the northern frontier. Indeed, the submission of the settlers of Wells, Cape Porpoise, and Saco was probably directly related to the great Indian scare that spread through northern New England in the spring of 1653. When thousands of Indians appeared in the Piscataqua region at spring planting time, many settlers were extremely frightened and "much distracted and taken off their employments at that busy time of year." The arrival of armed men from Ipswich and Rowley under the command of Daniel Dennison (a major general in the Massachusetts militia as well as a member of the Maine commissions) showed one great advantage of union.[20]

The Struggle for Power, 1658-1674

By 1658 the Massachusetts Bay Colony, founded as "a shelter and a hiding place" from God's vengeance on a wicked world, had absorbed all of the settlements on the coast and the rivers between Hampton Harbor in New Hampshire and Casco Bay in Maine. Within the borders of the colony there were now men of many different religious persuasions, some abhorrent to pious Puritans; nevertheless, they were freemen of God's city upon a hill, and many could vote and hold office.

Various motives induced the Massachusetts General Court to support the policy that led to this situation. Many legislators feared that independent colonies on their northern borders would threaten the Puritan way of life. They, and many ministers, were determined that neither the Anglicans nor any other non-Puritans should gain a foothold in northern New England. Other legislators greatly feared the introduction of despotic royal power into adjacent territory. And still others—perhaps only a minority within the General Court—believed that northeastward expansion was essential to obtain a continuous supply of exportable timber and timber products.

The motivation of those who executed the policy, however, was primarily economic. Almost all of the commissioners sent to Maine were merchants involved in the timber trade. They, and others like them, invested heavily in the region northeast of the Piscataqua in order to meet the rising demand of West Indian planters and English mast agents for timber products. Because of their exploitation, lumbering became the most important industry in almost all the settlements of northern New England during the second half of the seventeenth century.[21]

By 1675 there were at least fifty sawmills operating in northern Massachusetts and in New Hampshire and Maine, each able to produce between 500 and 1,000 feet of white pine boards a day. If their combined output (during a season of 180 days) was between 4,500,000 and 9,000,000 feet annually, the total value of the lumber would have been between £6,750 and £13,500 at the mill sites or £13,500 and £27,000 in the West Indies. Oak staves, however, were much more valuable than white pine boards, and hundreds of thousands of raw staves were cut for the coopers of many lands. The mast trade, too, was big business: during the early 1670s, Sir William Warren, the great English timber merchant, had over 250 New England masts worth well over £35,000 stored in his timberyards. And annually during this same period New Hampshire alone exported 20,000 "Tons" of deals and pipe staves, 10,000 quintals of fish, 10 shiploads of masts, and several thousand beaver and other skins, while importing 300 "Tonns" of wine and brandy, 200 "Tonns" of goods from the Leeward Islands, and 2,000 "Tonns" of salt.[22]

The rapid development of forest resources in northern New England during the third quarter of the seventeenth century did not ease the economic, social, and religious tensions that had plagued the settlements north of the Merrimack since the Great Migration. Indeed, the exploitation of the timberland of New Hampshire and Maine after 1660 apparently increased them. The power of the Massachusetts merchants was based primarily on their relations with agents in foreign ports and on their ability to control almost all imports and exports in New England. These merchants, who extracted large commissions for their services, not only monopolized the distribution of clothing and other essential English manufactures; they also controlled the sale and distribution of almost all northern timber. And, because they extended large amounts of credit to the settlers of the north, a debtor class soon emerged in New Hampshire and Maine.

An English visitor to New England during this period claimed that Massachusetts merchants sold English goods in Maine at excessive prices while complaining loudly of low profits. This visitor described some of the settlers on the northern frontier as "of a droanish disposition" and prone to "taking Tobacco, sleeping at noon, sitting long at meals some-times four times in a day, and now and then drinking a dram of the bottle extraordinarily." But it was clear to this Englishman that even "restless pains takers"—those who fenced their grounds, sowed their corn, provided for their cattle, and spent a good deal of time fishing, fowling, and cutting clapboards and pipe staves—were in constant danger of going into debt and losing their possessions. For Massachusetts merchants were always ready to seize debtors' cattle and plantations and even to turn men out of their homes.[23]

Many in the north resented the power of the Bay Colony merchants and the growing power of their agents, some of whom settled along the northern frontier. And because many of these agents were staunch Puritans, religious friction complicated the problems of economic exploitation and political rights. Anglicans, Antinomians, Anabaptists, and religious liberals, as well as many who ignored all formal religion, soon saw that the concessions granted on the religious test for voting and holding public office were not effective guarantees of religious or political freedom. The deputies from the north had a very small voice in the Massachusetts General Court, and they and their constituents had to obey many laws that they bitterly opposed.

By the end of the sixth decade, the missionary work of the Quakers brought on even greater religious strife. Quaker missionaries who had come to the Piscataqua region in September 1659 were arrested a few weeks later by the Massachusetts authorities and hanged on Boston Common. In 1662, however, Quakers were again active in New Hampshire and Maine, converting a number of people at Dover; at Kittery, they converted Major Nicholas Shapleigh, a merchant and the commander of the regional militia. When two women of the missionary group returned to Dover, Richard Waldron, the deputy magistrate, applied the Cart and Whip Act, stripping the two women to the waist and forcing them to trudge through deep snow tied to the tail of a cart. They were to receive ten lashes in each town through which they passed, but at Salisbury, Walter Barefoot, a Kittery resident who operated a sawmill at Exeter, set them free. Undaunted, they immediately returned to the Piscataqua; and after visiting Major Shapleigh, they were arrested again at Dover and subjected to barbarous treatment.[24]

Many settlers looked to England for a solution to these grave economic, political, and religious problems. While the Puritans prevailed in England, Massachusetts had de facto independence and could freely carry out an imperialistic policy. But after the Restoration, Charles II and his ministers received a series of petitions against the rulers of Massachusetts Bay. English businessmen who had invested in the Saugus ironworks and in timberland in northern New England claimed that Bay Colony courts had unjustly awarded their property to others. Samuel Maverick, representing a group of Anglican merchants who had settled in Boston during the 1650s, complained that a minority in Massachusetts conspired to deprive the majority of political rights. English Quakers sent urgent petitions to the king concerning the torture, imprisonment, and execution of their fellow-believers in Boston. The heirs of John Mason complained of being dispossessed of their property in New Hampshire. And Ferdinando Gorges the younger petitioned for the restoration of his grandfather's patent and, even before receiving an answer, appointed a temporary government in Maine.[25]

These petitions encouraged those in New Hampshire and Maine who had opposed the authority of the Bay Colony to denounce Massachusetts ministers, merchants, and their allies. Moreover, political and religious divisions widened within some Massachusetts towns and in the General Court, where many still believed that the Bay Colony government and the wilderness churches that it nurtured were the only sources of light and truth in a wicked and degenerate world. Such Puritans were firmly opposed to royal interference and willing to fight to retain their political and religious independence. On the other hand, moderate Puritans in Massachusetts realized that New England could not grow and flourish without maintaining close relations with the royal government and were willing to relax some religious strictures to this end.[26]

Many Bay Colony merchants, especially those concerned with developing New Hampshire and Maine timberland, advocated moderation. They believed that their access to the forest resources of the north and the trading system that they had established after the Great Migration depended upon royal favor. They appear to have looked upon the Navigation Act of 1660, whose careless wording led them to believe that it prohibited the direct shipment of timber and fish to the Continent, as the harbinger of a series of adverse economic regulations. That these merchants requested a specific exemption for direct trade in timber and fish, posting bonds at the port of Boston in conformity with the new law even though there were no royal collectors in the colony, clearly shows that they thought that their fortunes would be jeopardized by mercantilists in the new English government.[27]

Working with a surprising number of allies in the Massachusetts back country, merchants like Simon Bradstreet, Thomas Clarke, John Hull, Hezekiah Usher, and Joshua Scottow were able to present the moderate view to the king. And although such zealous merchants as William Hawthorne and Richard Waldron advocated vengeance against those who supported royal or proprietary interests in the north and complained that Massachusetts was imperialistic and failed to guarantee religious freedom, Bradstreet and his allies succeeded in limiting direct confrontation. And in 1665—while the royal commission that had been sent to New England by Charles II was creating an independent government in Maine and appointing a temporary governing body for that region—the moderates elected Thomas Clarke, perhaps the most important timber merchant in New England, Speaker of the Massachusetts House of Deputies. Subsequently, the moderate merchants and their allies defeated those in the House who sought to punish northerners for "tumultuous" or seditious practices.[28]

The same moderates also acted to reduce tensions after the king, having read his commissioners' highly critical report on Massachusetts, summoned to his court a number of Bay Colony leaders, who claimed that Massachusetts was totally independent of Parliament and the crown. In 1667 and 1668, hoping for a "continuance of our precious liberties without interruption," the

Massachusetts General Court, in which these moderates prevailed, sent to the royal dockyards a total of thirty masts. The masts cost several thousand pounds to prepare and ship and were especially welcome because they came while England was still at war with the French, although peace with the Dutch was at hand. This gift also made it clear to English merchants and royal officials that New Englanders could play an important part in the defense of the empire.[29]

But the royal government, wearied by war, plague, and the Great Fire of 1666, did not exert its authority over New England or seek to exploit the forest resources. And in 1668 the Massachusetts General Court, taking advantage of royal preoccupation, annexed Maine again. Six years later, claiming that the duke of York had abandoned his claims to the land between the Kennebec and the Saint Croix rivers, Massachusetts assumed jurisdiction over additional territory, the region between the Kennebec River and Penobscot Bay. A new county, Devonshire, was organized, and the fishermen who lived on the rim of the forest world became residents of God's commonwealth.[30]

War with the Indians, 1675-1678

Inclusion within the boundaries of Massachusetts failed to protect the settlers of the northern frontier. In the fall of 1675, the Abnaki Indians, realizing that the lumbermen were slowly destroying the forest in which their ancestors had lived for centuries, accepted French arms. While King Philip's War was raging in southern New England, they made surprise attacks on many communities in New Hampshire and Maine, forcing the English settlers to abandon Falmouth and burning twenty-seven houses at Scarborough. Saco was partly destroyed, and before the end of the year the Indians had attacked Wells and the settlements along the Piscataqua.[31]

Englishmen who had lived in the forest for decades and had cut and shipped thousands of tons of timber to foreign ports were now faced with "the skulking way of war" in the forest, in the course of which, even while under siege, they rarely saw their attackers, who went "Creeping deckt with Fearnes and boughs." The Indians, according to a colonial official, rarely stood and fought, but would "come upon some of our out plantationes and burne some of the remote houses and kill one or two and take there scalps and get away that our souldiers can rarely find any of them." In the more heavily populated regions one could see the "smoking funeral piles of wildred towns pitcht distant many miles." By the time a peace treaty was signed at Falmouth in April 1678, over 260 persons had been killed in Maine alone.[32]

The Indian attacks seriously affected the timber trade. Sawmills were particularly vulnerable, and a number were burned to the ground. Although many millwrights were forced to abandon lumbering operations, some mills, especially in the Piscataqua region, were able to continue production even in the midst of war. Sawmills at Quamphegan Falls (now Salmon River Falls) alone had already cut 266,281 feet of boards before the middle of August 1676.[33]

After the fighting was over, many millwrights returned and, with the financial backing of Boston merchants, erected sawmills at Falmouth and farther north at Wesgustogo (North Yarmouth). By 1685 the twenty-four mills at Kittery, York, Wells, Cape Porpoise, Saco, Black Point, and Casco Bay alone were capable of producing between 2 and 4 million feet of boards a year. Since boards sold at about thirty shillings a thousand feet at the mills, the value of the Maine output was probably somewhere between £3,000 and £6,000 a year or between £6,000 and £12,000 in the West Indies. The production of the New Hampshire mills in this period appears to have been substantial, too, for forty-seven trading vessels entered Portsmouth Harbor between 15 June 1680 and 12 April 1681.[34]

In 1677, in the midst of the fighting, Massachusetts had purchased the rights of the Gorges heirs and reconstituted Maine as a province of the Bay Colony, with a president and an upper house (standing council) appointed by the Massachusetts authorities and a lower house elected by the towns in Maine. Shortly after the signing of the peace treaty with the Indians in 1678, Scarborough and the settlements at Casco Bay and beyond were reestablished under this jurisdiction. And to protect Wesgustogo and the settlements farther south, as well as to encourage people to "replant themselves" in the more remote regions of Maine, the Massachusetts General Court built a fort at Falmouth Neck.[35]

The Struggle for Power, 1679-1692

With the recovery of the lumber industry in Maine and New Hampshire after the Indian warfare of 1675–78, the struggle for economic and political power entered a new phase. In 1676, while the fighting was still going on, the Lords of Trade and Plantations had sent Edward Randolph, a timber merchant, to New England to investigate violations of the Navigation Act of 1673. And from the replies of the Massachusetts General Court to Randolph's charge that New Englanders were heavily involved in illegal trade, the Lords of Trade discovered that many deputies to the court refused to acknowledge the authority of the king or Parliament. In spite of attempts by moderate Puritan merchants to avoid a direct confrontation with the British government, the Lords of Trade began proceedings that eventually led to the revocation of the Massachusetts Charter.[36]

In the meantime, the Lords of Trade recognized the land claim of Robert Mason (the heir of the original proprietor) in New Hampshire and ordered the Massachusetts General Court to withdraw its government from that region. In September 1679 a new royal government was created for New Hampshire, consisting of a president, council, and assembly. Many of the members of the council, however, were appointed at the recommendation of Sir William Warren, the most powerful timber merchant in England. Among them were John Cutts, William Vaughan, and Richard Waldron—men who had strong commercial ties with Massachusetts Bay, were large landowners, were deeply involved in the timber trade, and who refused to accept the claim that all unimproved land (that is, all New Hampshire timberland) was under the direct control of the proprietor. They had also refused to accept the authority of Edward Randolph and his deputy collector at Portsmouth, Walter Barefoot. It is probable that most of these men, despite the religious differences some of them had with the more zealous Congregationalists in Massachusetts Bay, would have preferred to remain under the government of Massachusetts.[37]

The trade of the province, the New Hampshire Council reported in 1682, was in masts, planks, boards, staves, and other lumber. Since ships rarely called at Portsmouth unless they intended to take on such products, a proprietor who controlled the timberland and the port of entry could control most of the economy. It was not to be expected that men who had developed a savage wilderness and made great sacrifices to defend it would welcome a powerful proprietor, and when Robert Mason came to New Hampshire in 1680 to supervise his holdings, he was abused and intimidated and barely escaped arrest. He soon returned to England in disgust, first mortgaging his lands to Edward Cranfield, who had been appointed royal governor of New Hampshire in March 1682.[38]

Cranfield gradually replaced Massachusetts-oriented councilors with Royalists and those loyal to the proprietor, and the governor and his assistants used packed juries to deprive timber merchants of their land. Then, claiming that the Massachusetts government protected and encouraged those who flouted the Navigation Acts and used the ports of Maine for the importation of "all foreign prohibited commodities," Cranfield and his council required small Massachusetts vessels entering New Hampshire waters to have a special license. This was apparently part of a carefully planned extortion scheme to force Massachusetts ships entering the Piscataqua for timber to pay tribute, for vessels coming from other plantations were to have "free liberty to load and carry away any boards, timber, other commodities, to any other his Majesty's plantations." The order was ignored by the majority of the settlers of New Hampshire; nevertheless, Cranfield set up a license office and proceeded to stop timber carriers entering the Piscataqua. Before long the Massachusetts General Court complained to Cranfield that his officers were forcing Maine timber traders to pay tribute on their way to market even when they sailed well outside New Hampshire waters. Finally, when he attempted to force the Anglican religion on all the inhabitants of New Hampshire and to collect taxes by force without the approval of an assembly, Cranfield stirred up so much opposition that in 1685 he was obliged to flee to the West Indies.[39]

While these controversies were raging in New Hampshire, Massachusetts residents learned that the Massachusetts Charter had been voided. Since this deprived the General Court of its authority, in October 1685 an interim government was created for Massachusetts, Maine, New Hampshire, and the Narragansett country. The new government, headed by Joseph Dudley, a moderate Puritan, included Robert Mason, Edward Randolph, and a number of merchants who had been deeply involved in exploiting timber in northern New England.[40]

These men, governing without an elected assembly, seem to have taken advantage of every opportunity to increase their economic power. Joseph Dudley, Samuel Shrimpton, Richard Wharton, and others came into control of a huge tract of Indian land in the Merrimack valley. Richard Wharton made large land purchases in Maine and presented numerous schemes for developing naval stores to the royal government. And Edward Randolph entered the mast trade; he had been appointed surveyor of woods and timber in Maine and had successfully cultivated Samuel Pepys and perhaps others on the Admiralty Board during frequent visits to England. The twenty-three white pine masts in Randolph's first shipment to the royal dockyards were so large that he had to send them in a 500-ton Dutch vessel, "there being never a ship long enough for Stowage of the said Masts to be had in England."[41]

The Massachusetts councilors continued to grant one another large tracts of northern New England timberland even after Sir Edmund Andros arrived in December 1686, instructed by the Lords of Trade to organize the colonies between Pennsylvania and Maine under one government that was to be called the Dominion of New England. Andros, who had been governor of New York, gradually replaced the original members of Dudley's council with New Yorkers. He also established an Anglican church in Boston, questioned the validity of land titles, and collected taxes without the consent of an elected assembly. In 1688, however, he was arrested and imprisoned by a Boston mob after it learned that James II had been deposed.[42]

In England, the Glorious Revolution insured the supremacy of Parliament. But the American phase of this revolution meant disaster once again for the lumbermen on the northern frontier. The garrisons of the forts that Andros had built at Wells, at Kennebunk, on the Saco, at Casco Bay, and on the Kennebec, as well as the forces that he had stationed on the upper Merrimack, withdrew when they heard of the uprising against the royal governor. And the Indians—urged on by the French, who were now prepared to make war against the British everywhere—again set the whole frontier aflame. All settlements in Maine except Kittery, York, and Wells, had to be abandoned, and the axes and the crude sawing machines in the vast wilderness beyond the Kennebunk were stilled once more. By September 1689, according to Randolph, the war damage in the north already amounted to £60,000: "The fisheries and lumber (our principal commodities) are quite destroyed, besides the loss of a fruitful country; all the masts for the Royal Navy are in the hands of the French or Indians."[43]

After Andros's overthrow, delegates from the four New Hampshire towns asked the royal authorities to reunite their communities with Massachusetts Bay. But some settlers in New Hampshire and Maine blamed the military disasters on Massachusetts, which, they believed, had exploited the northern New England forests but had failed to defend the frontier against the Indians. In Maine, for instance, it was claimed that most of the inhabitants were "either killed or carried away captives by the Indians or else fled to Boston for the preservation of their lives." The inhabitants of Great Island (New Castle), New Hampshire, complained to William III in May 1690, that they were in a "deplorable condition," threatened by French and Indians and abandoned by "the self-styled Government of Massachusetts."[44]

In 1692 William and Mary appointed Samuel Allen, a London merchant, royal governor of New Hampshire, and the colony was never again under the jurisdiction of Massachusetts. But neither the war nor the petitions of disgruntled settlers ended the influence of Massachusetts in Maine. A new royal charter issued in 1691 incorporated Maine (including the Sagadahoc territory) as well as Plymouth Colony within Massachusetts. The charter, however, provided for a governor appointed by the crown. And although the citizens of Massachusetts were granted liberty to cut trees on public land, "for the better provideing and furnishing of Masts for Our Royall Navy," trees twenty-four or more inches in diameter could no longer be cut without permission. This prohibition was soon superseded by more stringent mast laws enacted by Parliament, and the conflict between colonists and Englishmen over the northern timberland continued until Americans had won independence.[45]

Chapter 7

The Wilderness Transformed

By the late seventeenth century, much of New England was still covered by a vast forest, and thousands of settlers were clearing the woodlands, killing rattlesnakes, and building traps to catch the wolves that were destroying cattle. Even where the dangerous animals had been driven out, there were still "vast numbers of Frogs, toads, owls, batts, and other Vermin" at the edge of the uncleared land. But a short distance from the frontier —and especially in Boston—there were streets "full of Girles and Boys sporting up and downe, with a continued concourse of people," and crafts that depended on timber products were thriving.[1]

The shipbuilders of Boston were producing over half the shipping tonnage launched in New England, and shipbuilding had created a prosperous local trade in white and black oak, chestnut, larch, and red cedar framing timbers, in spruce and white pine trees for masts, and in pitch and tar. (Unlike their English counterparts, who were often forced to purchase timber abroad, Boston shipwrights could easily obtain even specially shaped trees for stems, sterns, and ribs.) Shipbuilding encouraged the development of a number of specialized woodworking industries as well—to build superstructures, install fittings, and decorate the vessels.[2]

Cooperage also thrived in Boston and other seacoast towns. Because vast amounts of staves were collected at Boston for shipment overseas, it was never a problem to procure supplies there, and coopers made thousands of casks each year for shipbuilders, brewers, distillers, fishermen, and merchants. They also made wooden pails, churns, tubs, and other utensils for foreign markets and for the settlers.[3]

As a meat-packing center and the major port of entry for hides from the West Indies, Boston was the tanning center of New

England. The bark of young white oak trees was preferred for tanning cowhides, and although large numbers of such oaks could not be found everywhere in New England, enough tanbark was available in the coastal regions, especially south of Boston. The hemlock was unknown in England, and its bark was probably not used by tanners in the seventeenth century, for hides were expensive and tanners could not afford to experiment.[4]

Other industries that depended on the forest were less successful in seventeenth-century New England. The need for a large capital investment, a cold climate, a shortage of skilled workers, and the high cost of shipping the product to England meant that only a small amount of potash could be produced, and that contained many impurities. (Purer grades were still imported from England even in the eighteenth century.) Because of the high cost of imported potash, window glass was not produced, although glass bottles were made at Salem for two or three decades after 1639, subsidized by the town of Salem and the Massachusetts General Court. Efforts to smelt copper near Danvers and to mine graphite and silver near Sturbridge also failed, and as late as 1680 "no great quantity" of iron was being produced in Massachusetts, for iron bars from Spain or iron goods from England were cheaper than those produced in New England.[5]

Agriculture was far more important to the economy of seventeenth-century New England than manufacturing, and by the end of the century, over half a million acres of woodland had been cleared for farming. In some regions sheep grazed on peaceful meadows reminiscent of the gentle English countryside, and English fruits, grains, and vegetables grew where dank, murky forests or swamps had been. In the open areas, such English plants as the daisy, buttercup, clover, chickory, hawkweed, and dandelion had replaced the native wild flowers, which, no longer protected by the trees, died from exposure to the sun.[6]

The forest was the greatest obstacle to the expansion of agriculture, but it was also the source of timbers for houses, outbuildings, and fences—and of firewood, the ashes of which served as a fertilizer. And in many settlements farmers supplemented their meager incomes by producing timbers, staves, hoops, and shingles for the artisans and merchants of the port towns. They also made feeding troughs from elm logs, and plows, harrows, shovels, flails, and pitchforks of ash and oak. Ink was made from oak galls, and dyes from many species, among them the sumac, hickory, butternut, hemlock, ash, sassafrass, dogwood, alder, birch, oak, and maple. Maple sugar and honey were also taken from the forest, for West Indian sugar was expensive. Wild cherries, wild plums, blueberries, and currants added variety to the settlers' diet. From the forest, too, came the bark and wood of the walnut, spruce, birch, and sassafras for making beer; nut oils for purgatives; the bark of the willow, oak, alder, and birch for suppuratives; cherry bark for cough remedies; and the sap of the white pine and hemlock for astringents.[7]

On the edge of the forest there was good hunting, and game was part of the New England diet. The passenger pigeons and blackbirds that often attacked the cornfields were killed and eaten in large numbers, and in Connecticut so many deer were killed by 1698 that the General Court limited the hunting season. Whereas in England most people were forbidden to hunt with a gun, marksmanship was essential for survival in the New England forest.[8]

Warfare with the Indians prevented the expansion of the frontier for almost a generation after 1675, but after 1713 the frontier was extended again, and in many regions land clearing, agriculture, and lumbering provided income for those who could not acquire land in developed communities. To meet an apparently unlimited demand for wood in New England port towns and abroad, almost all inhabited regions in New England were stripped of their original forest cover by the end of the eighteenth century. Because of clear-cutting—especially of the white cedar and the white pine—the composition of the original forest was irrevocably changed.[9]

Pollution of the environment and waste of natural resources are often considered consequences of the Judeo-Christian belief that man should have dominion over all nature. And indeed, before John Winthrop set out for the American colonies, he wrote: "The whole earth is the Lords garden, and he hath given it to the sonnes of men, and with a gen[eral] Commission: Gen: 1: 28: increace and multiplie, and replenish the earth and subdue it." But the seventeenth-century colonists' attitude toward nature was not as simple as that. Town records show that south of the Merrimack, where settlers were not wholly dependent on the sale of timber products they themselves could make, the cutting of timber trees was restricted by various laws. The system of land ownership in the early New England towns encouraged preservation of timber, for townships were granted to groups of men known as proprietors, who distributed land among themselves and other settlers but had the sole right to large tracts of common, or undivided, land held in reserve. Although the proprietors of a town allowed all of its inhabitants to take some building timber, fuel, and other essential wood from the common land, much of the valuable timber was reserved for the proprietors.[10]

The laws against cutting timber on common land were not enacted entirely to protect the rights of the proprietors, however. Many settlers had bitter memories of timber shortages in England and looked upon forest land not as ground to be leveled for planting at the first opportunity but as a natural resource to be preserved and cherished. They also thought that the wanton destruction of timberland was "displeasing to Almightie God, who abhorreth all willfull waste and spoile of his good Creatures."[11]

On the other hand, in a society in which the virtue of labor was extolled, material success was widely believed to be the just reward of pious diligence. And in a forested land during an Age of Wood, there were few ways to succeed without exploiting timber. By 1640, when the Great Migration ended, large quantities of staves, boards, and other timber products were being produced for Catholic wine makers and English slave masters. To meet the demands of these profitable markets, the Puritan merchants and their allies in the Massachusetts General Court became economic and political imperialists, expanding into New Hampshire and Maine and granting religious and political concessions to non-Puritan communities in exchange for control over the valuable northern timberland. Not only was conservation often subordinated to profit, but even land speculation, which all early political and religious leaders in New England had thought a great evil, eventually became a significant part of the economy north of the Merrimack.[12]

As the forest and the commerce that exploited it transformed the Puritans themselves and forced them to sacrifice some of their ideals, religious leaders deplored change that seemed to subvert the original purpose of the Puritan settlement. Roger Williams, among them, thought that society was being torn apart by "a depraved appetite after the great vanities, dreams and shadows of this vanishing life, great portions of land, land in this wilderness." Increase Mather complained that, whereas the first planters of Massachusetts Bay had been satisfied with twenty acres, later settlers "coveted after the earth, that many hundreds, nay thousands of Acres, have been engrossed by one man." Yet few seem to have been troubled by these contradictions in the Puritan ethic, and no one called for an end to trade, proposed a general conservation plan, or condemned the expansion of the frontier. And so devastation of the woodland continued unabated as the settlers, at first almost helpless before the forces of nature, learned by trial and error to survive in their forest world and to exploit its timber.[13]

Once the memory of the English timber crisis faded, and large sections of the common lands were divided among the proprietors, conservation legislation was passed less frequently, and existing laws were not obeyed. It was even assumed that the forests were "furnished by the author of nature with the means of perpetual self restoration." Late in the seventeenth century, and even in the eighteenth century, after hundreds of thousands of acres of timberland had been destroyed, New Englanders seem to have noticed only a few of the many significant changes that resulted from the clear-cutting of the forests: drier air, stronger winds, the disappearance of small streams, and a decline in the number of wolves, bears, and other wild animals. They considered most of these changes beneficial: "Clearing a new Country of Wood," one physician wrote, "conduces to its being more healthful: the Damp of Wood Lands produces intermitting, Pleuritick, Peripneumonick, Dysenterick, and Putrid Fevers."[14]

Devout Puritans may have regarded every leaf in the forest as evidence of God's being, but they did not worship the wilderness. Familiar with the ugly and vicious aspects of nature, they believed that God manipulated natural forces to reward and punish men in this life through special providences. The "dangers, and travails" that are over for the pilgrim in one of Anne Bradstreet's poems reflect her own experiences in the New England wilderness —and those of many others:

> The burning sun no more shall heat,
>   Nor stormy rains on him shall beat.
> The briars and thorns no more shall scratch,
>   Nor hungry wolves at him shall catch.
> He erring paths no more shall tread,
>   Nor wild fruits eat instead of bread.
> For waters cold he doth not long

For thirst no more shall parch his tongue.
No rugged stones his feet shall gall,
Nor stumps nor rocks cause him to fall.[15]

The society that grew up in the forests of New England remained wedded to many English customs and practices. But the colonists inevitably developed views, interests, and ways of living distinct from those who remained at home in the treeless English country-side. New Englanders were proud of their trade with the West Indies and its role in the development of the British Empire: "The other American Plantations cannot well subsist without New England," one New Englander wrote. But the value of the wooded land 3,000 miles away was not always appreciated in England, where the influence of the forest on the New England economy was never fully understood. Even the New England timber trade with the West Indies was undervalued or even thought to be a hindrance to English trade with the "Southern Plantations."[16]

In the slow break between New England and the mother country, the New Englanders' struggle against a hostile environment—and the inability of the English to understand this struggle—surely played a part. When Sir Edmund Andros was overthrown, many New Englanders already believed that the government should belong to those who "at vast charges of their own conquered a wilderness" and created a "pleasant land." The British imperial system was already too rigid for some pioneers. And less than a century later, when British power was resisted by arms, many in Massachusetts were mindful of the heritage left them by their ancestors, who had conquered a savage land with little help from England: "To our care and protection they consigned it, and the most sacred obligations are upon us to transmit the glorious purchase, unfettered by power, unclogged with shackles, to our innocent and beloved offspring."[17]

The struggle against great odds is a recurring theme in early American history. And New Englanders, searching for traditions in a country still very young, were not merely sermonizing when they remembered those who once stood helpless and dismayed before the forest world and yet dared to enter in, change old customs and ways, and transform the wilderness.

Appendixes

A. Shipping Tonnage
and the Timber Trade

Shipbuilding was a major part of the New England economy after 1640, when the Puritan leaders relied on the profits of
the timber trade to purchase essential manufactured goods in
England. The large timber requirements of a few distant wine
ports and the great amount of shipping space required for timber products led to the construction of many large vessels. At
least thirty vessels are known to have been built in New England
during the 1640s: fifteen at Boston, four at New Haven, two each
at Cambridge and Salem, one each at Plymouth Colony, Dorchester, Gloucester, and Portsmouth (Rhode Island), and three in
"Massachusetts Bay." The tonnage of these vessels ranged from
about 25 tons to 400 tons, with twelve ships rated at 200 tons or
more and nine ships rated at 100 tons or more.[1]

Although trade in fish, provisions, and horses created additional demands for vessels after 1650, the greatest part of the
tonnage of New England–built ships was used in the timber
trade. But as the number of vessels in New England greatly increased, their average tonnage greatly decreased. Of 27 vessels
that departed from the port of Boston between 16 August 1661
and 25 February 1662, 13 were registered there, and they averaged just over 61 tons. Between 25 March 1687 and 29 September
1687, the average size of 119 vessels with New England registry
departing from Boston averaged just over 43 tons, and during
the same period in 1688 the average tonnage for all departures
from Boston was around 47 tons. In 1698, 163 of 180 vessels
registered in Massachusetts (a total of 8,660 tons) were rated at
less than 100 tons, and the average size was a little over 49 tons.[2]

The dramatic increase in the number of trading vessels and the
significant reduction in their size can be attributed to increased
demand for timber, fish, and provisions on Barbados and other
sugar islands, the rise of North American coastal trade, and the

frequent loss of large vessels. In the West Indian trade, it was more efficient and profitable to use small vessels because of the seasonal nature of the trade, the inability of the small West Indian ports to absorb much cargo, and the lack of bulky return products. And as the continental colonies to the south of New England grew, merchants purchased small vessels to carry the products of these colonies and to distribute sugar, molasses, wine, and other goods from the West Indian trade. (The growth of the permanent population of Newfoundland similarly increased the demand for small trading craft.) Finally, ocean voyages—never very safe in the age of sailing ships—appear to have been more than usually perilous for large New England trading vessels during the 1640s. These vessels, often built hastily from green and unseasoned timber in a desperate attempt to save a damaged economy, performed poorly in storms and on unfamiliar or uncharted seas.[3]

Piracy was unchecked in this era, and a number of New England trading vessels were attacked or captured in the 1640s. After 1642, there was danger from warships of the Royal Navy, for the Puritans of Massachusetts Bay were known to be sympathetic to the Parliamentary party. After the leaders of the Bay Colony allowed the naval forces of Parliament to seize two royal vessels in Boston Harbor in 1644, the king's ships harassed a number of large Massachusetts-built vessels trading with the wine islands. Of the thirty known trading vessels built in New England in the 1640s, at least eight (27 per cent) were wrecked or captured by Royalists or pirates soon after they were launched, and nine (30 per cent) were seriously damaged or nearly lost at sea. The eight vessels lost or captured averaged over 127 tons; the nine vessels seriously damaged or nearly lost averaged over 151 tons. Of all the vessels lost, attacked by Royalists or pirates, or seriously damaged by the sea, 43 per cent were larger than 100 tons. Of the total of 4,645 tons recorded or estimated in this period, 1,020 tons (22 per cent) were lost, and 1,365 tons (over 29 per cent) were attacked or damaged.[4]

If the cost of building ships in early New England was about £4 a ton, £4,080 of a total investment of £18,580 was lost, and vessels worth £5,460 were attacked or damaged. At some point in the late 1640s or early 1650s, therefore, New England merchants must have decided not to build large ships, in spite of the availability of huge construction timbers and the continued growth of the trade in timber and other bulky cargoes. Accordingly, during the second half of the seventeenth century, most New England shipwrights specialized in trading vessels that rarely exceeded 100 tons. To build such vessels did not require large numbers of specially-trained craftsmen or large amounts of imported manufactures; thus shipyards could be built near the timber supplies in many of the bays, rivers, and small harbors along the New England coast. During the 1640s, twenty-three of the thirty vessels recorded had been launched near Boston or Salem, but by the 1670s there were shipyards at Portsmouth, Kittery, Dover, and Exeter in the Piscataqua region, at Salisbury, Amesbury, Newbury, Rowley, Ipswich, Gloucester, Beverly, Lynn, Milton, and Weymouth in Massachusetts, and at Hingham, Scituate, Taunton, Plymouth, Swansea, and Bristol in Plymouth Colony. New London, Connecticut, the best deep-water harbor between Newport and New York, had four shipwrights among its thirty permanent settlers in 1650, and a few years later sixteen of the sixty residents were employed in shipbuilding.[5]

However, the largest part of the registered tonnage launched in New England in the late seventeenth century was built at Boston, Charlestown, Salem, and Scituate. In 1698 these four towns accounted for 7,775 tons (almost 73 per cent) of the registered tonnage of New England. The craftsmen in the other shipbuilding towns built very few vessels or else specialized in vessels for the coastal and river trade or for the coastal fishery.[6]

New England shipwrights did not again construct many large vessels until early in the eighteenth century. And the launching of large vessels can be related, to a great extent, to the demands of English merchants—especially London merchants. Between 1698 and 1714, the merchants of the British Isles purchased 187 New England vessels totaling at least 20,601 tons and averaging over 110 tons. The tonnage of vessels built for the overseas trade of New England merchants during this period did not significantly increase.[7]

The shipbuilding patterns that emerged in New England after the trial-and-error period of the 1640s changed very little over seven decades. Even when demand for larger vessels in England increased after 1700, most New England shipwrights continued to specialize in relatively small vessels. The huge oaks and white pines that grew along New England streams were often sent to English shipwrights, who fashioned them into great English

merchant vessels and ships of the line; but New England shipwrights were unable to make full use of the great natural resources that surrounded them.

B. Tables

The figures on which table 1 is based are probably incomplete, and some may be inaccurate: it cannot be determined whether some ships departed without registering, whether the tonnage of all ships was recorded accurately, or whether all ships carried a full cargo. Although the recorder apparently intended to include the activity of all Massachusetts ports, the only Massachusetts-owned vessels listed are from Boston, which strongly suggests that other ports are not included. A total of twenty-seven departures from the port of Boston in six and one-half months in the early 1660s was somewhat below average, although the export tonnage from Boston apparently varied from year to year. In 1663, it was said, "there came into Boston harbor sixty ships and barks, besides ketches, etc.," and, during the following year, "near one hundred sail of ships . . . of our and strangers, and all laden hence" ("Diaries of John Hull," *AAS Trans.* 3 [1857]: 210, 214). The products carried by the vessels departing during the period covered by table 1 were recorded only for two vessels, one of which carried fish, the other fish and pipe staves.

Tables 2–6 are based on records in the Massachusetts Archives (7:16–64) and "Abstracts of English Shipping Records Relating to Massachusetts Ports. From Original Records in the Public Record Office, London. Compiled for the Essex Institute . . ." ("Mass. Shipping Abstracts"). These sources sometimes duplicate, supplement, or contradict each other, and when there are discrepancies, figures from the latter have been used. Vessels that departed in ballast are not recorded in the tables.

The records in the Massachusetts Archives cover many more months than those abstracted from the Public Record Office. The documents in the Public Record Office are for intermittent periods but are more complete; they also list the cargoes of all vessels, sometimes in great detail. Probably neither source includes information on shipping outside the port of Boston—indeed, during the seventeenth century almost all long-distance shipments from New England left from Boston. (Edward Randolph's report for 1687 was signed "Custom House Boston in New England," and his report in 1688 was called "An Account of Vessells entered out of Boston.")

Table 4 is included because in 1687, for the first time, the sources give some information for almost a full calendar year. However, the information in table 4 is incomplete, for Edward Randolph's report in the abstract from the Public Record Office, covering the period 25 March to 29 September 1687, contains entries for twenty vessels (746 tons) not recorded in the documents in the Massachusetts Archives. Since the Massachusetts Archives is the sole source for table 4 for the periods 3 January to 24 March 1687 and 30 September to 29 December 1687, there may be many departures and hundreds of tons missing from the table.

The average tonnage for the vessels in table 4 is almost 42 tons. If the twenty-four vessels without recorded tonnage were each assigned the average tonnage, the total tonnage for all vessels recorded in the table would be 10,852 tons. If there are as many vessels missing from the records in the Massachusetts Archives for the periods that cannot be checked against the shipping abstracts as in the periods that can, the number of departures listed in table 4 might be increased from 259 to about 279, and the tonnage from 10,852 to 11,690. These estimates, although admittedly conjectural, conform reasonably well with what is known about the activity of the port of Boston.

The three vessels that departed for Ireland, Surinam, and a fishing voyage (table 4) have no recorded tonnage, and therefore there are no categories for these voyages in table 6. The Bahamas and the "Spanish Wreck" (the site of sunken Spanish treasure off the Bahamas) are calculated in table 6 as part of the West Indies.

TABLE 1

Departures from the Port of Boston
16 August 1661–25 February 1662 (194 Days)

Destination	Departures	Tonnage
Barbados	7	540
London	4	360
Bilbao	4	320
Virginia	4	156
Málaga	1	150
Canaries	1	150
Azores	2	130
Newfoundland	1	60
Jamaica	1	40
Madeira	1	40
Maryland	1	20
Total	27	1,966

SOURCE: "The Names of such ships & masters that have Come in and gone out of our Harbours and Given bond for His Majesty's Customes," Massachusetts Archives, 60:33.

TABLE 2

Departures from the Port of Boston
18 May 1686–29 September 1686 (135 Days)

Destination	Departures	Tonnage
Barbados	32	1,760
London	6	780
Bilbao	9	465
Jamaica	7	280
Nevis	7	238
Newfoundland	7	220
Saint Kitts	4	155
Virginia	9	138
Madeira	2	115
Antigua	3	100
Portugal	1	40
Canaries	1	30
Montserrat	1	30
Total	89	4,351

SOURCE: "Mass. Shipping Abstracts," pt. 1, vol. 1, pp. 22–41.
NOTE: The entries begin on 18 May 1686, the day after Joseph Dudley and his council assumed office, and end on 29 September 1686 (Michaelmas), the date for closing out semiannual reports under the Julian calendar. There are many omissions on this list, and the official probably failed to record well over 1,000 tons. Departures for ports on the North American continent are notably lacking.

There is a list of twenty departures in the Massachusetts Archives, 7:15–16, for 17 Dec. to 30 Dec. 1686: six for Barbados, three for London, two each for Jamaica, Antigua, and Virginia, one each for North Carolina, Montserrat, Saint Kitts, and Madeira, and one unknown.

TABLE 3

Departures from the Port of Boston
25 March 1687–29 September 1687 (189 Days)

Destination	Departures	Tonnage
Barbados	40	2,084
London	9	760
Jamaica	11	611
Nevis	10	560
Bilbao	7	315
Virginia	15	311
Madeira	7	213
Pennsylvania	7	203
Newfoundland	6	175
Antigua	7	171
Saint Kitts	5	163
Leeward Islands	4	115
New York	4	103
Carolinas	5	100
Bermuda	5	96
Azores	2	85
Montserrat	1	80
Portugal	1	70
Curaçao	3	48
Maryland	3	36
Cádiz	1	30
Spanish Wreck	1	30
Connecticut	1	16
Providence	1	16
Total	156	6,391

SOURCES: "Mass. Shipping Abstracts," pt. 1, vol. 1, pp. 41–76, and Massachusetts Archives, 7:16–41.
NOTE: The document in the Massachusetts Archives records departures representing more than 158 tons not recorded in the Shipping Abstracts. Two vessels with no recorded tonnage, departing for London and Curaçao, respectively, are included in the departure column.

TABLE 4

Departures from the Port of Boston
3 January 1687–29 December 1687

Destination	Departures with recorded tonnage	Departures without recorded tonnage	Tonnage recorded
Barbados	57	6	3,083
Jamaica	19	2	1,036
London	10	2	1,010
Nevis	15	2	773
Leeward Islands	13		530
Virginia	25	1	513
Saint Kitts	14	1	449
Bilbao	8		350
Antigua	10		276
Madeira	9		268
Pennsylvania	9		261
Montserrat	3	1	175
Newfoundland	6		175
Carolina	8	2	154
Portugal	2		150
New York	5		133
Azores	3	2	120
Maryland	6		99
Bermuda	5		96
Curaçao	3	1	73
Bahama Islands	1		30
Cádiz	1		30
Spanish Wreck	1		30
Connecticut	1	1	16
Providence	1		16
Ireland		1	
Surinam		1	
Fishing voyage		1	
Total*	235	24	9,846

SOURCES: "License Granted by his Excellency Edmund Andros Knt. Govor," Massachusetts Archives, 7:16–41, and "Mass. Shipping Abstracts," pt. 1, vol. 1, pp. 41–76.
* See the discussion of the tables for higher estimates.

TABLE 5

Departures from the Port of Boston
25 March 1688–29 September 1688

Destination	Departures	Tonnage
Barbados	32	1,975
Great Britain	9	781
Bilbao	11	670
Jamaica	13	587
Antigua	11	557
Nevis	8	432
Maryland	6	200
Pennsylvania	9	192
New York	6	190
Bermuda	9	152
Saint Kitts	3	140
Madeira	4	125
Montserrat	3	100
Cádiz	1	100
Curaçao	2	94
Carolinas	5	92
Newfoundland	3	90
Portugal	1	70
Canaries	1	70
Virginia	4	63
Providence	2	55
Alicante	1	45
Azores	1	20
Total	145	6,800

SOURCE: "Mass. Shipping Abstracts," pt. 1, vol. 1, pp. 93–127.
NOTE: The title of the document is "Port of Boston In New England.
An Account of Vessels entered out of Boston In His Majesty's Territory
of New England from the 25th March 1688 to the 29th September
1688." An endorsement reads "New England An Account of Ships entered outwards in six months ending the 29 of September Rec'd 15th
January 1688/89."

TABLE 6

Percentage of Shipping Tonnage from the Port of Boston to the Principal New England Markets

Market	8/16/1661–2/25/1662 (27.5)	5/18/1686–9/29/1686 (40.5)	3/25/1687–9/29/1687 (32.6)	1/3/1687–12/29/1687 (31.3)	3/25/1688–9/29/1688 (29.0)	1714–1717
Barbados West Indies (including Barbados)	29.5	58.9	60.4	65.6	57.1	53.0
Great Britain	18.3	17.9	11.9	10.3	11.5	19.2
Wine Ports	40.2	14.9	11.2	9.3	16.2	5.7
Continent of North America	9.0	3.2	12.3	12.1	11.7	17.2
Newfoundland	3.0	5.1	2.7	1.8	1.3	4.3*
Bermuda			1.5	1.0	2.2	0.6

SOURCES: Calculated from tables 1–5. The percentages for 1714–17 are based on annual averages for years ending 23 June and appear in Stuart Bruchey, ed., *The Colonial Merchant: Sources and Readings* (New York, 1966), p. 16. For the years 1714–1717, 138 tons for unknown ports does not appear in the percentages.
* Probably includes Nova Scotia.

 Notes

Abbreviations Used in the Notes

AAS Procs.   *Proceedings of the American Antiquarian Society* (Worcester, Mass., o.s., 1843–1880, n.s., 1880–)

AAS Trans.   *Transactions and Collections of the American Antiquarian Society,* 12 vols. (Worcester, Mass., 1820–1911)

AHR   *American Historical Review*

Aspinwall Recs.   *A Volume . . . Containing the Aspinwall Records from 1644 to 1651 (Thirty-Second Report of the Record Commissioners of the City of Boston)* (Boston, 1903)

Conn. Recs.   J. H. Trumbull and L. W. Labaree, eds., *The Public Records of the Colony of Connecticut, 1636–1776,* 15 vols. (Hartford, Conn., 1850–90)

CSM Pubs.   *Publications of the Colonial Society of Massachusetts* (Boston, 1895–)

CSPC   *Calendar of State Papers, Colonial,* 44 vols. (London, 1860–)

CSPD   *Calendar of State Papers, Domestic,* 89 vols. (London, 1856–)

Doc. Hist. Me.   *Documentary History of the State of Maine,* 24 vols. (Portland, Me., 1869–1916)

EIHC   *Essex Institute Historical Collections* (Salem, Mass., 1859–)

Essex Court Recs.	George Francis Dow, ed., *Records and Files of the Quarterly Courts of Essex County, Massachusetts,* 8 vols. (Salem, Mass., 1911–21)
Mass. Recs.	Nathaniel B. Shurtleff, ed., *Records of the Governor and Company of Massachusetts Bay in New England,* 5 vols. (Boston, 1853–54)
"Mass. Shipping Abstracts"	"Abstracts of English Shipping Records Relating to Massachusetts Ports. From Original Records in the Public Record Office, London. Compiled for the Essex Institute, Salem, Massachusetts," 5 vols., typescript, 1931–49
Me. Court Recs.	Charles T. Libby et al., eds., *Province and Court Records of Maine,* 5 vols. (Portland, Me., 1928–)
MeHS Colls.	*Maine Historical Society Collections,* 22 vols. (Portland, Me., 1831–1906)
MHS Colls.	*Massachusetts Historical Society Collections* (Boston, 1792–)
MHS Procs.	*Proceedings of the Massachusetts Historical Society* (Boston, 1791–)
NEHG Reg.	New England Historic Genealogical Society, *New England Historical and Genealogical Register* (Boston, 1847–)
NEQ	*New England Quarterly*
N.H. Docs.	Nathaniel Bouton et al., eds., *Documents and Records Relating to the Province of New Hampshire,* 40 vols. (Concord, N.H., 1867–1943)
Plym. Recs.	N. B. Shurtleff et al., eds., *Records of the Colony of New Plymouth in New England,* 12 vols. (Boston, 1855–61)
R.I. Recs.	J. R. Bartlett, ed., *Records of the Colony of Rhode Island and Providence Plantations in New England,* 10 vols. (Providence, 1856–65)

Abbreviations Used in the Notes

WJ	James Kendall Hosmer, ed., *Winthrop's Journal*, 2 vols. (New York, 1908)
WP	*Winthrop Papers, 1498–1649,* 5 vols. (Boston, 1929–47)

Notes

1. The Timber Shortage in England

1. Winifred Pennington, *The History of British Vegetation* (London, 1969), pp. 55–77; Cyril E. Hart, *Royal Forest: A History of Dean's Woods as Producers of Timber* (Oxford, 1966), pp. xix, xxiii, 1–3; A. G. Tansley, *The British Islands and Their Vegetation* (Cambridge, 1939), pp. 149, 172; Robert Greenhalgh Albion, *Forests and Sea Power: The Timber Problem of the Royal Navy, 1652–1862* (Cambridge, Mass., 1926), pp. 98, 107–8; J. F. S. Stone, *Wessex before the Celts* (London, 1958), pp. 13–19; A. G. Smith, "The Influence of Mesolithic and Neolithic Man on British Vegetation: A Discussion," and Judith Turner, "Post-Neolithic Disturbance of British Vegetation," in D. Walker and R. G. West, eds., *Studies in the Vegetational History of the British Isles: Essays in Honour of Harry Godwin* (Cambridge, 1970), pp. 81–96, 97–116; Collin R. Tubbs, *The New Forest: An Ecological History* (Devon, 1968), pp. 25–26, 30.

For a description of the shifting forest zones in western Europe, see J. H. D. Clark, *Prehistoric Europe: The Economic Basis* (London, 1952), pp. 9–14.

2. I. A. Richmond, *Roman Britain*, 2d ed. (Baltimore, 1963), pp. 9–17; Caesar, *The Gallic War*, Loeb Classical Library (London, 1917), pp. 204–7, 244–47, 252–55, 258–59; *The Geography of Strabo*, 8 vols., Loeb Classical Library (London, 1917–32), 2:255–57; Pennington, *History of British Vegetation*, pp. 92–93; Hart, *Royal Forest*, pp. 3–5.

3. F. M. Stenton, *Anglo-Saxon England*, 2d ed. (Oxford, 1947), pp. 279–83; H. G. Richardson, "Some Remarks on British Forest History," *Transactions of the Royal Scottish Arboricultural Society* 35 (1921): 158–59; Doris Mary Stenton, *English Society in the Early Middle Ages* (Baltimore, 1951), pp. 99–101.

4. Hart, *Royal Forest*, pp. 5–7; Richard Koebner, "The Settlement and Colonization of Europe," and M. M. Postan, "England," in M. M. Postan, ed., *The Agrarian Life of the Middle Ages* (1966), vol. 1 in M. M. Postan and H. J. Habakkuk, eds., *The Cambridge Economic History of Europe*, 2d ed. (Cambridge, 1966–), pp. 43–52, 548–50; R. E. Prothero, *English Farming Past and Present*, 6th ed. (London, 1961), pp. 26–27; Albion, *Forests and Sea Power*, p. 121; H. L. Edlin, *Woodland Crafts in Britain* (London, 1949), p. 175; Pennington, *History of British Vegetation*, pp. 88–95.

5. Hart, *Royal Forest*, pp. 39–41; Reginald Lennard, "The Destruction of Woodland in the Eastern Counties under William the Conquerer," *Economic History Review* 15, nos. 1 and 2 (1945): 36–43; Postan, "England," in Postan, ed., *Agrarian Life*, pp. 549–50; Helen Cam, *England before Elizabeth* (New York, 1960), p. 100.

Estimates of English population vary widely because of the lack of statistics. There may have been as many as 3,000,000 people in England in 1086 or as few as 1,750,000. In the thirteenth century there may have been as many as 7,000,000 or as few as 3,700,000 (Postan, "England," in Postan, ed., *Agrarian Life*, pp. 551–56, 561–63, 569–73).

Britain had only three coniferous trees. The fir was the *Pinus sylvestris*, the Scotch pine. The yew (*Taxus baccata*), good for bows, grew in many sections of Britain, but not in large numbers; it was not used for timber. The juniper (*Juniperus communis*), useful only for Dutch gin or English spice, also grew in some areas of Britain (Edlin, *Woodland Crafts*, pp. 124, 127–29, 135). American trees have been introduced to England in recent centuries (J. H. Clapham, *An Economic History of Modern Britain: The Early Railway Age, 1820–1850* [Cambridge, 1964], p. 12).

6. F. M. Stenton, *Anglo-Saxon England*, pp. 28, 675; J. Charles Cox, *The Royal Forests of England* (London, 1905), pp. 1–2; Hart, *Royal Forest*, pp. 7–52; Charles Petit-Dutaillis, *Studies and Notes Supplementary to Stubbs' Constitutional History*, 3 vols. (London, 1923–29), 2:147–60, 194–95; Prothero, *English Farming*, p. 44; Richardson, "British Forest History," 35:162–64; Maurice Keen, *The Outlaws of Medieval Legend* (Toronto, 1961), p. 140.

7. J. F. D. Shrewsbury, *A History of the Bubonic Plague in the British Isles* (Cambridge, 1970), pp. 1–156; Postan, "England,"

in Postan, ed., *Agrarian Life*, pp. 556–70; A. R. Myers, *England in the Late Middle Ages*, rev. ed. (Baltimore, 1956), pp. 46–47.

8. Petit-Dutaillis, *Studies and Notes*, 2:155–56, 210–12, 232, 239–49; Prothero, *English Farming*, p. 58; S. T. Bindoff, *Tudor England* (Baltimore, 1950), p. 10; Myers, *England in the Late Middle Ages*, pp. 137–38; G. M. Trevelyan, *English Social History: A Survey of Six Centuries, Chaucer to Victoria* (London, 1942), pp. 132, 279.

9. Cam, *England before Elizabeth*, pp. 156–57; Myers, *England in the Late Middle Ages*, pp. 132–33, 211–12; Edlin, *Woodland Crafts*, p. 176; Robert Trow-Smith, *A History of British Livestock Husbandry to 1700* (London, 1957), pp. 5, 16, 75; Postan, "England," in Postan, ed., *Agrarian Life*, p. 570; V. M. Wadsworth, "Country Life and Economics," in J. E. Morpurgo, ed., *Life under the Tudors* (London, 1950), pp. 72, 74, 76; John U. Nef, *The Rise of the British Coal Industry*, 2 vols. (London, 1932), 1:190.

The population is estimated to have been 4,123,708 in 1570; 4,811,718 in 1600; 5,600,517 in 1630; 5,773,646 in 1670; and 6,045,008 in 1700 (Karl F. Helleiner, "The Population of Europe from the Black Death to the Eve of the Vital Revolution," in E. E. Rich and C. H. Wilson, eds., *The Economy of Expanding Europe in the Sixteenth and Seventeenth Centuries* [1967], vol. 4 in J. H. Clapham and Eileen Power, eds., *The Cambridge Economic History of Europe from the Decline of the Roman Empire* [Cambridge, 1941–67], pp. 32, 52–53). The number of sheep is even more difficult to estimate. Bindoff, *Tudor England*, pp. 11–12, says that "Five centuries ago sheep may have numbered about 8,000,000, that is, there were about three sheep to every human." Trow-Smith, *British Livestock Husbandry*, p. 233, accepts Gregory King's estimate of 1696 that there were 12,000,000 sheep and 4,500,000 cattle in England and Wales. But if one sheep in that period required 7 to 8 acres of grassland, as Trow-Smith claims, it is difficult to understand how 57,000,000 acres in Britain or 32,000,000 acres in England could have supported so many millions of sheep. (See Prothero, *English Farming*, pp. 16–17, 145.)

10. Carl Bridenbaugh, *Vexed and Troubled Englishmen, 1590–1642* (New York, 1968), pp. 70–82, 133–34; Christopher Morris, "England under the Tudors," in Morpurgo, ed., *Life under the Tudors*, p. 25; Mildred Campbell, *The English Yeoman*

under Elizabeth and the Early Stuarts (New Haven, 1942), pp. 223–24, 228; William Harrison, *The Description of England,* ed. Georges Edelen (Ithaca, N.Y., 1968), pp. 195, 200–201; Wallace Notestein, Frances Helen Relf, and Hartley Simpson, eds., *Commons Debates, 1621,* 7 vols. (New Haven, Conn., 1935), 7:274; Henry Best, *Rural Economy in Yorkshire in 1641* . . . , Publications of the Surtees Society, no. 33 (London, 1857), p. 156.

11. John U. Nef, "The Progress of Technology and the Growth of Large-Scale Industry in Great Britain, 1540–1640," *Economic History Review* 5 (1934–35): 3–24.

12. Trevelyan, *English Social History,* p. 217.

13. Ralph Davis, *The Rise of the English Shipping Industry in the Seventeenth and Eighteenth Centuries* (London, 1962), pp. 5–15, 22; George Lewis Beer, "The Early English Colonial Movement," *Political Science Quarterly* 23 (1908): 248; Trevelyan, *English Social History,* p. 189; John U. Nef, *The Conquest of the Material World* (Chicago, 1964), pp. 160, 166.

English merchant shipping reached 115,000 deadweight tons in 1629, 150,000 tons in 1640, and 200,000 tons in 1660 (Davis, *English Shipping Industry,* p. 15).

14. "During the eighty years between the end of Henry VIII's reign and the beginning of Charles I's, the tonnage of the British Navy about doubled" (Nef, *Conquest,* p. 160). It doubled again between 1649 and 1651 (G. J. Marcus, *A Naval History of England,* 2 vols. [London, 1961], 1:136).

15. We actually use more wood and wood products today for construction, paper, chemicals, and plastic. But wood and forest products cannot be called the basic materials of our industries. In the seventeenth century almost every industry and craft was dependent upon the forest and forest products.

The clothmaking industry was the greatest consumer of soap in England, using from 5,000 to 10,000 tons annually by the early seventeenth century.

16. *CSPD, 1631–33,* p. 390; E. S., "Britain's Buss . . ." [London, 1615], in Andrew Lang, ed., *Social England Illustrated: A Collection of Seventeenth-Century Tracts* (New York, 1905), pp. 284, 286; Nef, *Coal Industry,* 1:191–92; Bindoff, *Tudor England,* p. 9; G. P. B. Naish, "Ships and Shipbuilding," in Charles Singer et al., *A History of Technology,* 5 vols. (London, 1954–58), 3:482–93.

17. Nef, *Coal Industry*, 1:222; Nef, *Conquest*, p. 135; Maurice Ashley, *England in the Seventeenth Century*, 3d ed. (Baltimore, 1961), p. 15; Allen French, *Charles I and the Puritan Upheaval: A Study of the Causes of the Great Migration* (Boston, 1955), p. 120; Prothero, *English Farming*, p. 110; John Evelyn, *Sylva: A Discourse of Forest Trees and the Propagation of Timber in His Majesty's Dominions*, ed. Alexander Hunter (York, 1776), pp. 577–78; Campbell, *English Yeoman*, pp. 224–25; J. N. L. Baker, "England in the Seventeenth Century," in H. C. Darby, ed., *An Historical Geography of England before A.D. 1800* (Cambridge, 1936), p. 419; Richardson, "British Forest History," 36 (1922): 182; G. H. Kenyon, *The Glass Industry of the Weald* (New York, 1967), p. 47; Leo Francis Stock, ed., *Proceedings and Debates of the British Parliaments Respecting North America*, 5 vols. (Washington, 1924–41), 4:353.

18. Nef, *Coal Industry*, 1:193, n. 7; Rhys Jenkins, "Ironmaking in the Forest of Dean," *Newcomen Society Transactions* 6 (1925–26): 57; H. R. Schubert, *History of the British Iron and Steel Industry from c. 450 B.C. to A.D. 1775* (London, 1957), p. 220.

19. Pennington, *History of British Vegetation*, p. 98.

The area of some woodland in Essex can be estimated from John Norden's map in *Speculi Britanniae Pars: An Historical and Chorographical Description of the County of Essex, 1594*, ed. Sir Henry Ellis, Camden Society Publication no. 9 (London, 1840). See also Harrison, *Description*, pp. 275–76; Albion, *Forests and Sea Power*, pp. 97, 108–9; A. L. Rowse, *The England of Elizabeth: The Structure of Society* (New York, 1951), p. 67; Ashley, *England in the Seventeenth Century*, pp. 67, 69; Joan Thirsk, "The Farming Regions of England," in Joan Thirsk, ed., *The Agrarian History of England and Wales, 1500–1640* (Cambridge, 1967), pp. 1–112. The meager results of a survey of Quernmore Forest are cited in Cox, *Royal Forests*, pp. 73–74.

20. Nef, *Coal Industry*, 1:190; Samuel Hartlib, *His Legacy of Husbandry* (London, 1655), p. 46; Sumner Chilton Powell, *Puritan Village: The Formation of a New England Town* (Middletown, Conn., 1963), pp. 11–13; Edlin, *Woodland Crafts*, p. 176.

G. Hammersley, "The Crown Woods and their Exploitation in the Sixteenth and Seventeenth Centuries," *Bulletin of the Institute of Historical Research* 30 (1957): 136–61, denies that there was a timber crisis in England, but does not stress the rising demand for timber or mention the growing dependence on other nations for timber products. Tubbs, *New Forest*, p. 76, believes that the timber crisis did not occur until the second half of the seventeenth century, but the only evidence he presents concerns shipbuilding. The population of England in the very early seventeenth century was somewhere between 4,000,000 and 4,500,000. This number had increased to almost 5,500,000 by 1640 (Bridenbaugh, *Vexed and Troubled Englishmen*, pp. 16, 79, 119, 164–65; Trevelyan, *English Social History*, p. 283; Ashley, *England in the Seventeenth Century*, p. 12. Helleiner, "Population of Europe," in Rich and Wilson, eds., *The Economy of Expanding Europe*, pp. 32, 52, estimates the English population at 4,123,708 in 1570, 4,811,718 in 1600.

21. Clapham, *Economic History*, p. 10, Albion, *Forests and Sea Power*, pp. 103–4; E. Lipson, *The Economic History of England*, 12th ed., 3 vols. (London, 1959), 2:445–46; *Hartlib Legacy*, p. 47.

For the problems of water transportation, see Best, *Rural Economy*, pp. 111–12.

22. Nef, *Coal Industry*, 1:158; Nef, *Conquest*, pp. 263, 265; Notestein, Relf, and Simpson, eds., *Commons Debates, 1621*, 7 vols. (New Haven, 1935), 7:91–96, 104; Ashley, *England in the Seventeenth Century*, p. 24; Trevelyan, *English Social History*, p. 188; Rowse, *England of Elizabeth*, p. 354.

For timber and agricultural price indexes in the sixteenth and seventeenth centuries, see Peter Bowden, "Statistical Appendix," table 13, in Thirsk, ed., *Agrarian History*, p. 862. For the sufferings of the poor, see Bridenbaugh, *Vexed and Troubled Englishmen*, pp. 50, 51, 144, 375–82.

23. "Suspending Statute on Fuel," in Paul L. Hughes and James F. Larkin, eds., *Tudor Royal Proclamations*, 3 vols. (New Haven, 1964–69), 1:325; Richardson, "British Forest History," 36 (1922): 176; Nef, *Coal Industry*, 1:196; "The Great Frost, 1608," in Lang, ed., *Social England Illustrated*, pp. 172–73.

24. Harrison, *Description*, p. 431; William Vaughan, *The Golden Fleece Divided into Three Parts* (London, 1626), pt. 3, p. 13; Wallace Notestein, *The English People on the Eve of Colonization, 1602–1630* (New York, 1954), pp. 83–84, 220; Campbell, *English Yeoman*, p. 127; Nef, *Coal Industry*, 1:191; Bridenbaugh, *Vexed and Troubled Englishmen*, pp. 98–101; John

Smith, *England's Improvement Revivd: Digested into Six Books* ([London], 1670), p. 18.

25. Notestein, Relf, and Simpson, eds., *Commons Debates, 1621,* 7:472; Raymond W. K. Hinton, *The Eastland Trade and the Common Weal* (Cambridge, 1959), p. 88; Nef, *Coal Industry,* 1:192, 195; Nef, *Conquest,* pp. 133, 174, 264; Henry Oldenburg to John Winthrop, Jr., received 6 May 1669, "Correspondence of the Founders of the Royal Society with Governor Winthrop of Connecticut," *MHS Procs.* 16 (1878): 241.

26. Nef, *Coal Industry,* 1:195, citing royal proclamation of 1615; Albion, *Forests and Sea Power,* p. 95, citing the *Naval Tracts of Sir William Monson,* 5:268; *The Trades Increase* (London, 1615), pp. 17–18; *CSPD, 1631–33,* pp. 372, 390, 491, 566.

27. The conservation statute is 35 Henry VIII, c. 17; Nef, *Coal Industry,* 1:161, 191; J. Nisbet, "History of the Forest of Dean," *English Historical Review* 21 (1906): 446–47; Cox, *Royal Forests,* p. 73; A. C. Forbes, *English Estate Forestry* (London, 1904), p. 9; Thomas Southcliffe Ashton, *Iron and Steel in the Industrial Revolution* (Manchester, 1924), pp. 8–9; H. Neilson, "Early English Woodland and Waste," *Journal of Economic History* 2 (1942): 54–62; John Croumbie Brown, *The Forests of England and the Management of Them in Bye-Gone Times* (Edinburgh, 1883), p. 230; Schubert, *British Iron and Steel Industry,* p. 221; Richardson, "British Forest History," 36 (1922): 183; John Smith, *England's Improvement Revivd,* p. 8; *Hartlib Legacy,* p. 47.

Some of the other conservation statutes are: 1 & 2 Philip and Mary c. 5; 1 Eliz. c. 15; 23 Eliz. c. 5; 27 Eliz. c. 19; 35 Eliz. c. 11.

28. Albion, *Forests and Sea Power,* pp. 108–14; Josiah Child, *A New Discourse of Trade* (London, 1693), p. 209.

29. Albion, *Forests and Sea Power,* pp. 123–24, 131–32; Forbes, *English Estate Forestry,* pp. 10–11; Evelyn, *Sylva,* p. 3.

30. Albion, *Forests and Sea Power,* pp. 132–33; Marcus, *Naval History,* 1:182; Nef, *Coal Industry,* 1:399–400; Carew Reynel, *The True English Interest, or an Account of the Chief Natural Improvements* . . . (London, 1674), p. 40.

31. Campbell, *English Yeoman,* pp. 223–28; Notestein, Relf, and Simpson, eds., *Commons Debates, 1621,* 7:274; Davis, *English Shipping Industry,* p. 19; Harrison, *Description,* pp. 195–96, 356.

32. Davis, *English Shipping Industry*, pp. 18, 212, 214.

33. Schubert, *British Iron and Steel Industry*, p. 225.

34. Nef, *Coal Industry*, 1:20, 197–99; Nef, *Conquest*, pp. 169, 262; F. Sherwood Taylor and Charles Singer, "Pre-Scientific Industrial Chemistry," in Singer, *History of Technology*, 2:369–70; Lipson, *Economic History*, 2:113; Harrison, *Description*, p. 363; Baker, "England in the Seventeenth Century," in Darby, ed., *Historical Geography*, p. 421.

35. Nef, *Coal Industry*, 1:200–201; Nef, *Conquest*, pp. 133–36, 169–70, 187; J. U. Nef, "Coal Mining and Utilization," in Singer, *History of Technology*, 3:74–81; Ashton, *Iron and Steel*, p. 9.

36. Nef, *Coal Industry*, 1:197, n. 6; Trevelyan, *English Social History*, pp. 188–89, 286–87.

37. Christina Hole, *The English Housewife in the Seventeenth Century* (London, 1953), p. 66; Trevelyan, *English Social History*, pp. 286–87; Nef, *Coal Industry*, 2:391–93, 400–403; Lipson, *Economic History*, 2:113, 144; French, *Charles I*, p. 120; *The Diary of John Evelyn*, ed. E. S. DeBeer, 6 vols. (Oxford, 1955), 4:363. A chaldron of coal would have been equivalent to any amount from 32 to 36 bushels, or about 1.25 tons.

38. Nef, *Coal Industry*, 1:128–29, 160; Nef, *Conquest*, pp. 160, 164, 167; Nef, "Progress of Technology," pp. 20–21; Baker, "England in the Seventeenth Century," in Darby, ed., *Historical Geography*, p. 421; Davis, *English Shipping Industry*, p. 4; Lawrence A. Harper, *The English Navigation Laws* (New York, 1939), p. 339; Hinton, *Eastland Trade*, p. 51.

39. Nef, *Conquest*, pp. 170, 184–85; Trevelyan, *English Social History*, p. 189; Hole, *English Housewife*, p. 66; *Hartlib Legacy*, p. 49. A method of coking coal for the malt industry was discovered as early as the 1640s; but coke was not used in smelting until the late seventeenth century, or commonly in blast furnaces before the 1780s (Nef, "Coal Mining and Utilization," in Singer, *History of Technology*, 3:80–81; Ashton, *Iron and Steel*, pp. 9–12; Nef, *Conquest*, p. 133).

40. The value of the Danish rix-dollar varied from four shillings and sixpence to two shillings and three pence. Imports of timber and naval stores to England amounted to 28,000 rix-dollars by 1646. Timber and naval stores entering the port of London were valued at 74,000 rix-dollars in 1663, and 157,000

rix-dollars in 1669 (Hinton, *Eastland Trade*, pp. 39, 105, app. 5; Davis, *English Shipping Industry*, pp. 212–14; Nef, *Coal Industry*, 1:159–60).

41. C. F. Innocent, *The Development of English Building Construction* (Cambridge, 1916), pp. 102–4; Evelyn, *Sylva*, pp. 256–57; Davis, *English Shipping Industry*, p. 19; Violet Barbour, "Dutch and English Merchant Shipping in the Seventeenth Century," *Economic History Review* 2 (1930): 269–70; Richardson, "British Forest History," 36 (1922): 196.

42. Between 1699 and 1701, 359,000 tons of shipping were used to carry imports to England, of which 190,000 tons (53 per cent) were required for timber and timber products. Between 1752 and 1754, 562,000 tons of shipping were used for imports to England, of which 303,000 tons (54 per cent) were required for timber and other forest products. One cannot accurately derive the tonnage for the earlier years of the seventeenth century from these figures: in the eighteenth century, the English imported large amounts of forest products from Africa and North America, and the greater distance traveled required additional ships. Nevertheless, these figures suggest that the shipping tonnage required by the timber trade was always very large.

All of the figures are from Davis, *English Shipping Industry*, pp. 182, 184. Davis gives tonnage in terms of tons burden (carrying capacity). Tons burden differs significantly from displacement tonnage (the actual weight of the materials loaded on a ship), and from measured tonnage (the formula used by shipwrights to establish the measurement and selling price of a vessel). According to Davis (pp. 7, 74), the relationship between tons burden and measured tonnage differed from ship to ship, but tons burden was usually from 70 to 75 per cent of measured tonnage. For further information on the problems of the measurement of shipping tonnage, see Davis (p. 7), and James F. Shepherd and Gary M. Walton, *Shipping, Maritime Trade, and the Economic Development of Colonial North America* (Cambridge, 1972), pp. 237–40.

Parry, "Transport and Trade Routes," in Rich and Wilson, eds., *Economy of Expanding Europe*, p. 179, states that timber could be shipped safely by sea only in the summer. Timber carriers were usually fairly large (200 to 400 tons, by seventeenth-century reckoning). "Timber was reckoned in 'loads' of fifty cubic feet. A load corresponded roughly to a ton of shipping, assuming a judiciously mixed cargo of oak and lighter, bulkier fir, so that most ships carried from 200 to 400 loads."

43. Davis, *English Shipping Industry*, pp. 14–15.

Davis says that "a ship built entirely of foreign materials . . . would call for the transport services of as many as two or three ships of its own size to carry the materials" (p. 19). For the Dutch flyboat, see Davis, pp. 212–14. Parry, "Transport and Trade Routes," in Rich and Wilson, eds., *Economy of Expanding Europe*, p. 180, claims that Baltic timber was carried "almost entirely in Dutch ships" in the seventeenth century.

44. Davis, *English Shipping Industry*, pp. 14–15, 212–15; Child, *New Discourse on Trade*, p. 98.

Child complained that the carriage of timber by foreign shippers was increasing and advocated a heavy tax on all such commerce.

45. Evelyn, *Sylva*, p. 527.

Parry, "Transport and Trade Routes," in Rich and Wilson, eds., *Economy of Expanding Europe*, states that the cost of timber on the stump was "usually about 5 per cent of the delivered price" and that transportation "accounted for at least two-thirds of the price of imported timber at its final destination" (pp. 178–80).

For a discussion of wages, see Bridenbaugh, *Vexed and Troubled Englishmen*, pp. 51, 79, 211.

46. Davis, *English Shipping Industry*, pp. 185–88, 213–14; Reynel, *True English Interest*, p. 9.

The cloth goods that were carried from England to northern Europe had a high value in relation to shipping space, and one cargo of such goods might be worth that of fifty to sixty timber ships. But even cloth goods did not offset the unfavorable balance of trade (Parry, "Transport and Trade Routes," in Rich and Wilson, eds., *Economy of Expanding Europe*, pp. 177–81, and George Louis Beer, "Early English Colonial Movement," pp. 242–43).

47. "Sir Thomas Roe His Speech in Parliament" (1641), in William Huse Dunham, Jr., and Stanley Pargellis, eds., *Complaint and Reform in England, 1436–1714* (New York, 1938), pp. 605–6; Theodore J. Kreps, "Vicissitudes of the American Potash Industry," *Journal of Economic and Business History* 3 (1930–31): 634–45.

48. Parry, "Transport and Trade Routes," in Rich and Wilson,

eds., *Economy of Expanding Europe*, pp. 180–81; Albion, *Forests and Sea Power*, pp. 96, 164–68, 218, 224.

Albion believes that if an English fleet had been really crushed at sea in either the second or third Dutch War, "it is extremely doubtful if the stores on hand could have provided for a new force to regain the seas from the Dutch" (p. 224).

2. The Presettlement Forests of New England

1. Henry David Thoreau, *The Maine Woods* (New York, 1955), p. 320.
2. John W. Barrett, "The Northeastern Region," in John W. Barrett, ed., *Regional Silviculture of the United States* (New York, 1962), p. 45.
3. Walter Prescott Webb, *The Great Plains* (Boston, 1931), pp. 205–318; Stanley W. Bromley, "The Original Forest Types of Southern New England," *Ecological Monographs* 5 (1935): 65.
4. Barrett, "Northeastern Region," p. 30.
5. Eugene V. Zumwalt, "Taxation and Other Factors Affecting Private Forestry in Connecticut" (Ph.D. diss., Yale University, 1951), pp. 1–3; Bromley, "Original Forest Types," p. 65.
6. Herbert I. Winer, "History of the Great Mountain Forest, Litchfield County, Connecticut" (Ph.D. diss., Yale University, 1956), pp. 60–61; Marston Bates, *The Forest and the Sea: A Look at the Economy of Nature and the Ecology of Man* (New York, 1960), p. 117; Joseph A. Miller, "The Changing Forest: Recent Research in the Historical Geography of American Forests," *Forest History* 9 (1965): 19; Margaret B. Davis, "Phytogeography and Palynology of Northeastern United States," in H. E. Wright, Jr., and David G. Frey, eds., *The Quaternary of the United States* (Princeton, N.J., 1965), pp. 386–97.
7. Winer, "Great Mountain Forest," p. 36.
8. Barrett, "Northeastern Region," p. 44; Victor E. Shelford, *The Ecology of North America* (Urbana, Ill., 1963), pp. 22–26.
9. Susan Tarrow, "Translation of the Cèllere Codex," in Lawrence C. Wroth, *The Voyages of Giovanni da Verrazzano, 1524–1528* (New Haven, 1970), p. 140; "The Voyages of the Sieur de Champlain of Saintonge, Captain in ordinary for the King in the Navy" [Paris, 1613], trans. and ed. W. F. Ganong, in

H. P. Biggar, ed., *The Works of Samuel de Champlain in Six Volumes* (Toronto, 1922–36), 1:281–83, 334. See also James Rosier, *A True Relation of the most prosperous voyage made this present yeere 1605, by Captaine George Waymouth* . . . [London, 1605], no pagination; Francis Higginson, "A True Relation of the last voyage to New England . . . 1629," in Thomas Hutchinson, *A Collection of Original Papers Relative to the History of the Colony of Massachusetts Bay,* 2 vols. (Albany, 1865; originally published Boston, 1769), 1:47.

10. "The Voyages of the Sieur de Champlain," in Biggar, ed., *Works of Samuel de Champlain,* 1:331; John Josselyn, *An Account of Two Voyages to New-England* (London, 1674), pp. 196–97; Betty Flanders Thomson, *The Changing Face of New England* (New York, 1958), pp. 41–42; William Wood, *New Englands Prospect* (London, 1634), pp. 10–11; Bromley, "Original Forest Types," p. 67; Thomas Pownall, *A Topographical Description of the Dominions of the United States of America,* ed. Louis Mulkearn (Pittsburgh, 1949), p. 23.

According to Sumner Chilton Powell, *Puritan Village: The Formation of a New England Town* (Middletown, Conn., 1963), pp. 78–79, there were thousands of acres of grassland along the Concord River in the Concord-Sudbury region.

In the interior of Aquidneck Island Verrazzano found large fields "open and free of any obstacles or trees." His statement that the fields extended for thirty to thirty-five leagues is an exaggeration, but the open landscape in the Newport area is confirmed by a timber shortage in the seventeenth century (Tarrow, "Translation of the Cèllere Codex," in Wroth, *Voyages of Giovanni da Verrazzano,* p. 139). The absence of timber allowed the settlers of Rhode Island to produce agricultural surpluses very quickly.

11. "The Voyages of the Sieur de Champlain," in Biggar, ed., *Works of Samuel de Champlain,* 1:323–30, 338, 341, 395, 397–98; Edward Pierce Hamilton, *A History of Milton* (Milton, Mass., 1957), pp. 12–13; Rosier, *True Relation,* no pagination; Christopher Levett, "A Voyage into New England Begun in 1623 and Ended in 1624," *MHS Colls.,* 3d ser. 8 (1843): 165; Clarence A. Day, *A History of Agriculture in Maine, 1604–1860,* University of Maine Studies, 2d ser., no. 68 (Orono, Me., 1954), pp. 19–20.

The amount of land cleared in the Narragansett country is uncertain. Ralph H. Brown, *Historical Geography of the United States* (New York, 1948), pp. 31–33, suggests that the Indians farmed the land from the bay all the way back to the Connecticut border. Lyman Carrier, *The Beginnings of Agriculture in America* (New York, 1923), pp. 39–40, 189, says that the lands of the Narragansetts "for eight or ten miles distant from the seashore were cleared of wood."

12. Carrier, *Beginnings of Agriculture*, p. 40.

Gordon M. Day, "The Indian as an Ecological Factor in the Northeastern Forest," *Ecology* 34 (1953): 329–31, argues that the Indians greatly influenced the forest by clearing land for farming and using the wood for fuel, building material, canoes, weapons, furniture, and many other items. However, Day admits that scholars cannot determine the true influence of the Indians on the northeastern forest without some way to estimate their number (pp. 341–42). Bromley, "Original Forest Types," p. 64, believes that "there was probably a sufficient population to bring about an annual burning of most of the country [of southern New England] sufficiently dry for a conflagration." Charles C. Willoughby, *Antiquities of the New England Indians* (Cambridge, Mass., 1935), p. 282, believes that there were many Indian clearings in southern New England. Brown, *Historical Geography*, pp. 11–17, holds that the number of Indian clearings was significant. He accepts Willoughby's estimate that there were 24,000 Indians in southern New England at the beginning of the seventeenth century. See Brown's note on Indian populations, ibid., p. 541.

13. Tarrow, "Translation of the Cèllere Codex," in Wroth, *Voyages of Giovanni da Verrazzano*, p. 140; Bates, *Forest and the Sea*, pp. 119–20; Richard G. Wood, *A History of Lumbering in Maine, 1820–1861* (Orono, Me., 1935), pp. 17–18; Hugh M. Raup, "Old Field Forests of Southeastern New England," *Journal of the Arnold Arboretum* 21 (1940): 266–73, discusses the composition of the forest in the twentieth century.

The New England forest has a bewildering variety of coniferous and deciduous trees, and regions where particular species once prevailed cannot be neatly delineated; moreover, there are many variations within broad regions. The factors that affect the various species are extremely complex. See Davis, "Phytogeography," p. 381, and the maps in Lucy E. Braun, *Deciduous*

Forests of Eastern North America (New York, 1964), pp. 249–50.

14. See the vegetation maps in Barrett, ed., *Regional Silviculture of the United States*, pp. 20, 41; Thomson, *Changing Face of New England*, p. 102; Bromley, "Original Forest Types," pp. 70, 77; Braun, *Deciduous Forests*, pp. 249–50.

To make an accurate estimate of the predominance and distribution of species in this region one would need to know the influence of animals and insects and the number, movement, and activity of the Indians. Most ecologists now believe that animals (especially deer and beavers) significantly influence the composition of a forest—and there are about sixty species of insects that seriously damage climax trees. Some investigators believe that if the Indians were numerous and continually burned the woods, not many shallow-rooted, fire-sensitive trees could have survived (Shelford, *Ecology*, pp. 32–33; Bromley, "Original Forest Types," pp. 66–67).

15. Bromley, "Original Forest Types," pp. 66–67; Davis, "Phytogeography," pp. 382–83.

There is disagreement among ecologists, foresters, and phytogeographers about the amount of hemlock in the presettlement forest of central and southern New England. Winer, "Great Mountain Forest," pp. 78–79, notes that the use of the word *pine* for conifers or evergreens was common in England. "Among the common trees that foreign travellers saw in America, hemlock was the most important that lacked a European equivalent and, in consequence, a European name." In Europe, "hemlock" was a poisonous umbelliferous herb. John Josselyn was the first visitor to America who specifically mentioned hemlock trees.

16. Bromley, "Original Forest Types," pp. 72–73; Thomas Morton, *New English Canaan* (Amsterdam, 1637), p. 63; Wood, *New Englands Prospect*, p. 17.

The early records of the Connecticut River town of Northampton, Massachusetts, speak of a large "pine plain" that was divided among the early settlers (Northampton Town Records, no. 1, 1654–1754, Office of the City Clerk, City Hall, Northampton, Mass., passim); Zumwalt, "Taxation," pp. 73–74, says that the Connecticut valley from Hartford north was covered with a mixture of white pine and hemlock, with some beech, chestnut, and black birch.

17. Raup, "Old Field Forests," pp. 271–72; George B. Emerson, *A Report on the Trees and Shrubs Growing Naturally in the Forests of Massachusetts*, 4th ed., 2 vols. (Boston, 1887), 1:10; Bates, *Forest and the Sea*, p. 146; F. Andrew Michaux, *The North American Silva*, 3 vols. (Philadelphia, 1859), 1:28.

18. "The Voyages of the Sieur de Champlain," in Biggar, ed., *Works of Samuel de Champlain*, 1:291, 323–24; "Copy of a Narrative of the Commissioners from England, about New-England" [1665], in Hutchinson, *Original Papers*, 2:153; Josselyn, *Two Voyages*, p. 169; Raup, "Old Field Forests," pp. 271–72. Only white or black oak was used for ship timbers.

19. David M. Smith, "The Forests of the United States," in Barrett, ed., *Regional Silviculture*, p. 72; Zumwalt, "Taxation," pp. 73–74; Bromley, "Original Forest Types," pp. 66–67, 70–71; Raup, "Old Field Forests," pp. 271–72; J. Frederick Kelly, *The Early Domestic Architecture of Connecticut* (New Haven, Conn., 1924), passim; John Winthrop, Jr., to Henry Oldenburg, 25 July 1668, "Winthrop Papers," *MHS Colls.*, 5th ser. 8 (1882): 124–25.

20. Bromley, "Original Forest Types," pp. 71–72.

21. Morton, *New English Canaan*, pp. 52–53.

According to the *Oxford English Dictionary*, the word *swamp* was "originally and in early use only in the North American colonies" in the sense of "marsh or bog." The word was probably used in England, but apparently not in this sense. As late as 1675 John Josselyn thought it necessary to define the word for his readers (*Two Voyages*, p. 44). In 1676 Nathaniel Saltonstall included the word in a glossary "for the better Understanding [of] some Indian Words, which are necessarily used in the Following Narrative" (*A New and Further Narrative of the State of New England* [London, 1676]). A swamp, said Saltonstall, was "a Moorish Place overgrown with Woods and Bushes, but soft like a Quagmire or Irish Bogg, over which Horse cannot at all, nor English Foot (without great difficulty) passe."

22. Samuel Clark, *A Mirrour or Looking-Glass Both for Saints, and Sinners . . .* , 2 vols. (London, 1671), 1:31; Josselyn, *Two Voyages*, p. 44; Bromley, "Original Forest Types," pp. 70, 79; Jeremy Belknap, *The History of New-Hampshire*, 3 vols. (Dover, N.H., 1812), 3:89.

23. Josselyn, *Two Voyages*, p. 44; William Pinhorne and N. Bayard to Governor Fletcher of New York, 24 July 1694, in

Seymour Dunbar, *A History of Travel in America,* 4 vols. (Indianapolis, 1915), 1:14–15; Adolph B. Benson, ed., *The America of 1750: Peter Kalm's Travels in North America,* 2 vols. (New York, 1937), 1:36; Edward Winslow to John Winthrop, Sept. 1640, in *WP,* 4:262.

24. Thoreau, *Maine Woods,* pp. 317–18; G. E. Nichols, "The Vegetation of Connecticut: II, Virgin Forests," *Torreya* 13 (1913): 201–5; Benson, ed., *Kalm's Travels,* 1:219, 370; Donald Culross Peattie, *A Natural History of Trees of Eastern and Central North America* (Boston, 1950), p. 168.

According to Nichols (p. 205), in a virgin forest "every stage in development and deterioration is present—from the slender saplings to the rotting logs with which the ground is strewn on all sides."

25. Tarrow, "Translation of the Cèllere Codex," in Wroth, *Voyages of Giovanni da Verrazzano,* p. 139; "The Voyages of the Sieur de Champlain," in Biggar, ed., *Works of Samuel de Champlain,* 1:329; Josselyn, *Two Voyages,* p. 44.

Some of the reports that stress the parklike quality of the early New England countryside were published to attract investors and settlers, who would be discouraged by reports of impenetrable woodlands. Moreover, those who described the early landscape were more likely to visit and inhabit open forest regions.

26. Morton, *New English Canaan,* pp. 52–54; Roger Williams, *A Key into the Language of America* (London, 1643), pp. 117–18. See also Sir Ferdinando Gorges, "A Description of New England," pp. 44–45, in Ferdinando Gorges, *America Painted to the Life . . .* (London, 1659); Martin Pring, "A Voyage Set out from the Citie of Bristoll at the charge of the chiefest Merchants and inhabitants of the said Citie . . ." [1603], in Henry S. Burrage, ed., *Early English and French Voyages, Chiefly from Hakluyt, 1534–1608* (New York, 1906), p. 351; Adriaen van der Donck, *A Description of the New Netherlands,* ed. Thomas F. O'Donnell (Syracuse, N.Y., 1968), pp. 20–21; and Brown, *Historical Geography,* p. 11.

Although there is no proof in New England records that large trees caused an open forest, several travelers in the Middle Colonies noted the effect of the large trees on the forest floor. A settler in New Netherland observed that the young woodlands were thick and almost impassable. But as the trees matured, they

shaded the underwood, which eventually died. Peter Kalm noticed the same phenomenon a century later. In 1806 a traveler
in the Pennsylvania forest saw sections entirely free from
underbrush, which, he believed, resulted from "the extraordinary
height, and spreading tops of the trees; which thus prevent the
sun from penetrating to the ground, and nourishing inferior
articles of vegetation" (van der Donck, *Description of the New
Netherlands*, p. 20; Benson, ed., *Kalm's Travels*, 1:60; Bates,
Forest and the Sea, pp. 117–18). Jasper Jacob Stahl, *History of
Old Broad Bay and Waldoboro*, 2 vols. (Portland, Me., 1956),
1:4, believes that the forests in the Broad Bay area were open
because the giant trees shaded the forest floor. The author of
American Husbandry, ed. Harry J. Carman (Port Washington,
N.Y., 1964) notes that in part of the Canadian forest, "the under-
wood is thick, in others there is none at all" (p. 19).

27. Bromley, "Original Forest Types," pp. 65–66; Day,
"Indian as Ecological Factor," p. 355; Pring, "Voyage," in
Burrage, ed., *Early English and French Voyages*, p. 351.

Colonial legislation shows that the Indians burned the woods
and that many settlers believed this endangered their property
(see *Mass. Recs.*, 5:230–31, and *R.I. Recs.*, 1:107). Indian fires
in the Middle Colonies apparently were not extensive. Peter
Kalm believed that since the Indians in this region lived chiefly
by hunting and fishing, "the woods therefore had never been
meddled with, except that sometimes a small part had been destroyed by fire" (Benson, ed., *Kalm's Travels*, 1:60). Andrew
Burnaby, *Travels through the Middle Settlements in North-
America* . . . , 2d ed. (Ithaca, N.Y., 1960), pp. 108–9, mentions a
fire confined to "a circle of several miles." See also van der
Donck, *Description of the New Netherlands*, pp. 20–22.

28. John Winthrop, Jr., to Henry Oldenburg, 25 July 1668,
"Winthrop Papers," *MHS Colls.*, 5th ser. 8 (1882): 124–25.

For accounts of storm damage, see the comments of the
Reverend William Adams (1671) in F. M. Caulkins, ed., "Memoir
of the Rev. William Adams, of Dedham, Mass., and of the Rev.
Eliphalet Adams, of New London, Conn.," in *MHS Colls.*, 4th
ser. 1 (1852): 14, and those of Wigglesworth (1654) in *The Diary
of Michael Wigglesworth, 1653–1657*, ed. Edmund S. Morgan
(New York, 1965), p. 74.

29. "The Voyages of the Sieur de Champlain," in Biggar, ed.,
Works of Samuel de Champlain, 1:291; John Winthrop, Jr., to

Henry Oldenburg, 25 July 1668, "Winthrop Papers," *MHS Colls.,*
5th ser. 8 (1882): 124–25.
30. Rosier, *True Relation,* no pagination.
31. Lawrence Henry Gipson, *The British Empire before the
American Revolution,* 14 vols. (Caldwell, Idaho, 1936–68), 3:40;
Timothy Dwight, *Travels in New-England and New York,* 4 vols.
(New Haven, 1821), 1:36; Thoreau, *Maine Woods,* p. 276;
Bromley, "Original Forest Types," p. 73; Robert Greenhalgh
Albion, *Forests and Sea Power: The Timber Problem of the Royal
Navy, 1652–1862* (Cambridge, Mass., 1926), p. 234; James E.
Defebaugh, *History of the Lumber Industry of America,* 2 vols.
(Chicago, 1906–7), 2:73, 130; Wood, *Lumbering in Maine,* p. 20.
32. *The New England Farmer* 4 (1826): 242.
One of the largest oaks standing in the United States is the
400-year-old white oak at Wye Mills, Maryland. It is 95 feet tall,
has a horizontal spread of 165 feet, and a trunk circumference of
21 feet. Michaux, *North American Sylva,* 1:17–30, 76–86, presents much information on the varieties of oak.
33. William Douglass, *A Summary, Historical and Political of
the . . . British Settlements in North America,* 2 vols. (Boston,
1749–51), 2:53–54; Stahl, *Old Broad Bay,* 1:4; Thoreau, *Maine
Woods,* p. 301; Nichols, "Vegetation of Connecticut," p. 203.
34. Nichols, "Vegetation of Connecticut," p. 203.
Nichols says that there is no exact relation between the age of
a tree and the diameter of its trunk. In the eighteenth century,
Peter Kalm found that the largest trees in the Middle Colonies
were only two hundred years old, and many of the younger trees
were decayed (Benson, ed., *Kalm's Travels,* 1:219).

3. English Exploration and Settlement, 1602–1628

1. Louis B. Wright, *The Dream of Prosperity in Colonial
America* (New York, 1965), pp. 1–20.
2. Richard Hakluyt, *The Principall Navigations Voiages and
Discoveries of the English Nation,* 2 vols. (London, 1589; photo-
lithographic facsimile, New York, 1965), vol. 1, par. 4 of the
"Epistle Dedicatorie to Sir Francis Walsingham"; Richard Hakluyt, "Discourse on Western Planting," *Doc. Hist. Me.,* 2 (1877):
105–6; John Brereton, *A Briefe and true Relation of the Dis-*

coverie of the North part of Virginia (London, 1602), pp. 25–26, 34–36.

3. Hakluyt "Discourse on Western Planting," *Doc. Hist. Me.*, 2 (1877): 21–22; John Frampton, *Joyfull Newes out of the new founde world* (London, 1577), pp. 46–55; "A short and brief narration . . ." [Cartier's Second Voyage"], in Henry S. Burrage, ed., *Early English and French Voyages, Chiefly from Hakluyt* (New York, 1906), pp. 75–77; Donald Culross Peattie, *A Natural History of Trees of Eastern and Central North America* (Boston, 1950), pp. 67–68.

For the numerous maladies endured by Englishmen in the sixteenth and seventeenth centuries, see Carl Bridenbaugh, *Vexed and Troubled Englishmen, 1590–1642* (New York, 1968), pp. 8, 26–27, 101–6, 150–52, 186–87: "He was a rare individual in early Stuart days who did not have to nurse along a chronic disability in addition to contracting some kind of fever and a number of other maladies" (p. 102).

4. "An account of the particularities of the imployments of the Englishmen left in Virginia . . ." ["Lane's Account of the Englishmen Left in Virginia"], in Burrage, ed., *Early English and French Voyages*, p. 257; Lawrence C. Wroth, "An Elizabethan Merchant and Man of Letters," *Huntington Library Quarterly* 17 (1954): 308–9.

For problems concerning the background, objectives, and accounts of the Gosnold-Gilbert expedition, see Warner F. Gookin and Philip L. Barbour, *Bartholomew Gosnold, Discoverer and Planter: New England—1602, Virginia—1607* (Hamden, Conn., 1963), pp. 64–70, and D. B. Quinn, "Edward Hayes, Liverpool Colonial Pioneer," *Transactions of the Historic Society of Lancashire and Cheshire* 3 (1959): 25–45.

5. Brereton, *Briefe and true Relation*, pp. 4–7; Charles Knowles Bolton, *The Real Founders of New England: Stories of Their Life along the Coast, 1602–1628* (Boston, 1929), pp. 17–18; "The Relation of Captaine Gosnold's Voyage to the North Part of Virginia . . . Delivered by Gabriel Archer . . ." and "Master Bartholomew Gosnold's Letter to His Father Touching His First Voyage to Virginia, 1602," in Herbert Levermore, ed., *Forerunners and Competitors of the Pilgrims*, 2 vols. (Brooklyn, 1912), 1:50, 56.

There is an excellent map of the route followed by the Gosnold expedition in Gookin and Barbour, *Bartholomew Gosnold.*

6. "The Relation of Captaine Gosnold's Voyage" and "Gosnold's Letter to His Father," in Levermore, ed., *Forerunners and Competitors of the Pilgrims*, 1:52–56; Brereton, *Briefe and true Relation*, pp. 10–12.

7. Wroth, "An Elizabethan Merchant," pp. 308–9; Norman Lloyd Williams, *Sir Walter Raleigh* (London, 1962), p. 163; Edward Thompson, *Sir Walter Raleigh: Last of the Elizabethans* (New Haven, Conn., 1936), p. 146; Charles Manning and Merrill Moore, "Sassafras and Syphilis," *NEQ* 9 (1936): 473. See Burrage's introduction to Brereton's "Briefe and true Relation" in *Early English and French Voyages*, p. 327; Samuel Eliot Morison, *Builders of the Bay Colony*, rev. ed. (Boston, 1962), pp. 6–7.

8. Martin Pring, "A Voyage set out from the Citie of Bristoll ..." ["The Voyage of Martin Pring, 1603"], in Burrage, ed., *Early English and French Voyages*, pp. 343–52; Bolton, *Real Founders*, pp. 21–22; David B. Quinn, "Martin Pring at Provincetown in 1603?" *NEQ* 40 (1967): 79–91; Henry David Thoreau, *Cape Cod* (Boston, 1914), pp. 298–99.

Manning and Moore, "Sassafras and Syphilis," p. 474, say that "because syphilis was considered by many to have come from America, it was only natural, according to the medical thought of the day, that its cure should be found there." For the search for sassafras in Virginia after the settlement at Jamestown, see Wright, *Dream of Prosperity*, pp. 46–47, and Thomas Hughes, *Medicine in Virginia, 1607–1699* (Williamsburg, Va., 1957), pp. 47–49. According to *The Genesis of the United States*, ed. Alexander Brown, 2 vols. (Boston, 1890), 1:384, small sassafras roots drawn in the winter were worth at least £50 a ton in 1619.

9. James Rosier, *A True Relation of the most prosperous voyage made this present yeere 1605, by Captaine George Waymouth ...* ["Rosier's Relation"] (London, 1605), no pagination; A. L. Rowse, *The Elizabethans and America* (New York, 1959), pp. 62, 95; Bolton, *Real Founders*, p. 22.

At least one white pine was planted at Longleat, the estate of the Thynne family in Wiltshire. But these "Weymouth pines" did not grow very well in England (Peattie, *Natural History of Trees*, p. 6).

10. Rowse, *Elizabethans and America*, pp. 61–98.

11. Bolton, *Real Founders*, p. 24; Rowse, *Elizabethans and America*, pp. 99–101; "Relation of a Voyage to Sagadahoc,

1607–1608" in Burrage, ed., *Early English and French Voyages*, pp. 399–419; Charles M. Andrews, *The Colonial Period of American History*, 4 vols. (New Haven, Conn., 1934–38), 1:92.

12. Sir Ferdinando Gorges to Sir Robert Cecil, Dec. 1607, Feb. 1608, *MeHS Colls.*, 2d ser. 2 (1891): 282, 292; Sir William Alexander, *Map and Description of New England* [1630], cited by John Gorham Palfrey, *History of New England*, 3 vols. (Boston, 1890), 1:84n.; William Strachey, *The Historie of Travell into Virginia Britania*, ed. Louis B. Wright and Virginia Freund (London, 1953), p. 35; Andrews, *Colonial Period*, 1:93–94; Bolton, *Real Founders*, p. 24; Rowse, *Elizabethans and America*, pp. 100–101.

For Sir Ferdinando Gorges's efforts to encourage more settlers to come to New England, see his work, "A Briefe Narration of the Originall Undertakings of the Advancement of Plantations Into the parts of America" [London, 1658], pp. 1–57 in Ferdinando Gorges, *America Painted to the Life* . . . (London, 1659), and Rowse, *Elizabethans and America*, pp. 63, 90–122.

13. Bolton, *Real Founders*, pp. 9–12, 25–29, 56–57; Morison, *Builders of the Bay Colony*, pp. 25–26.

14. William Bradford, *Of Plymouth Plantation, 1620–1647*, ed. Samuel Eliot Morison (New York, 1952), pp. 1–27, 58–63; *A Relation Or Journall of the beginning and proceedings of the English Plantation settled at Plimoth in New England* . . . [commonly called "Mourt's Relation"] (London, 1622), pp. 1–4; George D. Langdon, Jr., *Pilgrim Colony: A History of New Plymouth, 1620–1691* (New Haven, Conn., 1966), pp. 1–11; Samuel Eliot Morison, "Plymouth Colony Beachhead," *U.S. Naval Institute Proceedings* 80 (1954): 1352.

For the background of many Plymouth settlers, see Charles Edward Banks, *The English Ancestry and Homes of the Pilgrim Fathers* . . . (Baltimore, 1962). Banks, in his foreword, says that "the large majority of the 'Passengers' of the first four ships . . . came from the great city of London where they had lived in its vast network of lanes and alleys."

15. Bradford, *Of Plymouth Plantation*, pp. 62–65; *Relation Or Journall of the English Plantation at Plimoth*, pp. 2–5.

16. Thoreau, *Cape Cod*, pp. 306–11.

17. Ibid., pp. 2, 251, 308–10; "The Voyages of the Sieur de Champlain of Saintonge, Captain in ordinary for the King in the Navy" [Paris, 1613], trans. and ed. W. F. Ganong, in H. P.

Biggar, ed., *The Works of Samuel de Champlain in Six Volumes* (Toronto, 1922–36), 1:347–48. "The Relation of Captaine Gosnold's Voyage" (in Levermore, ed., *Forerunners and Competitors of the Pilgrims*, 1:46) describes one section of Cape Cod as "all champaine and full of grasse, but the Ilands somewhat wooddie." Modern scientific investigation shows that the older dune tract behind Provincetown was "well anchored by the growth of scrub trees peculiar to the district." Many Cape Cod swamps and offshore waters contain submerged trees (J. B. Woodworth and Edward Wigglesworth, *Geography and Geology of the Region Including Cape Cod . . .* , Memoirs, Museum of Comparative Zoology at Harvard College, 52 [Cambridge, 1934]: 77–79, 296–98).

18. Bradford, *Of Plymouth Plantation*, p. 64; *Relation Or Journall of the English Plantation at Plimoth*, pp. 2–4; "Purchas His Pilgrims," *MHS Colls.* 1st ser. 8 (1802): 206.

19. *Relation Or Journall of the English Plantation at Plimoth*, pp. 16–20; Bradford, *Of Plymouth Plantation*, pp. 65, 69–70.

20. *Relation Or Journall of the English Plantation at Plimoth*, pp. 7–8.

21. Bradford, *Of Plymouth Plantation*, pp. 70–72.

22. *Relation Or Journall of the English Plantation at Plimoth*, pp. 20–23; Bradford, *Of Plymouth Plantation*, pp. 72, 92.

Morison ("Plymouth Colony Beachhead," pp. 1352–53) and Langdon (*Pilgrim Colony*, pp. 12–14) point out that the Pilgrims selected a good site for settlement.

23. William Hilton to his cousin, 1621, in Captain John Smith, *New Englands Trials* (London, 1622), no pagination; *Relation Or Journall of the English Plantation at Plimoth*, pp. 8–10, 15, 18, 23; E. W. [Edward Winslow], *Good Newes From New-England: Or A true Relation of things very remarkable at the Plantation of Plimoth in New-England* (London, 1624), pp. 64–65.

In many sections of Britain, the common people had neither hunting and fishing rights nor access to ponds and woods. See A. R. Myers, *England in the Late Middle Ages (1307–1536)*, rev. ed. (Baltimore, 1956), pp. 137–38. But G. E. Fussell, "Social and Agrarian Background of the Pilgrim Fathers," *Agricultural History* 7 (1933): 183–202, argues that the *Mayflower* passengers were prepared for the new environment merely because some had experience in farming. He also believes that they hunted and fished in spite of the game laws. However, "A Decliration of the

Afaires of the Einglish People [that first] Inhabited New Eingland"
["Narrative of Phinehas Pratt"], in Levermore, ed., *Forerunners
and Competitors of the Pilgrims*, 2:808–9, states that "som
Indescret men, hoping to incoridg thayr friends to Come to them,
writ Letters Conserning the great plenty of Fish fowle and deare,
not considering that the wild Salvages weare many times hun-
grye, that have a better scill to catch such things then Einglish
men have."

The Pilgrims hoped to procure timber and firewood from the
islands in Plymouth Harbor, "wherein are nothing but woods,
Okes, Pines, Wal-nuts, Beech, Sasifras, Vines, and other trees
which wee know not" (*Relation Or Journall of the English Plantation at Plimoth*, pp. 20–21). But since they had no boats, they
could not use the island timber. The Pilgrims were not the only
settlers in North America to misjudge the availability of timber.
(See Marc Lescarbot, *The History of New France*, trans. and ed.
W. L. Grant, 3 vols. [Toronto, 1907–14], 2:255–58.)

24. *Relation Or Journall of the English Plantation at Plimoth*,
pp. 24–25, 27–30; Bradford, *Of Plymouth Plantation*, pp. 76–84,
95, 130; Nathaniel Morton, *New Englands Memorial* (Cambridge, Mass., 1669), p. 22; "Narrative of Phinehas Pratt," in
Levermore, ed., *Forerunners and Competitors of the Pilgrims*,
2:810.

25. *Relation Or Journall of the English Plantation at Plimoth*,
pp. 27–28, 36–37; "Purchas His Pilgrims," *MHS Colls.*, 1st ser.
8 (1802): 225.

26. *Relation Or Journall of the English Plantation at Plimoth*,
pp. 30, 64; Hugh Morrison, *Early American Architecture, from
the First Colonial Settlements to the National Period* (New
York, 1952), pp. 8–11, 136–37; Bradford, *Of Plymouth Plantation*, pp. 94, 103, 107; John Smith, *New Englands Trials*, no
pagination.

According to Martin Shaw Briggs, *The Homes of the Pilgrim
Fathers in England and America (1620–1685)* (New York, 1932),
"only John Alden . . . is known to have any connexion with one
of the crafts, for he was taken on—probably at Southampton—
as a cooper, being then 21 years of age. It has been stated, though
perhaps on inadequate evidence, that he was responsible for
most of the early wooden building" (p. 120).

Samuel Eliot Morison, *The Story of the "Old Colony" of
New Plymouth* (New York, 1956), p. 87, believes that the clap-

boards the Pilgrims shipped to England were "cedar clapboard (in demand in England for wainscoting rooms)," but it is more likely that they were oak staves for barrels. In the early seventeenth century, *clapboard* meant a board of split oak for making casks. Because of the timber shortage in England, few houses with clapboard siding were built, if any.

27. Bradford, *Of Plymouth Plantation*, pp. 90, 97, 111; Nathaniel Morton, *New Englands Memorial*, pp. 27, 32; John Pory to the earl of Southampton, 13 Jan. 1623 and later, in Sidney V. James, Jr., ed., *Three Visitors to Early Plymouth* (Plimoth Plantation, 1963), p. 11; Winslow, *Good Newes From New-England*, p. 4; Harold R. Shurtleff, *The Log Cabin Myth* (Cambridge, Mass., 1939), pp. 10–12; Morrison, *Early American Architecture*, pp. 11–12.

28. Emmanuel Altham to Sir Edward Altham, Sept. 1623, and Isaack de Rasieres to Samuel Blommaert, ca. 1628, in James, ed., *Three Visitors to Early Plymouth*, pp. 24, 26, 28, 76–77; Bradford, *Of Plymouth Plantation*, pp. 125, 127–28, 132.

Bradford does not mention shipments of timber other than clapboard, but other forms of timber were shipped in 1621 and 1623. Of the shipment made in 1623 (aboard the *Anne*, a ship of 140 tons), Bradford says only that the ship was "in a short time laden with clapboard by the help of many hands." Altham's samples were of cedar, beech, pine, oak, and other species, and sassafras may also have been in the cargo. Altham believed that an ambitious person could develop a valuable sassafras trade in the plantation in spite of the exploitation of the tree in Virginia. Sassafras was still selling for two shillings a pound on the English market.

29. *Plym. Recs.*, 11:3–4; Bradford, *Of Plymouth Plantation*, pp. 140, 146, 163, 178, 183, 373; Morton, *New Englands Memorial*, p. 61.

30. *Plym. Recs.*, 11:4; Morrison, *Early American Architecture*, p. 11; Bradford, *Of Plymouth Plantation*, p. 155.

For the craftsmen at Plymouth Colony, see Banks, *English Ancestry and Homes of the Pilgrim Fathers*, passim; Briggs, *Homes of the Pilgrim Fathers*, pp. 120–21; *MHS Colls.*, 2d ser. 4 (1816): 239–40.

31. Emmanuel Altham to Sir Edward Altham, Sept. 1623, in James, ed., *Three Visitors to Early Plymouth*, p. 24; Bradford, *Of Plymouth Plantation*, pp. 187–88; *Plym. Recs.*, 12:9–13.

32. Emmanuel Altham to Sir Edward Altham, Sept. 1623, and Isaack de Rasieres to Samuel Blommaert, ca. 1628, in James, ed., *Three Visitors to Plymouth*, pp. 28, 74–75; Bradford, *Of Plymouth Plantation*, pp. 193, 202, 232, 244, 245–46, 257–60; Morrison, *Early American Architecture*, pp. 90–91; Langdon, *Pilgrim Colony*, p. 36.

For the Pilgrim leaders' difficulties in the fur trade, see Ruth A. McIntyre, *Debts Hopeful and Desperate: Financing the Pilgrim Colony* (Plimoth Plantation, 1963), pp. 47–57.

Because of the danger of attack by the Indians and Dutch, craftsmen prepared the frame and boards for the post at Windsor in advance at Plymouth. These materials, nails, and provisions were then stowed in a large new bark so that when the traders arrived at Windsor they could finish the house quickly, land their provisions, and send the bark home. Safely inside their prefabricated fortress, which by then was protected by palisades, the small band withstood the "warlike manner" of seventy armed men from New Netherland.

33. Bradford, *Of Plymouth Plantation*, pp. 109–10, 116, 117–18; Morton, *New Englands Memorial*, pp. 36, 40–41, 42; "Narrative of Phinehas Pratt," in Levermore, ed., *Forerunners and Competitors of the Pilgrims*, 2:814, 817; Bolton, *Real Founders*, pp. 45–46; Winslow, *Good Newes From New-England*, pp. 13–15, 23–25, 34–46; Christopher Levett, "A Voyage into New England, Begun in 1623, and Ended in 1624," *MHS Colls.*, 3d ser. 8 (1843): 182; James Truslow Adams, *The Founding of New England* (Boston, 1921), pp. 104–5.

34. Bradford, *Of Plymouth Plantation*, pp. 133–38; *Plym. Recs.*, 11:4; "[William] Morell's Poem on New England" [London, 1625], *MHS Colls.*, 1st ser. 1 (1792): 128.

35. Levett, "Voyage into New England," *MHS Colls.*, 3d ser. 8 (1843): 82, 180; Bradford, *Of Plymouth Plantation*, p. 134; Bolton, *Real Founders*, pp. 66, 109, 155.

36. Levett, "Voyage into New England," *MHS Colls.*, 3d ser. 8 (1843): 180; Bolton, *Real Founders*, mentions most of the settlements started along the New England coast during the 1620s.

In August 1622 the Council for New England granted almost all the land between the Merrimack and Kennebec rivers to Captain John Mason and Sir Ferdinando Gorges, who divided their holdings in 1629. Gorges received the land north of the Piscataqua, and Mason that between the Piscataqua and the Merrimack (*Capt. John Mason: The Founder of New Hampshire*, ed. John W. Dean [Boston, 1887], pp. 11–22). For Sir Ferdinando Gorges's attempt at commercial lumbering, see his "Briefe Narration," pp. 39–40, 49–50, in Ferdinando Gorges, *America Painted to the Life*.

37. Levett, "Voyage into New England," *MHS Colls.*, 3d ser. 8 (1843): 180; Bradford, *Of Plymouth Plantation*, pp. 205–10; Thomas Morton, *New English Canaan* (Amsterdam, 1637), p. 132.

4. The Great Migration, 1630-1640

1. Edmund S. Morgan, *The Puritan Dilemma: The Story of John Winthrop* (Boston, 1958), p. 29; [Edward Johnson], *Good news from New-England: With An exact relation of the first planting that Countrey: A description of the profits accruing by the Worke* (London, 1648), pp. 1–3; Joshua Scottow, *A Narrative of the Planting of the Massachusetts Colony Anno 1628* (Boston, 1694), p. 9.

2. "The Diaries of John Hull, Mint-master and Treasurer of the Colony of Massachusetts Bay," *AAS Trans.* 3 (1857): 167; Carl Bridenbaugh, *Vexed and Troubled Englishmen* (New York, 1968), pp. 394–433; Morgan, *Puritan Dilemma*, pp. 18–53; Nellis M. Crouse, "Causes of the Great Migration, 1630–1640," *NEQ* 5 (1932): 8–36; George C. Homans, "The Puritans and the Clothing Industry in England," *NEQ* 13 (1940): 519–29; T. H. Breen and Stephen Foster, "Moving to the New World: The Character of Early Massachusetts Immigration," *William and Mary Quarterly*, 3d ser. 30 (1973): 189–222; Allen French, *Charles I and the Puritan Upheaval: A Study of the Causes of the Great Migration* (Boston, 1955), pp. 230–32, 320, 339, 361; *WP*, 1:296–98; Sumner Chilton Powell, *Puritan Village: The Formation of a New England Town* (Middletown, Conn., 1963), pp. 41, 55–57.

A curious combination of Puritan piety and a desire for a refuge from creditors brought Jonathan Edwards's ancestors to New England (Ola Winslow, *Jonathan Edwards, 1703–1758* [New York, 1940], pp. 5–14).

3. John White, *The Planters Plea, Or The Grounds of Planta-*

tions Examined, And Usuall Objections answered (London, 1630), pp. 21–22; Scottow, *Narrative*, p. 12; [Francis] Higgeson [Higginson], *New-Englands Plantation, or a Short and True Description of the Commodities and Discommodities of that Countrey*, 3d ed. (London, 1630), no pagination; Joshua 17:15, in *The Geneva Bible: A Facsimile of the 1650 Edition* (Madison, Wis., 1969); "Papers of Sir John Eliot," *MHS Procs.* 8 (1864–65): 418–26.

4. Samuel Eliot Morison, *Builders of the Bay Colony*, rev. ed. (Boston, 1962), pp. 21–50; White, *Planters Plea*, pp. 9–69; *Mass. Recs.*, 1:54, 384, 395; "A Letter from Matthew Craddock, to Captain John Endicott" (17 Apr. 1629), *MHS Colls.*, 2d ser. 8 (1819): 117–18; "Records of the Company of the Massachusetts Bay, to the Embarkation of Winthrop and His Associates for New England, as contained in the First Volume of the Archives of the Commonwealth of Massachusetts," *AAS Trans.* 3 (1857): 91–92; George D. Phippen, "The 'Old Planters' of Salem, Who Were Settled Here before the Arrival of Governor Endicott, in 1628," *EIHC* 1 (1859): 97–110, 145–53, 185–99; George Cheever, "Some Remarks on the Commerce of Salem from 1626 to 1741, with a Sketch of Philip English—A Merchant in Salem from about 1670 to about 1733–4," *EIHC* 1 (1859): 67–76.

5. Morgan, *Puritan Dilemma*, pp. 18–53; Bridenbaugh, *Vexed and Troubled Englishmen*, pp. 410n., 434–73; Morison, *Builders of the Bay Colony*, pp. 49–79; Darret B. Rutman, *Winthrop's Boston: Portrait of a Puritan Town, 1630–1649* (Chapel Hill, N.C., 1965), pp. 178–79.

6. For interpretations of the Puritan attitudes toward expansion into the wilderness, see Alan Heimert, "Puritanism, the Wilderness, and the Frontier," *NEQ* 26 (1953): 361–82, and Peter N. Carroll, *Puritanism and the Wilderness: The Intellectual Significance of the New England Frontier, 1629–1700* (New York, 1969), esp. pp. 140–47. For an analysis of the patterns of settlement, see Glenn T. Trewartha, "Types of Rural Settlement in Colonial America," *Geographical Review* 36 (1946): 568–80.

7. *WJ*, 1:47; Johnson, *Good news from New-England*, pp. 5–7; J. Franklin Jameson, ed., *Johnson's Wonder-Working Providence, 1628–1651* (New York, 1910), p. 85; Powell, *Puritan Village*, pp. 77–79.

8. Johnson, *Good news from New-England*, p. 6; Carroll, *Puritanism and the Wilderness*, pp. 11, 137–39; Robert E. Moody,

"Thomas Gorges, Proprietary Governor of Maine, 1640–1643,"
MHS Procs., 3d ser. 75 (1963): 14.
   9. George B. Emerson, *A Report on the Trees and Shrubs Growing Naturally in the Forests of Massachusetts*, 4th ed., 2 vols. (Boston, 1887), 2:576–78; Jameson, ed., *Johnson's Wonder-Working Providence*, p. 112.
   10. William Wood, *New Englands Prospect* (London, 1634), p. 46; Robert E. Moody, *A Proprietary Experiment in Early New England History: Thomas Gorges and the Province of Maine* (Boston, 1963), p. 21; John Josselyn, *An Account of Two Voyages to New England* (London, 1674), pp. 118–20.
   11. William Harrison, *The Description of England*, ed. Georges Edelen (Ithaca, N.Y., 1968), pp. 324–25, 327, 333–35; Scottow, *Narrative*, p. 35; Jameson, ed., *Johnson's Wonder-Working Providence*, p. 112; Daniel Neal, *The History of New-England*, 2 vols. (London, 1720), 2:574; Wood, *New Englands Prospect*, pp. 19–20, 23–24, 44; Capt. John Smith, *Advertisements for the unexperienced Planters of New-England, or any where* (London, 1631), pp. 29–30; Victor E. Shelford, *The Ecology of North America* (Urbana, Ill., 1963), pp. 28–29.
   In England the wooded regions were the traditional retreats of outlaws, thieves, fugitives from justice, and runaways, as well as elves, nickers and other spirits. For a discussion of popular English attitudes toward the wooded regions, see Maurice Keen, *The Outlaws of Medieval Legend* (Toronto, 1961), esp. pp. 1–7. G. E. and K. R. Fussell, *The English Countrywoman: A Farmhouse Social History, A.D. 1500–1900* (London, 1953), pp. xi–xii, also recognize the Englishman's fear of the forest, as does Gilbert Chinard, "The American Philosophical Society and the Early History of Forestry in America," *Proceedings of the American Philosophical Society* 89 (1945): 445.
   In the seventeenth and eighteenth centuries, forested regions were thought to be extremely unhealthful, because the trees prevented the sunlight from reaching the ground (Marc Lescarbot, *The History of New France*, trans. and ed. W. L. Grant, 3 vols. [Toronto, 1907–14], 2:262–65, 306–7, 345–46, and Jeremy Belknap, *The History of New-Hampshire*, 3 vols. [Dover, N.H., 1812], 3:171–72).
   12. William Bradford, *Of Plymouth Plantation, 1620–1647*, ed. Samuel Eliot Morison (New York, 1952), p. 260; Wood, *New Englands Prospect*, p. 46; Josselyn, *Two Voyages*, pp. 29, 117,

122; Edward Winslow to John Winthrop, Sept. 1640, *WP*, 4:262.

13. Christopher Levett, "A Voyage into New England, Begun in 1623, and Ended in 1624," *MHS Colls.*, 3d ser. 8 (1843): 181; Josselyn, *Two Voyages*, pp. 121–22; Wood, *New Englands Prospect*, pp. 46–47; Johnson, *Good news from New-England*, p. 8; Bradford, *Of Plymouth Plantation*, p. 144; Oliver Wendell Holmes, "Dissertation on Intermittent Fever in New England," in *Boylston Prize Dissertations for the Years 1836 and 1837* (Boston, 1838), pp. 1–134.

When Peter Kalm traveled through the forest between Albany and Canada in the mid-eighteenth century, he noted that the woods contained "immense swarms of gnats which annoy the travellers. To be in some measure secured against these insects some besmear their face with butter or grease, for the gnats do not like to settle on greasy places. The great heat makes boots very uncomfortable; but to prevent the gnats from stinging the legs they wrap some paper round them, under the stockings. Some travellers wear caps which cover the whole face, and some have gauze over the eyes. At night they lie in tents, if they can carry any with them, and make a great fire at the entrance so that the smoke will drive the pests away" (Adolph B. Benson, ed., *The America of 1750: Peter Kalm's Travels in North America*, 2 vols. (New York, 1937), 1:336–37).

14. Shelford, *Ecology*, p. 28; Wood, *New Englands Prospect*, pp. 49–52; Smith, *Advertisements*, pp. 28–29; Pond to William Pond, 15 Mar. 1631, *MHS Procs.*, 2d ser. 8 (1892–94): 471; *WP*, 1:165–66; Thomas Prince, "Annals of New England" [Boston, 1775], *MHS Colls.*, 2d ser. 7 (1818): 208; Morgan, *Puritan Dilemma*, pp. 9, 56.

It is probable that former game poachers made the best hunters. When John Winthrop wrote "Common Grevances Groaninge for Reformation" in 1623, he noted that "many handycraftes men in good townes and otherwise doe in the night tyme, with nettes doges and engines take what soever they can spie owte in the day whereby the game is utterly spoyled" (*WP*, 1:307–8).

The best article on the problems of the hunt is Alexander E. Bergstrom, "English Game Laws and Colonial Food Shortages," *NEQ* 12 (1939): 681–90.

15. Richard Eburne, *Plaine Pathway to Plantation* (London, 1624), p. 20; *WJ*, 1:54, 58; Jameson, ed., *Johnson's Wonder-Working Providence*, pp. 65, 113–14; Wood, *New Englands Pros-*

pect, p. 47; Prince, "Annals," p. 209; "Capt. Roger Clap's Memoirs," in Alexander Young, ed., *Chronicles of the First Planters of the Colony of Massachusetts Bay, from 1623 to 1636* (Boston, 1846), pp. 348–49, 351; Thomas Morton, *New English Canaan* (Amsterdam, 1637), pp. 24–25; Harold R. Shurtleff, *The Log Cabin Myth* (Cambridge, Mass., 1939), p. 23; Harry J. Carman, ed., *American Husbandry* (Port Washington, N.Y., 1964), p. 267; Edward Ward, *A Trip to New England* (London, 1699), p. 9; "Buildings and House Hardware: Gleanings from Eighteenth-Century Boston Newspapers," *Old Time New England* 17 (1926): 21; Cotton Mather, *Magnalia Christi Americana* (London, 1702), bk. 4:3; E. B. O'Callaghan, ed., *Documentary History of the State of New York*, 4 vols. (Albany, N.Y., 1849–51), 4:31; Hugh Morrison, *Early American Architecture: From the First Colonial Settlements to the National Period* (New York, 1952), p. 9; Edward Howes to John Winthrop, Jr., 26 Mar. 1632, *WP*, 3:73–74.

Thomas Dudley attributes much of the sickness during the winter of 1630–31 to the lack of warm lodging (Thomas Dudley to the Countess of Lincoln, 1631, *MHS Colls.*, 1st ser. 8 (1802): 43). Michael Wigglesworth, who imigrated to New England when he was a boy, later recalled his first miserable dwelling place at New Haven: "Winter approaching we dwelt in a cellar partly under ground covered with earth the first winter. But I remember that one great rain brake in upon us & drencht me so in my bed being asleep that I fell sick upon it; but the Lord in mercy spared my life & restored my health" ("Autobiography of Michael Wigglesworth," *NEHG Reg.* 17 [1863]: 137).

16. Smith, *Advertisements*, p. 27; Joseph Schafer, *The Social History of American Agriculture* (New York, 1936), pp. 38–39; *WJ*, 1:97, 115; Prince, "Annals," pp. 273–74, 278; Samuel Symonds to John Winthrop, Jr., 14 Dec. 1637, *WP*, 3:518; Jameson, ed., *Johnson's Wonder-Working Providence*, p. 196; Jared Eliot, *Essays upon Field-Husbandry in New England*, ed. Harry J. Carman and Rexford G. Tugwell (New York, 1934), p. 7; Percy W. Bidwell and John I. Falconer, *History of Agriculture in the Northern United States, 1620–1860* (Washington, 1925), p. 9.

17. Robert Trow-Smith, *A History of British Livestock Husbandry to 1700* (London, 1957), pp. 16–18, 41–42, 198, 233, 250–51; R. E. Prothero, *English Farming Past and Present*, 6th ed.

(London, 1961), p. 146; Joan Thirsk, "Farming Techniques," in Joan Thirsk, ed., *The Agrarian History of England and Wales, Volume IV, 1500–1640* (Cambridge, 1967), pp. 192–93; Wallace Notestein, Frances Relf, and Hartley Simpson, eds., *Commons Debates, 1621*, 7 vols. (New Haven, Conn., 1935), 7:514–15; R. J. Forbes, "Food and Drink," in Charles Singer et al., *History of Technology*, 5 vols. (London, 1954–58), 3:12, 23; Mildred Campbell, *The English Yeoman under Elizabeth and the Early Stuarts* (New Haven, Conn., 1942), pp. 206–7; G. E. Fussell, ed., *Robert Loder's Farm Accounts, 1610–1620*, Publications of the Camden Society, 3d ser. 53 (1936): xxiii.

18. Pond to William Pond, 15 Mar. 1631, p. 471; *A Treatise of New England Published in Anno Dom. 1637 and Now Reprinted* (n.p., 1650; photostat in the John Carter Brown Library, Brown University, Providence, R.I.), pp. 2–3. "Trelawny Papers," in *Doc. Hist. Me.*, 3 (1884): 30–32, 46, 57, 109, 141; Robert Earle Moody, "The Maine Frontier, 1607 to 1763" (Ph.D. diss., Yale University, 1933), pp. 18–19; Clarence A. Day, *A History of Agriculture in Maine, 1604–1860* (Orono, Me., 1954), pp. 11–12; *WP*, 3:121; William Hilton to John Winthrop, Jr., ca. 1633, *MHS Procs.*, 2d ser. 10 (1895–96): 361–62; Robert C. Black, *The Younger John Winthrop* (New York, 1966), pp. 70–71.

19. *WJ*, 1:105; "Trelawny Papers," in *Doc. Hist. Me.*, 3 (1884): 141; Powell, *Puritan Village*, p. 12; Wood, *New Englands Prospect*, p. 41; William B. Weeden, *Economic and Social History of New England, 1620–1789*, 2 vols. (Boston, 1890), 1:58–59; *Dorchester Town Records, Fourth Report of the Record Commissioners* (Boston 1880), pp. 1–2; *The Records of the Town of Cambridge (Formerly Newtowne) Massachusetts, 1630–1703* (Cambridge, Mass., 1901), p. 8; *Boston Town Records, 1634–1660: Second Report of the Record Commissioners of the City of Boston, 1877* (Boston, 1877), p. 3.

20. *Boston Town Records, 1634–1660*, pp. 67, 68; *Mass. Recs.*, 1:181–82, 188–89, 219–20, 238–39, 255, 285, 317; *Dorchester Town Records*, p. 37; *Records of the Town of Cambridge*, pp. 30–31; *Plym. Recs.*, 1:38–39.

21. "Some brief collections out of a letter that Mr. [Francis] Higginson sent to his friends in Leicester," in Thomas Hutchinson, *A Collection of Original Papers Relative to the History of the Colony of Massachusetts Bay*, 2 vols. (Albany, N.Y., 1865;

originally published Boston, 1769), 1:53; *WP*, 3:125; *WJ*, 1:112, 143–44; *Mass. Recs.*, 1:260, 291; Bernard Bailyn, *The New England Merchants in the Seventeenth Century* (Cambridge, Mass., 1955), p. 33.

For lists of carpenters and other craftsmen who came to New England during the 1630s, see *MHS Colls.*, 3d ser. 8 (1843): 252–320, 4th ser. 1 (1852): 97–100. The financial problems of John Scobell, a Boston carpenter, are set forth in "A Note-Book Kept by Thomas Lechford, Esq., Lawyer, in Boston, Massachusetts Bay, from June 27, 1638, to July 29, 1641," *AAS Trans.* 7 (1885): 342–49.

22. "Note-Book Kept by Thomas Lechford," pp. 58–59; *WJ*, 1:103–4; "Some brief collections that Mr. Higginson sent to his friends in Leicester," in Hutchinson, *Collection of Original Papers*, 1:53–55.

23. Morrison, *Early American Architecture*, pp. 12–15, 35; Bridenbaugh, *Vexed and Troubled Englishmen*, p. 77; *WJ*, 1:77, 90.

The settlers did not build log cabins. They were not familiar with such structures, and they came from regions that did not have large conifers. In the seventeenth century, English craftsmen used hardwood logs for forts, prisons, and the like, but they always hewed logs square and notched the corners—a process that required a great deal of skill, labor, and a variety of tools (Shurtleff, *Log Cabin Myth*, and H. L. Edlin, *Woodland Crafts in Britain: An Account of the Traditional Uses of Trees and Timbers in the British Countryside* [London, 1949], p. 136).

Sometimes the settlers nailed clapboards to the outer walls of their dwellings before filling the spaces between the studs with soft bricks or wattle and daub (*The Early Records of the Town of Dedham*, 6 vols. [n.p., 1886–1936], 3:25).

24. Moody, "Thomas Gorges," p. 13; Wood, *New Englands Prospect*, p. 52; Campbell, *English Yeoman*, pp. 231–32; Morton, *New English Canaan*, p. 92; *Mass. Recs.*, 1:101–2, 104, 129, 130; *Boston Town Records, 1634–1660*, pp. 2, 3, 4, 7, 13–14; *WJ*, 1:141, 258; *WP*, 4:10.

25. *WJ*, 1:59, 90; *WP*, 3:73–74; Johnson, *Good news from New-England*, pp. 7–8; Morrison, *Early American Architecture*, pp. 39–40; Thomas Dudley to the Countess of Lincoln, 1631, p. 43.

26. *WJ*, 1:63, 75, 207; *Records of the Town of Cambridge*, p. 23; Meyric R. Rogers, *American Interior Design* (New York, 1947), pp. 51–52.

27. Johnson, *Good news from New-England*, pp. 6–7, 9–10; *WP*, 4:51; *WJ*, 1:296; Joseph B. Felt, *The Annals of Salem, from Its First Settlement* (Salem, 1827), p. 120; William P. Upham, "An Account of the Dwelling-Houses of Francis Higginson, Samuel Skelton, Roger Williams, and Hugh Peter," *EIHC* 8 (1866): 256.

28. *WP*, 3:515.

A Cambridge ordinance of April 1636 forbidding the building of unauthorized structures assured residents that they would not be penalized for making additions "to their new dwellinge houses" (*Records of the Town of Cambridge*, p. 22).

29. *WP*, 4:11–12.

30. *A Treatise of New England*, p. 10; Johnson, *Good news from New-England*, pp. 9–10; *WP*, 3:515; "Note-Book Kept by Thomas Lechford," pp. 217–18; Francis Kirby to John Winthrop, 10 May 1637, "Winthrop Papers," *MHS Colls.*, 4th ser. 7 (1865): 19–20.

31. A barn seventy-four feet long and forty feet wide was built near Boston in 1639 ("Note-Book Kept by Thomas Lechford," pp. 94–100, 363–64). See also John Fitchen, *The New World Dutch Barn: A Study of Its Characteristics, Its Structural System, and Its Probable Erectional Procedures* (Syracuse, N.Y., 1968).

32. *WJ*, 1:99; *Boston Town Records, 1634–1660*, pp. 1, 11, 12–13; *Town Records of Salem*, 3 vols. (Salem, Mass., 1868–1934), 1:14; *Records of the Town of Cambridge*, pp. 6, 10, 29; "Hartford Town Votes," *Collections of the Connecticut Historical Society*, 7:9–10. *Lumber*, a word that signified disused articles of furniture and the like that might be found in a storage room or attic, took on a new meaning in the English colonies, where it came to mean timber sawn into planks and boards or otherwise roughly prepared for the market.

33. *WJ*, 1:98, 114; Weeden, *Economic and Social History*, 1:114.

34. "Records of the Company of the Massachusetts Bay, to the Embarkation of Winthrop and His Associates for New England, as Contained in the First Volume of the Archives of the Commonwealth of Massachusetts," *AAS Trans.* 3 (1857): 90,

101–2; *Mass. Recs.*, 1:396, 401; *Records of the Town of Dedham*, 3:37, 78; "Trelawny Papers," *Doc. Hist. Me.*, 3:69; *WP*, 3:167; Josselyn, *Two Voyages*, pp. 28–29; C. F. Innocent, *The Development of English Building Construction* (Cambridge, 1916), p. 92.

35. Robert R. Walcott, "Husbandry in Colonial New England," *NEQ* 9 (1936): 232–33; Sarah Knight, *The Private Journal of a Journey from Boston to New York, in the Year 1704 . . .* (Albany, 1865), pp. 26–27, 82–83.

The type of canoe built by the Indians and the colonists often depended on the species of trees available. In 1605 Champlain sighted Indians with birch bark canoes on the Merrimack. But south of Cape Ann the canoe birch did not grow big enough to make bark canoes, and in Massachusetts Bay Champlain found that the Indians built dugout canoes from white pines. Farther south, the Indians often fashioned dugouts from chestnut, white oak, or tulip trees. In some regions they also used white or red cedars. See "Of Savages, or Voyage of Samuel Champlain of Brouage" [Paris, 1603], trans. and ed. H. H. Langton, and "The Voyages of the Sieur de Champlain of Saintonge, Captain in ordinary for the King in the Navy" [Paris, 1613], trans. and ed. W. F. Ganong, in H. P. Biggar, ed., *The Works of Samuel de Champlain in Six Volumes* (Toronto, 1922–36), 1:104–5, 338–39. Verrazzano says that Indian dugouts in Narragansett Bay had room for fifteen men (Susan Tarrow, "Translation of the Cèllere Codex," in Lawrence C. Wroth, *The Voyages of Giovanni da Verrazzano* [New Haven, 1970], p. 139).

36. *WP*, 4:108, 145; Wood, *New Englands Prospect*, p. 43; *Records of the Town of Dedham* 1:37; *WJ*, 1:83, 115, 137; *Mass. Recs.*, 1:246; "[William] Hubbard's History of New England . . . ," *MHS Colls.*, 2d ser. 5 (1815): 197.

The large number of canoe accidents led to the first New England water-safety ordinances. Salem began testing canoes for safety in 1636 (Felt, *Annals of Salem*, p. 526), and in 1638 the Massachusetts General Court prohibited the use of canoes at ferries. In 1640 some members of the Court attempted to make the use of the canoe illegal (*Essex Court Recs.*, 1:21; *WP*, 4:254; *Mass. Recs.*, 1:292).

37. Wood, *New Englands Prospect*, pp. 25–26; Bailyn, *New England Merchants*, pp. 23–30.

38. *WP*, 3:134, 137–38, 149, 166–67; Edward Hopkins to John Winthrop, Jr., 16 Aug. 1634, "Winthrop Papers," *MHS Colls.*,

4th ser. 6 (1863):325–26; Richard Saltonstall to Emmanuel Downing, 4 Feb. 1632, *MHS Procs.*, 2d ser. 8 (1892–94): 208–9; *WJ*, 1:64; Wood, *New Englands Prospect*, p. 52; *Records of the Town of Dedham*, 3:47; *Mass. Recs.*, 1:253.

39. "Records of the Company of the Massachusetts Bay," *AAS Trans.* 3 (1857): 90, 101–2; *Mass. Recs.*, 1:394, 402; Felt, *Annals of Salem*, pp. 30–31; Pond to William Pond, 15 Mar. 1631, p. 471.

40. "Letter of the Rev. Thomas Welde, 1633," *CSM Pubs.* 13 (1910–11): 130; *WJ*, 1:65, 67, 68, 95, 111, 176, 187, 260, 331; Prince, "Annals," pp. 221, 253, 298–99; Felt, *Annals of Salem*, p. 64; William G. Saltonstall, *Ports of the Piscataqua* (Cambridge, Mass., 1941), p. 11; *MHS Colls.*, 3d ser. 8 (1843): 324–25; Wood, *New Englands Prospect*, p. 40; John W. Dean, ed., *Capt. John Mason, the Founder of New Hampshire* (Boston, 1887), p. 345.

41. *Town Records of Salem*, pp. 12, 40, 54, 107–8; James Duncan Phillips, *Salem in the Seventeenth Century* (Boston, 1933), pp. 96–97; Henry W. Belknap, "Philip English, Commerce Builder," *AAS Procs.*, n.s. 41 (1931): 19–20; "Trelawny Papers," *Doc. Hist. Me.*, 3:89–90, 109, 133, 140, 142, 161–62, 164–65, 176, 216, 243, 258, 279, 283.

A ship may have been built at Dorchester by Nehemiah Bourne or Thomas Hawkins (*Dorchester Town Records*, p. 20; "A Note-Book Kept by Thomas Lechford," pp. 193n., 210–14; Isaac J. Greenwood, "Rear Admiral Nehemiah Bourne," *NEHG Reg.* 27 [1873]: 26–36). In 1639 the Massachusetts legislature attempted to encourage shipbuilding by exempting "ship carpenters, which follow that calling," from militia duty. Probably many shipwrights, like many other craftsmen, gave up their calling and became farmers during the early years of settlement (*Mass. Recs.*, 1:258).

42. Bridenbaugh, *Vexed and Troubled Englishmen*, pp. 470–71; George Louis Beer, *The Origins of the British Colonial System, 1578–1660* (New York, 1908), p. 28on.; *WJ*, 1:126, Emmanuel Downing to Sir John Coke, 23 Aug. 1634, *MHS Procs.*, 2d ser. 8 (1892–94): 385–86; Dean, ed., *Capt. John Mason*, p. 284.

43. Dean, ed., *Capt. John Mason*, pp. 284, 322–28, 336, 344, 351; *N.H. Docs.*, 1:45; *WJ*, 1:129, 2:10–11; "First Settlers of New Hampshire," *NEHG Reg.* 2 (1848): 37–41; Belknap, *History*

of *New-Hampshire*, 1:28, 38; Charles Edward Banks, *History of York, Maine*, 2 vols. (Boston, 1931–35), 1:5, 64–65; Moody, *Proprietary Experiment*, pp. 29–30; Moody, "Thomas Gorges," p. 13; Morgan, *Puritan Dilemma*, pp. 134–47; John Gorham Palfrey, *History of New England*, 3 vols. (Boston, 1890), 1:515–16; John Heard, Jr., *John Wheelwright, 1592–1679* (Boston, 1930), pp. 66–80.

44. "Trelawny Papers," *Doc. Hist. Me.*, 3:71, 78–79, 80–81, 100, 147–49, 162–63; Moody, "Maine Frontier," pp. 17–18; *N.H. Docs.*, 2:530.

5. The Timber Trade, 1640-1688

1. *WJ*, 2:6, 17, 19; *Mass. Recs.*, 1:304.
2. *WJ*, 2:19, 31, 82, 306–7; "[William] Hubbard's History of New England," *MHS Colls.*, 2d ser. 5 (1815): 238–39; John R. Broadhead, *History of the State of New York*, 2 vols. (New York, 1853–71), 1:334–35; Charles M. Andrews, *The Colonial Period of American History*, 4 vols. (New Haven, Conn., 1934–38), 1:497–98; Nathaniel Ward, *The Simple Cobler of Aggawam in America* (London, 1647), p. 71; Edmund S. Morgan, *The Puritan Dilemma: The Story of John Winthrop* (Boston, 1958), pp. 174–84; *Conn. Recs.*, 1:59–61; *Mass. Recs.*, 1:292, 294, 305, 320, 322, 344, 2:137; William B. Weeden, *Economic and Social History of New England, 1620–1789*, 2 vols. (Boston, 1890), 1:169; A. P. Van Gelder and H. Schlatter, *History of the Explosives Industry in America* (New York, 1927), pp. 29–30; William Haynes, *American Chemical Industry: A History*, 6 vols. (New York, 1945–54), 1:53, 77–78; James Duncan Phillips, *Salem in the Seventeenth Century* (Boston, 1933), pp. 154–55; Bernard Bailyn, *The New England Merchants in the Seventeenth Century* (Cambridge, Mass., 1955), pp. 23–26, 49–74, 76–78.

Winthrop, *WJ*, 2:42, says that no fewer than 300,000 cod were caught in 1641. But much of this catch was probably brought in by fishermen who had been making similar catches all through the 1630s. According to Ralph Brown, *Historical Geography of the United States* (New York, 1948), p. 25, a dozen men could catch from 20,000 to 25,000 fish a month. Presumably only 150 men would be needed to catch 300,000 fish a month.

3. J. H. Parry, "Transport and Trade Routes," in E. E. Rich and C. H. Wilson, eds., *The Economy of Expanding Europe in the Sixteenth and Seventeenth Centuries* (1967), vol. 4 in J. H. Clapham and Eileen Power, eds., *The Cambridge Economic History of Europe from the Decline of the Roman Empire* (Cambridge, 1941–67), pp. 181–85; Francisco Morales Padron, *El Comercio Canario-Americano (Siglos XVI, XVII y XVIII)* (Seville, 1955), pp. 22–25, 297; Hans Sloane, *A Voyage to the Islands Madera, Barbados, Nieves, S. Christophers and Jamaica . . .* , 2 vols. (London, 1707–25), 1:9–10; Frédéric Mauro, *Le Portugal et L'Atlantique au XVII Siècle (1570–1670)* (Paris, 1960), pp. 183–89, 299, 352–56.

English trade with Spain in the late Elizabethan and early Stuart eras is discussed in John Browne, *The Merchants Avizo*, ed. P. McGrath, Kress Library Publication no. 11 (Cambridge, Mass., 1957), and Harland Taylor, "Price Revolution or Price Revision? The English Spanish Trade after 1604," *Renaissance and Modern Studies* 12 (1968): 5–32. Trade between the British Empire and Portugal in the eighteenth century is discussed by H. E. S. Fisher, *The Portugal Trade: A Study of Anglo-Portuguese Commerce, 1700–1770* (London, 1971). According to Fisher, New England merchants received few products direct from Portugal, "the American balances in the main being remitted to merchants' agents in England" (p. 19).

4. Darrett B. Rutman, *Winthrop's Boston: Portrait of a Puritan Town, 1630–1649* (Chapel Hill, N.C., 1965), pp. 184–85; *Aspinwall Recs.*, pp. 71–72; *WJ*, 2:68, 72, 126–27.

5. *WJ*, 2:68, 72, 126–27; Robert E. Moody, "Thomas Gorges, Proprietary Governor of Maine, 1640–1643," *MHS Procs.*, 3d ser. 75 (1963): 25.

6. *WJ*, 2:248–50; Bailyn, *New England Merchants*, pp. 83–84.

7. Gillian T. Cell, *English Enterprise in Newfoundland, 1577–1600* (Toronto, 1970), pp. 118–20, 124; *Aspinwall Recs.*, pp. 244–45.

During the same year Mr. Bruen in Funchal (Madeira) demanded that Thomas Mayhew of Massachusetts pay his obligation of 20,000 pipe staves.

8. *WJ*, 2:321; Harold A. Innis, *The Cod Fisheries: The History of an International Economy* (New Haven, Conn., 1940), p. 76.

9. *Aspinwall Recs.*, pp. 75–76, 244–45, 380; Massachusetts Archives, State House, Boston, 60:112; Weeden, *Economic and*

Social History, 1:158, n. 5. Shaken casks consisted of staves that had been formed into casks and subsequently broken down for shipment.

10. *Mass. Recs.*, 2:82, 87, 100, 106, 130, 152, 171, 173, 188, 215, 246, 253, 257, 258, 260, 276, 277; J. Leander Bishop, *A History of American Manufactures from 1608 to 1860*, 2 vols. (Philadelphia, 1864), 1:269–70.

11. Carl and Roberta Bridenbaugh, *No Peace beyond the Line: The English in the Caribbean, 1624–1690* (New York, 1972), pp. 10–14, 26–29; Sir Alan Burns, *History of the British West Indies* (London, 1954), pp. 188–245; *WP*, 1:345, 356–57, 361–62, 382, 405; *WJ*, 2:82, 84.

12. Vincent T. Harlow, *A History of Barbados, 1625–1685* (Oxford, 1926), p. 338; "Voyage of Henry Colt," in Vincent T. Harlow, ed., *Colonising Expeditions to the West Indies and Guiana, 1623–1667* (London, 1925), p. 69; Innis, *Cod Fisheries*, p. 78.

Father Andrew White visited Barbados in 1634 and noted that the trade of the island was "chiefly in corne and cotton, which it delighted us much to see grow upon trees in such plentie" ("A Briefe Relation of the Voyage unto Maryland, by Father Andrew White, 1634," in Clayton Colman Hall, ed., *Narratives of Early Maryland, 1633–1684* [New York, 1910], p. 35).

13. *Conn. Recs.*, 1:59–60, 64, 67, 75.

14. *Early Records of the Town of Portsmouth* (Providence, R.I., 1901), p. 10; *WJ*, 2:31, 73; *Mass. Recs.*, 1:294, 303, 2:105.

15. Harlow, *History of Barbados*, pp. 39–41; Bridenbaugh and Bridenbaugh, *No Peace beyond the Line*, chap. 3, passim, and p. 272; Richard S. Dunn, *Sugar and Slaves: The Rise of the Planter Class in the West Indies, 1624–1713* (Chapel Hill, N.C., 1972), pp. 60–62; Richard Ligon, *A True & Exact History of the Island of Barbados . . .* (London, 1657), pp. 85–86; Andrews, *Colonial Period*, 2:253; Richard S. Dunn, "The Barbados Census of 1680: Profile of the Richest Colony in English America," *William and Mary Quarterly*, 3d. ser. 26 (1969): 3–30; Ellen Deborah Ellis, *An Introduction to the History of Sugar as a Commodity* (Philadelphia, 1905), p. 98.

Barbadian tobacco—judged the worst in the world in Ligon's *History* (p. 113)—had been the most profitable crop in the 1630s and early 1640s, and tobacco growers were important consumers of New England staves, hoops, and heading.

16. Richard Blome, *A Description of the Island of Jamaica* (London, 1672), p. 85; Richard S. Dunn, *Sugar and Slaves,* pp. 67–76, 86–96; Bridenbaugh and Bridenbaugh, *No Peace beyond the Line,* p. 13.

Compare the statistics in these volumes with Harlow, *History of Barbados,* pp. 43–44, 338–40. For the early involvement of New England in the slave trade, see *WJ,* 2:227, and the contract of 13 Feb. 1644 in Massachusetts Archives, 60:290. See also Winthrop D. Jordan, *White over Black: American Attitudes toward the Negro, 1550–1812* (Chapel Hill, N.C., 1968), pp. 63–72, 105, 110, 113, 141–42, 145, 152, 175–76, 181. Bridenbaugh and Bridenbaugh, *No Peace beyond the Line,* pp. 33–34, believe that the shift from indentured white servants to black slave labor in Barbados started before the shift to large-scale sugar production. For the migrations of Europeans in the Caribbean, see ibid., chaps. 7 and 8.

17. Charles de Rochefort, *The History of the Caribby-Islands* (London, 1666), pp. 4, 29–49; "Voyage of Henry Colt," in Harlow, ed., *Colonising Expeditions,* pp. 69–70; "A Briefe Relation of the Voyage unto Maryland, by Father Andrew White, 1634," in Hall, ed., *Narratives of Early Maryland,* p. 37; Ligon, *Barbados,* pp. 22, 23, 25, 41, 66–79, 94; Blome, *Jamaica,* pp. 3, 11, 69–70, 77–78, 98; *CSPC, 1574–1660,* p. 374; David Watts, *Man's Influence on the Vegetation of Barbados, 1627 to 1800,* University of Hull Occasional Papers in Geography, no. 4 (Hull, 1966), chap. 3; Sir Dalby Thomas, *An Historical Account of the Rise and Growth of the West-India Collonies* (London, 1690), p. 16.

Bridenbaugh and Bridenbaugh, *No Peace beyond the Line,* p. 268, claim that land clearing was taking place in nearly every English colony in the West Indies between 1650 and 1665 and that this "may properly be called the era of the Great Clearing."

18. Bridenbaugh and Bridenbaugh, *No Peace beyond the Line,* pp. 269–70, 297–98.

One anonymous writer of 1648 suggested that the English sugar islands should send their crude sugar to Chesapeake Bay for refining to avoid importing fuel "at great expense" (cited by E. G. R. Taylor, *Late Tudor and Early Stuart Geography* [New York, 1968], pp. 126–28).

19. Thomas, *Rise and Growth of the West-India Collonies,* pp. 15–20; Dunn, "The Barbados Census of 1680," pp. 11, 16; Dunn, *Sugar and Slaves,* pp. 287–94.

A plantation of 200 acres required a capital investment of £8,000 and an additional £1,000 a year for operating expenses. 20. Ligon, *Barbados*, p. 113; Blome, *Jamaica*, p. 89; "Voyage of Henry Colt," and "A Briefe Description of the Illande of Barbados," in Harlow, ed., *Colonising Expeditions*, pp. 46–47, 68; Dunn, *Sugar and Slaves*, pp. 272–81.

21. Ralph Greenlee Lounsbury, *The British Fishery at Newfoundland, 1634–1763* (New Haven, 1934), pp. 1–2, 7, 15–18, 22, 40, 56–58; Daniel W. Prowse, *A History of Newfoundland, 1634–1763* (New Haven, Conn., 1895), pp. 103, 126–27, 130–31; Innis, *Cod Fisheries*, pp. 55, 57, 63; Cell, *English Enterprise in Newfoundland*, pp. 63–64.

22. *WJ*, 2:248; Prowse, *History of Newfoundland*, pp. 153, 198; Innis, *Cod Fisheries*, p. 80; Bailyn, *New England Merchants*, p. 129.

The interior of Newfoundland remained heavily wooded; but it was largely inaccessible, and its timber supplies were not exploited until the coming of the railroads in the nineteenth century.

23. *Conn. Recs.*, 1:67–68; Ralph Davis, *The Rise of the English Shipping Industry in the Seventeenth and Eighteenth Centuries* (London, 1962), pp. 217, 222–23; George Louis Beer, *The Origins of the British Colonial System, 1578–1660* (New York, 1908), pp. 247; V. J. Wycoff, "Ships and Shipping of Seventeenth Century Maryland," *Maryland Historical Magazine* 33 (1938): 342; 34 (1939): 59–60; Robert Greenhalgh Albion, *Forests and Sea Power: The Timber Problem of the Royal Navy, 1652–1862* (Cambridge, Mass., 1926), pp. 151–52.

24. Albion, *Forests and Sea Power*, pp. 29, 31, 234.

25. Leo Francis Stock, ed., *Proceedings and Debates of the British Parliaments respecting North America*, 5 vols. (Washington, 1924–41), 1:109.

26. *Aspinwall Recs.*, pp. 13–14, 143, 185; *CSPD, 1649–1650*, p. 317; *CSPD, 1651*, p. 507; *CSPD, 1653–1654*, pp. 163, 253, 317; Weeden, *Economic and Social History*, 1:56; Marion H. Gottfried, "The First Depression in Massachusetts," *NEQ* 9 (1936): 668–69.

27. Bailyn, *New England Merchants*, pp. 127, 219, n. 42; Innis, *Cod Fisheries*, p. 113; Weeden, *Economic and Social History*, 1:235; George Louis Beer, *The Old Colonial System, 1660–1754*, 2 vols. (New York, 1933), 1:73–74, 2:114.

28. Davis, *English Shipping Industry*, p. 182. Davis states that large masts required sixteen tons of shipping, but the largest New England masts required a much greater tonnage.

There is substantial information about the trade from Boston in this period, since port officials required that traders post bonds ensuring that their commodities would go to English ports; the record of these bonds covers departures for 194 days in 1661 and 1662. (See table 1, Appendix B.)

A rather detailed list of mast sizes and prices is given in William Sutherland, *Britain's Glory: Or, Ship-Building Unvail'd Being a General Director, for Building and Compleating The Said Machines* (London, 1717), p. 204. Much of the value of masts, probably 75 to 80 per cent, derived from transportation costs.

29. Noel Deerr, *The History of Sugar*, 2 vols. (London, 1949–50), 2:172; Samuel Winthrop to John Winthrop, Jr., 8 Nov. 1663, in "Winthrop Papers," *MHS Colls.*, 5th ser. 8 (1882): 251; C. S. S. Higham, *The Development of the Leeward Islands under the Restoration, 1660–1688* (Cambridge, 1921), pp. 144, 148; Dunn, *Sugar and Slaves*, pp. 117–87.

Although the population of Virginia reached 40,000 by the early 1660s, the population of Maryland was less than 15,000, and that of the Middle Colonies was still very small. The Dutch held New York, New Jersey, and the shores of Delaware Bay until 1664, and the population of this entire region probably did not exceed 7,000 when the Dutch surrendered to the forces of the duke of York. William Penn did not begin the colonization of the rich agricultural region of Pennsylvania until 1682, and the population of North Carolina in the 1660s was still very small. Permanent settlement in South Carolina did not begin until 1670, and Charleston was not founded until 1680 (Evarts B. Greene and Virginia D. Harrington, *American Population before the Federal Census of 1790* [New York, 1932], pp. 1, 88, 105, 113–14, 123–24, 136–37, 156, 172). For early commercial relations between Massachusetts and Virginia, see Massachusetts Archives, 40:21a, 100:36a. Bermuda is not mentioned in the shipping record of 1661–62, but according to Bailyn, *New England Merchants*, p. 85, New Englanders began to trade with that island in 1645.

30. R. N. Toppan and A. T. S. Goodrick, *Edward Randolph: Including His Letters and Official Papers . . . , 1676–1703*, 7 vols. (Boston, 1898–1909), 2:206; Benjamin Price to Hezekiah Usher et

al., 27 Apr. 1679, Jeffries Family Papers, 33 vols., Massachusetts Historical Society, Boston, 2:147; James G. Lyndon, "Fish and Flour for Gold: Southern Europe and the Colonial American Balance of Payments," *Business History Review* 39 (1965): 171–83.

R. Gravil, "Trading to Spain and Portugal, 1670–1700, *Business History* 10, no. 2 (July 1968): 69–88, presents a great deal of information on English trade with Spain, but New England merchants are not mentioned.

In 1665 the royal commissioners sent by the king and Privy Council to determine the nature of the trade carried on at Massachusetts Bay did not include statistics in their reports. "The commodities of the country," they wrote, "are fish, which is sent into France, Spain and the Streights, pipe staves, masts, firr boards, some pitch and tarr, pork, beef, horses, and corn, which they send to Virginia, Barbados, etc." In return for these products the Massachusetts merchants "take tobacko and sugar for payment, which they after send for England" ("Copy of a Narrative of the Commissioners from England, about New England" [1665], in Thomas Hutchinson, *A Collection of Original Papers Relative to the History of the Colony of Massachusetts Bay*, 2 vols. [Albany, 1865; originally published Boston, 1769], 2:150).

31. Dunn, "The Barbados Census of 1680," p. 4, n. 5; 6–8; Dunn, *Sugar and Slaves*, pp. 87, 126–31, 169, 203; Harlow, *History of Barbados*, p. 338; Deerr, *History of Sugar*, 1:193, 2:172; Edmund Hickeringill, *Jamaica viewed . . .* (London, 1661), p. 18; Frank Wesley Pitman, *The Development of the British West Indies, 1700–1763* (New Haven, Conn., 1917), p. 48, n. 25.

32. Dunn, *Sugar and Slaves*, pp. 210–11, states that the scattered shipping records for Nevis, Saint Kitts, and Montserrat for 1678–84 show that 107 vessels (an average of 15 a year) arrived in those islands from New England ports, 77 of them from Boston. For the development of the Leeward Islands in this period, see ibid., pp. 140–48.

33. *N.H. Docs.*, 17:515.
Not all of the mast ships went to England.

34. Beer, *Old Colonial System*, 2:225; Innis, *Cod Fisheries*, pp. 70, 100–101, 109; Lounsbury, *British Fishery at Newfoundland*, p. 119; Viola F. Barnes, *The Dominion of New England: A Study in British Colonial Policy* (New York, 1960), p. 146, n. 33.

35. Beer, *Old Colonial System*, 2:194–200; Frank Wesley

Craven, *The Southern Colonies in the Seventeenth Century,*
1607–1689 (Baton Rouge, La., 1949), pp. 184, 240, 241, 358,
401, 409; Carl Bridenbaugh, *Cities in the Wilderness: The First*
Century of Urban Life in America, 1625–1742 (New York,
1938), p. 33.

Both Barnes, *The Dominion of New England,* pp. 158–59, and
Michael Garibaldi Hall, *Edward Randolph and the American*
Colonies, 1676–1703 (Chapel Hill, N.C., 1960), pp. 110–11, hold
that by 1686 the strict enforcement of the Navigation Acts
had curtailed New England trade with the Continent and that
this, in turn, led to decreased trade with both the West Indies and
the Southern Colonies. This interpretation, however, is partially
based on Edward Randolph's allegation that there was a large
amount of illegal trade between New England and foreign ports.
In the early 1680s the New England tonnage to the Southern
Colonies was possibly much higher than tables 2–6 suggest. Trade
in this period seems to have been extremely complex and vari-
able, and there were apparently great shifts in the amount and
direction of the New England export tonnage. But shifts in trade
and the composition of cargo were not caused by the enforcement
of the Navigation Acts alone, for changes resulted from numerous, often unrelated, factors.

36. Lounsbury, *British Fishery at Newfoundland,* pp. 141–42.
According to Innis, *Cod Fisheries,* p. 118, Boston exported
50,000 quintals of dried fish in 1700, three-quarters of which went
to Bilbao. Raymond McFarland, *A History of the New England*
Fisheries (New York, 1911), p. 69, claims that Massachusetts
exported about 100,000 quintals of dried codfish at the close of
the seventeenth century. (A quintal weighed 100 to 112 pounds
and was made up of about 120 fish.) The Commissioners of the
United Colonies of New England declared in 1660 that fish was
"the most staple comoditie in this Countrey" (Ebenezer Hazard,
ed., *Historical Collections: Consisting of State Papers and Other*
Authentic Documents, 2 vols. [Philadelphia, 1792–94], 2:436).
See also Toppan and Goodrick, *Edward Randolph,* 2:208–9;
"Mass. Shipping Abstracts," pt. 1, vol. 1, pp. 22–127.

37. John Josselyn, *An Account of Two Voyages to New-*
England (London, 1674), pp. 210–11; "Mass. Shipping Abstracts," pt. 1, vol. 1, pp. 22–127.

38. *CSPC, 1669–1674,* p. 475; John Hull, "Letter Book," 1670–

85, typescript, American Antiquarian Society, Worcester, Mass., 1:118.

In 1671 the Assembly of Barbados complained that the land was becoming less productive because of inadequate fertilization and that timber and wood were being destroyed (Ellis, *Sugar as a Commodity*, pp. 107–8).

39. Bridenbaugh and Bridenbaugh, *No Peace beyond the Line*, pp. 297–98; *CSPC, 1675–1676*, p. 466; "Mass. Shipping Abstracts," pt. 1, vol. 1, pp. 22–127.

Two additional departures for the West Indies recorded in the Massachusetts Archives for 25 Mar. 1687–29 Sept. 1687 have no entry for cargo (Massachusetts Archives, 7:16–41). The estimates of timber needs are calculated from figures in Thomas, *Rise and Growth of the West-India Collonies*, p. 15; Dunn, "The Barbados Census of 1680," p. 4, n. 5; Deerr, *History of Sugar*, 1:193. Every ton of sugar required the equivalent of two 1,000-pound hogsheads. Additional hogsheads were needed for the molasses. One ton of molasses was the by-product of five tons of sugar.

40. "Mass. Shipping Abstracts," pt. 1, vol. 1, pp. 22–127.

It is possible that some goods labeled "provisions" actually were cheaper grades of fish. However, some entries make a clear distinction between fish and provisions. Two additional departures for the West Indies recorded in the Massachusetts Archives, 7:16–41, have no entries for cargo.

41. John Hull to William Stoughton and Peter Bulkeley, 22 Dec. 1677, in John Hull, "Letter Book," 2:365; *Conn. Recs.*, 3:297; Curtis P. Nettels, *The Money Supply in the American Colonies before 1720* (Madison, Wis., 1934), p. 95; "An Account of the Present State and Government of Virginia" [ca. 1696], *MHS Colls.*, 1st ser. 5 (1798): 126. Richard Forde, *New Map of the Island of Barbadoes* (London, ca. 1674), notes that "For Provisions they are chiefly furnished from other American Plantations." Harlow, *History of Barbados*, p. 283, believes that Barbados "received a considerable proportion of her foodstuffs from England and Ireland."

42. "Mass. Shipping Abstracts," pt. 1. vol. 1, pp. 22–127; Sloane, *Voyage*, 1:lxxxiv.

In this period almost all of the from 70,000 to 80,000 arable acres on Barbados were under cultivation. One horse was needed

for about 20 acres of sugar land. For the horse trade, see Bridenbaugh and Bridenbaugh, *No Peace beyond the Line*, pp. 97, 291.

43. Prowse, *History of Newfoundland*, p. 205; Lounsbury,
British Fishery at Newfoundland, p. 129; *CSPC, 1675–1676*, pp.
140, 157, 185; Innis, *Cod Fisheries*, p. 102.

44. "Mass. Shipping Abstracts," pt. 1, vol. 1, pp. 1–76; Bailyn,
New England Merchants, p. 130; Beer, *Old Colonial System*,
2:205, 225.

Most molasses received by New Englanders from the West Indies was used for sweetening, not for making rum (Gilman N. Os-
trander, "The Colonial Molasses Trade," *Agricultural History*
30 (1956): 77–85).

45. "Mass. Shipping Abstracts," pt. 1, vol. 1, pp. 22–76.

46. Ibid.

47. Richard Pares, *Yankees and Creoles: The Trade between
North America and the West Indies before the American Revolution* (Cambridge, Mass., 1956), pp. 104, 121, 150–52; Fisher,
Portugal Trade, pp. 71, 90–91; John Hull, "Letter Book," 1:121–
22; Toppan and Goodrick, *Edward Randolph*, 2:208–9; Bridenbaugh and Bridenbaugh, *No Peace beyond the Line*, pp. 340–41.

Figures on exports from the British West Indies in 1677–78
are in "An Account of all goods entered in H. M. Customs from
one plantation to another. Michaelmas 1677–Michaelmas 1678,"
reproduced in Higham, *Leeward Islands*, p. 210. Edward Randolph's records are in "Mass. Shipping Abstracts," pt. 1, vol. 1,
pp. 1–22, 77–92.

Some of the logwood collected by Yankee traders was sent
direct to France and the Netherlands.

48. Fisher, *The Portugal Trade*, pp. 90–91; Bailyn, *New
England Merchants*, pp. 145–46, 148–49, 152–53, 156–57; Beer,
Old Colonial System, 2:80; Josselyn, *Two Voyages*, pp. 211–12;
Forde, *New Map of the Island of Barbadoes*.

The Navigation Act of 1663 allowed New England ships to
take on salt in any part of Europe, wine in Madeira and the Azores,
and servants, horses, and provisions in Scotland and Ireland.

49. Forde, *New Map of the Island of Barbadoes*; *CSPC, 1675–
1676*, p. 381; *MHS Colls.*, 3d ser. 8 (1843): 338; Barnes,
Dominion of New England, pp. 140–41; Harlow, *History of
Barbados*, pp. 282–85.

The requirements and actual operation of the Navigation Acts
of 1660 and 1673 are unclear. The Navigation Act of 1660 required

the captains of all vessels sailing from England, Ireland, and Wales, for any English colony to post a substantial bond insuring that any enumerated goods picked up in any English colony would be unloaded in England, Ireland, or Wales. The captains of all other English vessels picking up enumerated goods in English colonial ports were required to post bond insuring that they would take these goods only to another English plantation, or to England, Ireland, or Wales. According to English merchants, Yankee traders were bringing sugar and tobacco to Boston and claiming that their bonds were discharged when the goods were landed. The Yankees then claimed that they could legally ship enumerated goods direct from Boston to the Continent.

The Navigation Act of 1673 was passed to limit the profits earned by the New England merchants in this allegedly unlawful trade. This act required the captains of all English vessels who did not take out a bond in England or Wales in conformity with the Navigation Act of 1660 to pay duties roughly equivalent to the duties imposed on the same goods upon entrance into England. The Customs Commissioners established by the Navigation Act of 1673 claimed that bonds were still required under the Navigation Act of 1660 for all those who loaded enumerated products. The New England merchants, however, claimed that if duties were paid in the colonies under the Navigation Act of 1673, no bonds were required, and consequently enumerated products could still be carried from Boston to the Continent.

Pares, *Yankees and Creoles*, p. 147, and Bailyn, *New England Merchants*, pp. 150–51, believe that under the Navigation Act of 1673 goods shipped from the West Indies to Boston for transshipment to England were subject to duty at the port of origin and in England. Andrews, *Colonial Period*, 4:122–23, believes that although double duties might have been paid, the second payment would probably have been refunded. Lawrence A. Harper, *The English Navigation Laws: A Seventeenth-Century Experiment in Social Engineering* (New York, 1939), gives extensive information about the operation of the Navigation Acts at the waterside but not about double duties. Additional duties placed on tobacco and sugar in 1685 were not aimed directly at New England trade (Beer, *Old Colonial System*, 1:160–67). For some complaints about violations of the Navigation Acts, see Massachusetts Archives, 126:53, 112, 115–16, 133, 134, 156, 164, 282, 367, 380, 127:150, 250, 295, 299, 128:91, 129:121,

288; Toppan and Goodrick, *Edward Randolph*, 4:164–65; "Dudley Records," *MHS Procs.*, 2d ser. 13 (1899–1900): 253, 271; Bailyn, *New England Merchants*, pp. 163–64.

6. Timber Imperialism, 1632-1692

1. "A Note-Book Kept by Thomas Lechford . . . 1638 to 1641," *AAS Trans.* 7 (1885): 92, 223; *WP*, 4:422; William B. Weeden, *Economic and Social History of New England*, 2 vols. (Boston, 1890), 1:129, 135; Charles E. Clark, *The Eastern Frontier: The Settlement of Northern New England, 1610–1763* (New York, 1970), pp. 36–89.

2. *Mass. Recs.*, 1:167, 236–37, 259, 289; John Gorham Palfrey, *History of New England*, 3 vols. (Boston, 1890), 1:516; Robert Earl Moody, "The Maine Frontier" (Ph.D. diss., Yale University, 1933), p. 42.

The Massachusetts General Court always claimed that the northern border of the Bay Colony was three miles north of the northernmost source of the Merrimack.

3. Palfrey, *History of New England*, 1:205, 516–21, 587–91; Moody, "Maine Frontier," pp. 34–48; Edmund S. Morgan, *The Puritan Dilemma: The Story of John Winthrop* (Boston, 1958), pp. 134–54; H. L. Osgood, *The American Colonies in the Seventeenth Century*, 3 vols. (New York, 1904–7), 1:374–75.

There were economic motives for the northern extension of the borders of Massachusetts Bay in the 1630s, too. See the letter of Emanuel Downing, 12 Dec. 1633, in *CSPC, 1675–76*, p. 159.

4. *N.H. Docs.*, 40, passim.

For an analysis of the favorable balance of trade enjoyed by Boston and other cities with the back country, see Carl Bridenbaugh, *Cities in the Wilderness: The First Century of Urban Life in America, 1625–1742* (New York, 1938), pp. 30–33, 40–41, and Curtis P. Nettels, *The Money Supply in the American Colonies before 1720* (Madison, Wis., 1934), pp. 99–102.

The lack of law and order in the region north of the Merrimack is probably exaggerated at times. Except for some of the fishing settlements, it is doubtful that New Hampshire and Maine had any more lawbreaking and commandment breaking than other frontier regions. Nevertheless, many residents in the north believed that their neighbors were more unruly than the settlers of Massachusetts Bay and that the northward extension of Massachusetts authority would insure the establishment of law and order. The apprehension of runaway servants—who always gathered where government was weak—was another reason for union with Massachusetts (N.H. Docs., 40:41–42). See also the comments of Thomas Lechford, Plain Dealing: Or Newes from New-England (London, 1642), p. 47.

5. Palfrey, History of New England, 1:587–92; Joseph B. Felt, The Annals of Salem (Salem, 1827), p. 130; WJ, 2:20, 23, 25–26, 27–28, 38–39; Raymond Phineas Stearns, The Strenuous Puritan: Hugh Peter, 1598–1660 (Urbana, Ill., 1954), p. 148; Samuel Eliot Morison, Builders of the Bay Colony, rev. ed. (Boston, 1962), pp. 235–37; Allen Johnson and Dumas Malone, eds., Dictionary of American Biography (New York, 1928–36), 2:579–80.

Hugh Peter had been at Piscataqua in Dec. 1640 when a great English ship, the 300-ton Charles, and another vessel took on a huge load of pipe staves for Mediterranean ports. Early in 1641 he was chosen to negotiate trade relations with merchants of England, New England, and the West Indies. A large timber carrier, rated at 300 tons, was built by merchants at Salem who had been inspired by his propaganda. Peter was one of the first to deal with the problems of economic growth in underdeveloped forest land.

Exeter joined Massachusetts when Wheelwright, whose Antinomian faction had grown weak, led a small group of followers to Wells, just outside the expanded jurisdiction of Massachusetts (John Heard, Jr., John Wheelwright, 1592–1678 [Boston, 1930], pp. 79–83, and Edmund M. Wheelwright, "A Frontier Family," CSM Pubs. 1 [1892–94]: 277, 280–83).

6. WJ, 2:42–43; Palfrey, History of New England, 1:589–92; Moody, "Maine Frontier," pp. 43–55.

According to Moody, p. 261, many of the original settlers of Ipswich and Newbury (Mass.) migrated northward. For the early attitude of the Puritans concerning land speculation, see E. A. J. Johnson, American Economic Thought in the Seventeenth Century (New York, 1961), p. 22.

7. Palfrey, History of New England, pp. 587–92; WP, 4:422; N.H. Docs., 40, passim.

8. Moody, "Maine Frontier," pp. 69–74, believes that the

Massachusetts leaders had designs on Maine from the beginning. He views Winthrop's refusal to intervene in disputes in the 1630s and 1640s as part of a calculated policy: "The tactics adopted by Winthrop were precisely those which would sooner or later put Massachusetts into the saddle in Maine. To try to claim that Massachusetts had no such intentions is to ignore entirely that Winthrop was an able diplomat who was never at a loss to justify his obedience, or as the case often was, disobedience to legal principle." William Willis, *The History of Portland*, 2 vols. (Portland, Me., 1831–33), 1:21–83, analyzes the conflict between Maine and Massachusetts solely in terms of religion. Neither author emphasizes economic factors.

9. *Aspinwall Recs.*, pp. 13–14, 143, 379, 380; *CSPD, 1649–1650*, pp. 317–18.

Those involved in the mast shipment of 1646 were Adam and Stephen Winthrop, Benjamin Gillam, Joshua Foote, Thomas Bell, and Emanuel Downing. There were mast shipments to England in 1647, 1648, and 1649.

In 1646 the Commissioners for Foreign Plantations awarded the region between the Kennebunk and Cape Elizabeth to Alexander Rigby, over the objection of Sir Ferdinando Gorges. George Cleeves, who administered this territory for Rigby, returned to England in 1650. For events in the life of Cleeves, see Moody, "Maine Frontier," chap. 3; Palfrey, *History of New England*, 1:594–95, 2:383; Willis, *History of Portland*, 1:21–83.

10. For more details on the government formed by Edward Godfrey in July 1649, see Palfrey, *History of New England*, 2:383–86; William D. Williamson, *The History of Maine from Its Discovery to the Separation (1607–1820)*, 2 vols. (Hallowell, Me., 1832), 1:325–27; Charles M. Andrews, *The Colonial Period in American History*, 4 vols. (New Haven, 1934–38), 1:426–29. Leading participants in this government were Nicholas Shapleigh, Thomas Withers, and Richard Leader, all of Kittery, and Edward Rishworth of Agamenticus (York). Clark, *Eastern Frontier*, pp. 48–49, suggests that legislation by the Godfrey government on 16 Oct. 1649 allowing residents to establish independent churches "contains substantial internal evidence of Puritan influence from southwest of the Piscataqua."

One tiny settlement in Maine—Pejepscot (Brunswick), settled by Thomas Purchas and his company at an early date—had been annexed by Massachusetts Bay in July 1639 (Palfrey, *History of New England*, 1:593).

For an estimate of the population of Maine in 1640, see Williamson, *History of Maine*, 1:267n.

11. *Mass. Recs.*, 3:247, 250–51; 4, pt. 1, 44, 64, 68, 70, 73, 188, 420–21, 437.

That the commissioners shared a common economic interest in the region north of Cape Ann does not mean that they were members of an "Essex County Junto." In 1644 William Hawthorne of Salem was elected Speaker of the House of Deputies and became the leading opponent of Governor John Winthrop and the oligarchical House of Assistants. Hawthorne publicly declared that if the House of Assistants did not limit its powers, it would not be obeyed, and he even threatened to appeal to the unenfranchised for support. Bradstreet, although a member of the House of Assistants, openly supported Hawthorne. The other members refused to relinquish their power, but Winthrop's loss of the governorship to another Essex County resident, John Endecott, and the election of Hawthorne and Bradstreet as delegates to the New England Confederacy in place of Winthrop and Dudley clearly demonstrated the growing political power of the Essex County towns. But the Essex deputies did not always agree among themselves, and, aside from the revolt against Winthrop and the Assistants in 1644, there was apparently no definite Essex County position embracing all matters of general interest. But the Essex County merchants were united in their determination to expand the political and economic influence of Massachusetts beyond the Merrimack (*Mass. Recs.*, 1:339; 2:12, 51–52, 58–59; 3:94, 247; *N.H. Docs.*, 40:12, 13; J. Franklin Jameson, ed., *Johnson's Wonder-Working Providence, 1628–1651* [New York, 1910], p. 143; *WJ*, 2:304–5; Palfrey, *History of New England*, 1:157–60, 303–4, 521, 591; 2:156–57, 316n., 362, 627; 3:329–32; Andrews, *Colonial Period*, 1:452; Morison, *Builders of the Bay Colony*, pp. 65, 95, 108, 135, 138, 235–37, 256, 319, 321, 325, 332, 372).

For the new outlook developing among most New England merchants in this period, see Bernard Bailyn, *The New England Merchants in the Seventeenth Century* (Cambridge, Mass., 1955), 103–9.

12. "Province of Maine's Petition to the Council of State in

England," in Ebenezer Hazard, ed., *Historical Collections: Consisting of State Papers and Other Authentic Documents*, 2 vols. (Philadelphia, 1792–94), 1:559; Palfrey, *History of New England*, 2:385; Marion Jacques Smith, *A History of Maine: From Wilderness to Statehood* (Portland, Me., 1949), p. 96.

For the difficulties of Richard Leader, see Edward Neal Hartley, *Ironworks on the Saugus* (Norman, Okla., 1957), pp. 135–37; Bailyn, *New England Merchants*, pp. 67–70; and Everett E. S. Stackpole, *Old Kittery and Her Families* (Lewiston, Me., 1903), pp. 128–29.

13. *Mass. Recs.*, 3:274, 288, vol. 4, pt. 2, p. 242; Lawrence Shaw Mayo, *John Endecott: A Biography* (Cambridge, Mass., 1936), pp. 222–24; Palfrey, *History of New England*, 2:385; Moody, "Maine Frontier," p. 83.

14. *Mass. Recs.*, 3:278, 288, vol. 4, pt. 1, pp. 109–10, vol. 4, pt. 2, p. 242; Mayo, *John Endecott*, pp. 222–24.

15. Stackpole, *Old Kittery and Her Families*, pp. 140–46.

For the career of Thomas Wiggin, see Palfrey, *History of New England*, 1:366n., 517, 613; 3:329; *Mass. Recs.*, 3:256; Charles Henry Pope, *The Pioneers of Maine and New Hampshire* (Boston, 1908), pp. 233–36. Apparently the two New Hampshire men, Pendleton and Wiggin, were added to the commission because they dealt with people on the northeastern side of the Piscataqua.

16. Hazard, ed., *Historical Collections*, 1:573–77 [including "Privileges of the Town of Kittery" (pp. 573–74), "The Retourne of the Commissioners . . . " (p. 570), and "Privileges of the Town of Agamenticus" (pp. 576–77)]; Stackpole, *Old Kittery and Her Families*, pp. 141–46; Smith, *History of Maine*, pp. 96–97; Palfrey, *History of New England*, 2:386; George Ernst, *New England Miniature: A History of York, Maine* (Freeport, Me., 1961), pp. 18–19, 106–7; Andrews, *Colonial Period*, 1:429n.

Godfrey went to England in 1655 and attempted to interest Cromwell and the Puritan Parliament in an independent colony in Maine, but as long as the Puritans were in power in England, his proposal was ignored.

17. *Mass. Recs.*, 3:361–63, vol. 4, pt. 1, pp. 157–65, 207; Mayo, *John Endecott*, p. 225; Palfrey, *History of New England*, 2:387.

18. *Mass. Recs.*, 2:335–38, vol. 4, pt. 1, pp. 357–62; Palfrey, *History of New England*, 2:387–89.

After 1658 Wesgustogo (North Yarmouth) was the first town northeast of the Massachusetts line.

19. Robert E. Moody, "Thomas Gorges, Proprietary Governor of Maine, 1640–1643," *MHS Procs.*, 3d ser. 75 (1963): 20.

20. *Mass. Recs.*, vol. 4, pt. 1, p. 165.

21. The merchants were also beginning to force out the undercapitalized entrepreneurs who had already exploited forest land and built mills in this region. By the sixth decade, some of these unfortunate pioneers owed large sums to the wealthy merchants of Boston, Salem, and Ipswich; there is little doubt that a number of these creditors sought political power in Maine to protect their investments (*Me. Court Recs.*, 2:33–34, 190, 250, 275, 279, 3:57–58, 62, 68, 83–84, 89; Charles Edward Banks, *History of York, Maine, Successively Known as Bristol (1632), Agamenticus (1641), Gorgeana (1642), and York (1652)*, 2 vols. [Boston, 1931–35], 2:246–48; *Essex Court Recs.*, 2:251, 3:92, 168–71; "Records of the Suffolk County Court, 1671–1680," *CSM Pubs.* 29 [1933]: 65–78, 30 [1933]: 899–900; Curwin Papers [1652–1889], Essex Institute, Salem, Mass., vols. 3 and 4; Miscellaneous Bound Papers, Massachusetts Historical Society, Boston, Mass., 2 [1663–74]; John Hull, "Letter Book," American Antiquarian Society, Worcester, Mass., 1:11, 14–15, 140, 142, 144, 150–51, 174–76, 188, 203–6, 241–42, 244, 250, 277–78).

In this period the fishing industry gradually moved away from the New England coast to the shoals off Cape Breton and Newfoundland (William G. Saltonstall, *Ports of the Piscataqua* [Cambridge, Mass., 1941], p. 14; Byron Fairchild, *Messrs. William Pepperrell* [Ithaca, N.Y., 1954], 13; Weeden, *Economic and Social History*, 1:371–72).

22. Robert Greenhalgh Albion, *Forests and Sea Power: The Timber Problem of the Royal Navy, 1652–1862* (Cambridge, Mass., 1926), pp. 51–52, 56, 218; Bailyn, *New England Merchants*, pp. 132–33; *N.H. Docs.*, 17:515.

In 1665 there were over twenty sawmills in the Piscataqua region alone ("Copy of a Narrative of the Commissioners from England, about New England" [1665], in Thomas Hutchinson, *A Collection of Original Papers Relative to the History of the Colony of Massachusetts Bay*, 2 vols. [Albany, 1865; originally published Boston, 1769], 2:152). The figures for sawmill production and the value of boards are estimates. In the seventeenth century a reciprocating saw powered by a mill wheel could produce from 500 to 1,000 feet of one-inch boards a day and probably operated 180 days a year. The cost of boards at the mill was about thirty shillings a thousand feet. However, the price of boards in the West Indies, estimated here at three pounds a thousand feet, fluctuated greatly in relation to supply and demand. In 1659 white pine boards were selling in Barbados for only two pounds ten shillings a thousand feet (Vincent T. Harlow, *A History of Barbados, 1625–1685* [Oxford, 1926], pp. 278–79). But in 1673 John Hull instructed his agent to sell boards in Jamaica at ten pounds a thousand feet (John Hull, "Letter Book," 1:121–22). Between 1714 and 1721 New England boards sold for from four to six pounds a thousand feet in Barbados (Byron Fairchild, "A Sea of Troubles: The Voyage of *Bonetta*, 1718," *The American Neptune* 9 [1949]: 136).

White oak pipe staves, which cost three or four pounds a thousand in New England, sold for eighteen or twenty pounds in the wine regions (*Aspinwall Recs.*, pp. 244–45, 374–75; *Me. Court Recs.*, 2:164).

23. John Josselyn, *An Account of Two Voyages to New-England* (London, 1674), pp. 207–12.

24. Rufus M. Jones, *The Quakers in the American Colonies* (New York, 1966), pp. 79–89, 101–5; *Mass. Recs.*, vol. 4, pt. 2, p. 69.

Walter Barefoot later became Edward Randolph's deputy collector at Portsmouth.

25. Moody, "Maine Frontier," pp. 107–9, 115–16; *Mass. Recs.*, vol. 4, pt. 1, p. 219; Bailyn, *New England Merchants*, pp. 114–15; Jones, *Quakers*, pp. 90–92; Andrews, *Colonial Period*, 1:429n.

26. The best discussion of political division in this period is Paul R. Lucas, "Colony or Commonwealth: Massachusetts Bay, 1661–1666," *William and Mary Quarterly*, 3d ser. 24 (1967): 88–107. (Lucas does not mention the Quaker problem, however.)

27. Bailyn, *New England Merchants*, pp. 127, 219, n. 42; Harold A. Innis, *The Cod Fisheries: The History of an International Economy* (New Haven, 1940), p. 113; Weeden, *Economic and Social History*, 1:235; George Louis Beer, *The Old Colonial System, 1660–1754*, 2 vols. (New York, 1933), 1:73–74; 2:114; "The Names of such ships & masters that have Come in and

gone out of our Harbours and Given bond for His Majesty's Customes," Massachusetts Archives, 60:33.

28. Palfrey, *History of New England*, 2:448–52, 521, 527, 576–82; Jones, *Quakers*, pp. 98–99; *Mass. Recs.*, vol. 4, pt. 2, pp. 99–100, 141–43, 304–5; Bailyn, *New England Merchants*, p. 125; Moody, "Maine Frontier," pp. 119–20, 140–45, 150–53. For the activities of the royal commissioners in Maine, see the *Clarendon Papers, Collections of the New-York Historical Society* (New York, 1869), pp. 71–72, 79–80, 138–39.

29. *Mass. Recs.*, vol. 4, pt. 2, pp. 318, 327–28, 368–70, 538; *The Early Records of the Town of Dedham, Massachusetts*, 6 vols. (n. p., 1886–1936), 4:156.

30. Palfrey, *History of New England*, 3:96–97. The immediate issue of the 1668 annexation seems to have been a conflict over land on the Piscataqua where giant mast trees grew. Richard Waldron, the deputy magistrate at Dover, still antagonistic toward Quakers, opposed Nicholas Shapleigh; the latter, representing the Mason interests, granted two friends large white pine tracts. Thereupon Waldron, supported by Puritan merchants, circulated petitions in Maine calling for a return to Massachusetts authority. In May 1668 a commission with a small armed force annexed Maine at York. At the first court only one case was heard, but it provided a sample of imperialistic justice: Elias Stileman, a Portsmouth selectman, won a case for Thomas Clarke, the Massachusetts timber merchant. In 1669 Clarke was again elected Speaker of the Massachusetts House. In the same year Maine sent three delegates to the Massachusetts General Court. Moody, "Maine Frontier," pp. 122, 156–69; *Me. Court Recs.*, 2:163.

31. Douglass Edward Leach, *Flintlock and Tomahawk: New England in King Philip's War* (New York, 1958), pp. 21–22; Moody, "Maine Frontier," p. 182; Major Richard Waldron to the Governor of Massachusetts, 25 Sept. 1675, *NEHG Reg.*, 7 (1853): 93–94; Edward E. Bourne, *The History of Wells and Kennebunk* (Portland, Me., 1875), pp. 139–43; Thomas Hutchinson, *The History of the Colony and Province of Massachusetts-Bay*, ed. Lawrence Shaw Mayo, 3 vols. (Cambridge, Mass., 1936), 1:261; William Hutchinson Rowe, *Ancient North Yarmouth and Yarmouth, Maine, 1636–1936: A History* (Yarmouth, Me., 1937), pp. 23–24.

32. Major Richard Waldron to the Governor of Massachusetts, 25 Sept. 1675, pp. 93–94; John Hull to Philip French, 2 Sept. 1675, in John Hull, "Letter Book," 1:271; Benjamin Tompson, "New England's Crisis" [Boston, 1676], in *Benjamin Tompson, 1642–1714: First Native-Born Poet of America: His Poems*, ed. Howard Judson Hall (Boston, 1924), pp. 54–57; *Me. Court Recs.*, 3:xx–xxi.

33. Rowe, *Ancient North Yarmouth and Yarmouth*, pp. 7, 30; Richard Waldron to the Governor of Massachusetts, 25 Sept. 1675, pp. 93–94; "Diary of Samuel Sewall," *MHS Colls.*, 5th ser. 1 (1878): 41; John Hull, "Letter Book," 1:203.

According to the *London Gazette* of 17 Nov. 1675, the whole Indian uprising in New England had "put a great stop to Trade and Commerce there" (cited in Russell Hawes Kettell, ed., *Early American Rooms, 1650–1858* [Portland, Me., 1936], p. 19).

34. *Me. Court Recs.*, 3:xxii, 163, 214; Willis, *History of Portland*, pp. 166–68; Jeremy Belknap, *The History of New-Hampshire*, 3 vols. (Dover, N.H., 1812) 1:152.

The figures for sawmill production are based on an average saw-mill producing 500 to 1,000 feet of one-inch boards a day operating for 180 days a year. For lumber prices, see chap. 6, n. 22.

35. Palfrey, *History of New England*, 3:400; "The Baxter Manuscripts," *Doc. Hist. Me.*, 4 (1889): 398–402; *Me. Court Recs.*, 3:xxiv–xxv; *Mass. Recs.*, 5:309–10, 326–27.

36. R. N. Toppan and T. S. Goodrick, *Edward Randolph: Including His Letters and Official Papers, 1676–1703*, 7 vols. (Boston, 1898–1909), 2:205–7, 230–31; Viola F. Barnes, *The Dominion of New England: A Study in British Colonial Policy* (New York, 1960), pp. 5–16.

Little is known about Randolph except that he was well acquainted with the timber trade. Many years before he became interested in the New World, he had felled the large oaks on his land in southeastern Kent and sold hewn timber to the navy. In 1661 he was a timber agent for the navy: "I am going into the Wild of Kent, and such places as may with most conveniency supply your wants," he told the Naval Commission in that year. But because of some financial disaster early in the 1660s, Randolph sold his timberland and left England. During the late 1660s he acted as timber agent in northern Scotland for the duke of Richmond and others. There he was deeply involved in controversy over the control of valuable timberland and shipped timber

to the London market. He was back in Kent by the early 1670s
and must have spoken frequently with Robert Mason (his wife's
cousin), heir to proprietary rights in New Hampshire. There is
little doubt that Mason and Randolph planned to exploit timber
in northern New England. The two men were probably interested
primarily in the production of stores for the British navy and
merchant marine, for several near disasters during the Dutch
Wars of 1664–67 and 1672–74 had convinced many officials
that the government should support North American forest industry. Many now argued that northern New England should supply England not only with masts, spars, yards, and oars, but
with ship timbers, tar, pitch, and resin as well (Toppan and
Goodrick, *Edward Randolph*, 2:188–89, 190–91, 196–99;
Michael Garibaldi Hall, *Edward Randolph and the American
Colonies, 1676–1703* [Chapel Hill, N.C., 1960], pp. 2–3.

37. Toppan and Goodrick, *Edward Randolph*, 3:39–40, 41, 47,
64, 104–8; Bailyn, *New England Merchants*, p. 161; H. L. Osgood,
The American Colonies in the Seventeenth Century, 3 vols.
(New York, 1904–7), 3:338–39; Clark, *Eastern Frontier*, pp.
58–60.

38. Belknap, *History of New-Hampshire*, 1:150–51, 318.

39. *N.H. Docs.*, 1:464, 568–69; Osgood, *American Colonies
in the Seventeenth Century*, 3:338–56; *Mass. Recs.*, 5:444.

40. Barnes, *Dominion of New England*, pp. 20–25, 49–54;
Bailyn, *New England Merchants*, pp. 110–11.

41. Viola F. Barnes, "Richard Wharton: A Seventeenth-
Century New England Colonial," *CSM Pubs.* 26 (1924–26):
238–70; "Dudley Records," *MHS Procs.*, 2d ser. 13 (1899–1900):
270–74; Bailyn, *New England Merchants*, pp. 173–74; Hall,
Edward Randolph, pp. 102–3; Toppan and Goodrick, *Edward
Randolph*, 4:34, 35, 42, 58–59, 64.

42. Bailyn, *New England Merchants*, pp. 175–76; Barnes,
Dominion of New England, pp. 76–100, 129–30, 174–211.

43. Barnes, *Dominion of New England*, pp. 218, 228–29;
Wheelwright, "A Frontier Family," pp. 288–90; "The Baxter
Manuscripts," *Doc. Hist. Me.*, 4 (1889): 446–75; *CSPC, 1689–
1692*, pp. 140–41; *N.H. Docs.*, 2:27–28.

44. Miscellaneous Bound Papers, 4 (1683–90), Massachusetts
Historical Society; *CSPC, 1689–1692*, pp. 262–63.

45. "Charter of the Province of the Massachusetts Bay, 1691,"
CSM Pubs. 2 (1913): 28–29.

For a short review of the conflicts over woodlands in the eighteenth century, see Bernhard Knollenberg, *Origin of the American Revolution, 1759–1766*, rev. ed. (New York, 1965), pp. 122–30.
The penalty for cutting trees over twenty-four inches in diameter without permission of the crown was £100 sterling a tree. The mast laws later enacted by Parliament conflicted with the Massachusetts Charter of 1691.

7. The Wilderness Transformed

1. Daniel Neal, *The History of New-England*, 2 vols. (London, 1720), 2:574; John Dunton, *Letters written from New England, 1686*, ed. W. H. Whitmore (Boston, 1867), p. 52; J. Franklin Jameson, ed., *Johnson's Wonder-Working Providence, 1628–1651* (New York, 1910), pp. 71, 108, 248.
A Huguenot refugee in Massachusetts reported in 1687 that there were "plenty of bears, and wolves in great number who commit ravages among the sheep, if good precautions are not taken. We also have here plenty of rattlesnakes" (E. T. Fisher, trans., *Report of a French Protestant Refugee, in Boston, 1687* [Brooklyn, 1868], pp. 38–39).
2. Bernard Bailyn and Lotte Bailyn, *Massachusetts Shipping, 1697–1714: A Statistical Study* (Cambridge, Mass., 1959), pp. 84–85, table 6; J. G. B. Hutchins, *The American Maritime Industries and Public Policy, 1789–1914* (Cambridge, Mass., 1941), pp. 82–83, 130–31; William Douglass, *A Summary, Historical and Political of the . . . British Settlements in North America*, 2 vols. (Boston, 1749–51), 2:59, 61; Contract between John Row and Nathaniel Newgate, Miscellaneous Bound Papers, Massachusetts Historical Society, Boston, Mass., 5 (1694–97); *Essex Court Recs.*, 3:284–85; *Mass. Recs.*, vol. 4, pt. 2, pp. 499–500; *Plym. Recs.*, 5:65; Capt. John Smith, *The Sea-man's Grammar and Dictionary* (London, 1699), pp. 8–9, 11. The Massachusetts Archives, 40:18, 61:129–30, contains lists of equipment necessary for fitting out a ship.
3. *Boston Town Records, 1634–1660 (Second Report of the Record Commissioners of the City of Boston, 1877)* (Boston,

1877), pp. 152–53, 156–57; *Boston Town Records, 1660–1701, A Report of the Record Commissioners of the City of Boston* (Boston, 1881), pp. 5, 21, 39, 80; *Mass. Recs.*, 2:98–99, 250–51, 3:133, vol. 4, pt. 1, pp. 39–40, pt. 2, pp. 107, 377; *Aspinwall Recs.*, pp. 75–76; Carl Bridenbaugh, *Cities in the Wilderness: The First Century of Urban Life in America, 1625–1742* (New York, 1966), pp. 36–37; Darrett B. Rutman, *Winthrop's Boston: Portrait of a Puritan Town, 1630–1649* (Chapel Hill, N.C., 1965), pp. 189, 199, 242, 251–52.

4. Rutman, *Winthrop's Boston*, pp. 188, 199, 200, 207, 247; "Records of the Suffolk County Court, 1671–1680," 2 vols., *CSM Pubs.* 29 (1933): 432; *CSM Pubs.* 30 (1933): 738–42, 1094; *Boston Town Records, 1634–1660*, pp. 61–62, 70, 72, 110–11, 144, 148, 155, 158; *Boston Town Records, 1660–1701*, p. 74; *Mass. Recs.*, 2:18 20, 215 16, 249 50; "A Note Book Kept by Thomas Lechford, Esq., Lawyer, in Boston, Massachusetts Bay, from June 27, 1638, to July 29, 1641," *AAS Trans.* 7 (1885): 408; Edgar M. Hoover, Jr., *Location Theory and the Shoe and Leather Industries* (Cambridge, Mass., 1937), pp. 125–28, 137.

John Josselyn, who made a voyage to New England in 1663, was the first to mention the hemlock by name. He said it was a "kind of spruce. The bark of this tree serves to dy tawny. The fishers tan their sails and nets with it" (John Josselyn, "New-England's Rarities Discovered" [London, 1672], *AAS Trans.* 4 [1860]: 200–201).

5. Theodore J. Kreps, "Vicissitudes of the American Potash Industry," *Journal of Economic and Business History* 3 (1930–31): 633–34; John Hull, "Letter Book," 1670–85, 2 vols., typescript, American Antiquarian Society, Worcester, Mass., 1:81, 2:619; William B. Weeden, *Economic and Social History of New England, 1620–1789*, 2 vols. (Boston, 1890), 1:171; *Mass. Recs.*, 3:256, vol. 4, pt. 1, pp. 65–66; Richard S. Dunn, *Puritans and Yankees: The Winthrop Dynasty of New England, 1630–1717* (Princeton, N.J., 1962), pp. 84–87, 94, 128, 201; "Simon Bradstreet to the Committee for Trade and Foreign Plantations, 1680," *MHS Colls.*, 3d ser. 8 (1843): 335–36.

For the complexity of potash manufacture, see Malachy Postlethwayt, *The Universal Dictionary of Trade and Commerce*, 2 vols. (London, 1751–55), 2:532–34, and *Directions for making calcined or Pearl-ashes, as practised in Hungary, &c. with A*

Copper-plate Drawing of a Calcining Furnace (Boston, 1766). The first volume of John Hull's "Letter Book" is full of references to imported Spanish iron "in barrs or bolts."

6. Neal, *History of New England,* 2:584; "Maverick's Description of New England" ("A Briefe Discription of New England and the Severall Townes Therein, Together with the Present Government thereof," ca. 1660), *NEHG Reg.* 39 (1885): 47; John Ogilby, *America: Being An Accurate Description of the New World* (London, 1670), p. 160; Betty Flanders Thomson, *The Changing Face of New England* (New York, 1958), pp. 46–47; Marston Bates, *The Forest and the Sea: A Look at the Economy of Nature and the Ecology of Man* (New York, 1960), pp. 242–43.

The estimate of 500,000 acres of cleared woodland in 1700 is based on an estimated population of 100,000 persons, each of whom required 5 acres of farm land for sustenance. However, one estimate of the amount of land cleared by 1700 is as high as 880,000 acres (Eugene V. Zumwalt, "Taxation and Other Factors Affecting Private Forestry in Connecticut" [Ph.D. diss., Yale University, 1951], pp. 8–9). For a discussion of the amount of land necessary to sustain the population of eighteenth-century America, see Charles S. Grant, *Democracy in the Connecticut Frontier Town of Kent* (New York, 1961), pp. 36–38; James Lemon, "Household Consumption in Eighteenth-century America," *Agricultural History* 41 (1967): 59–70; Kenneth A. Lockridge, *A New England Town, the First Hundred Years: Dedham, Massachusetts, 1636–1736* (New York, 1970), pp. 147–50. Population estimates are from Evarts B. Greene and Virginia D. Harrington, *American Population before the Federal Census of 1790* (New York, 1932), pp. 1, 8–9.

For the extensive interchange of plants and trees between the colonies and England in the eighteenth century, see June Rainsford Butler, "America—A Hunting Ground for Eighteenth-Century Naturalists, with Special Reference to Their Publications about Trees," *Papers of the Bibliographical Society of America* 32 (1938): 1–16, and E. G. Swem, ed., "Brothers of the Spade, Correspondence of Peter Collison, of London, and of John Custis, of Williamsburg, Virginia, 1734–1746," *AAS Procs.,* n.s. 58 (1948): 17–190.

7. Evangeline W. Andrews and C. M. Andrews, *Journal of a Lady of Quality* (New Haven, Conn., 1921), p. 164; Solon J. Buck and Elizabeth Hawthorne Buck, *The Planting of Civiliza-*

tion in Western Pennsylvania (Pittsburgh, Pa., 1939), pp. 268–70; *Me. Court Recs.,* 3:139; Lyman Carrier, *The Beginnings of Agriculture in America* (New York, 1923), pp. 263–67; R. E. Prothero, *English Farming Past and Present,* 6th ed. (London, 1961), p. 29; H. L. Edlin, *Woodland Crafts in Britain: An Account of the Traditional Uses of Trees and Timbers in the British Countryside* (London, 1949), pp. 147–49; Samuel Deane, *The New-England Farmer* (Worcester, Mass., 1790), pp. 23, 190, 192; Asa Ellis, Jr., *The Country Dyer's Assistant* (Brookfield, Mass., 1798), pp. 22–25, 37–38, 67–68; Paul Dudley, "An Account of the Method of Making Sugar from the Juice of the Maple Tree in New England," and "An Account of a Method Lately Found out in New-England, for Discovering Where the Bees Hive in the Woods, in Order to Get Their Honey," in Perry Miller and Thomas H. Johnson, eds., *The Puritans,* rev. ed. (New York, 1963), pp. 747–50; *Report of a French Refugee,* p. 220; *Aspinwall Recs.,* p. 229; A. H. Verrill, *Foods America Gave the World* (Boston, 1937), pp. 129–30, 134, 173, 176–78; Neal, *History of New-England,* 2:567–68; Douglass, *Summary of the British Settlements,* 2:56–57, 67, 72–73; Josselyn, "New-England's Rarities," *AAS Trans.* 4 (1860): 183–86, 198–201; John Tennent, "Every Man His Own Doctor: Or the Poor Planter's Physician," in George Fisher, *The American Instructor* (Philadelphia, 1770), pp. 350, 353–54, 357–59, 360–61, 368–69, 372–73; William N. Fenton, "Contacts between Iroquois Herbalism and Colonial Medicine," *Annual Report of the Board of Regents of the Smithsonian Institution . . . 1941* (Washington, 1942), pp. 508, 514, 523–26.

8. *WJ,* 2:92; "Forefathers' Song," in Louis Untermeyer, ed., *An Anthology of the New England Poets from Colonial Times to the Present Day* (New York, 1948), pp. 33–34; Samuel Danforth, *An Almanack for the Year . . . 1648* (Cambridge, Mass., 1648), no pagination; *Watertown Records,* 8 vols. (Watertown, Mass., 1894–1939), 1:93; Carrier, *Beginnings of Agriculture,* pp. 99–100, 258; *Conn. Recs.,* 4:248–49; Lincoln Smith, *The Power Policy of Maine* (Berkeley, Calif., 1951), pp. 1–9.

9. Edna Scofield, "The Origin of Settlement Patterns in Rural New England," *Geographical Review* 28 (1938): 660.

10. *WP,* 2:139; *Watertown Records,* 1:1–2, 14; *The Early Records of the Town of Dedham, Massachusetts,* 6 vols. (n.p., 1886–1936), 2:25, 32, 36; *The Records of the Town of Cam-*

bridge (Formerly Newtowne) Massachusetts, 1630–1703 (Cambridge, Mass., 1901), pp. 10, 25; *Town Records of Salem,* 3 vols. (Salem, Mass., 1868–1934), 1:17–18, 30–31; *Dorchester Town Records, Fourth Report of the Record Commissioners* (Boston, 1880), pp. 26, 41, 44, 45; Northampton Town Records, Number 1, 1654–1754, Office of the City Clerk, City Hall, Northampton, Mass., pp. 48–49, 129; *Mass. Recs.,* 1:101, 292; *R.I. Recs.,* 1:15–16, 97; Charles M. Andrews, "The River Towns of Connecticut," *Johns Hopkins Studies in Historical and Political Science,* 7th ser. (Baltimore, 1889), pp. 66–67; Roy H. Akagi, *The Town Proprietors of the New England Colonies* (Philadelphia, 1924), pp. 3–4, 71.

For an analysis of Judeo-Christian beliefs and their influence on man's attitudes toward the development of land and natural resources, see Roderick Nash, *Wilderness and the American Mind* (New Haven, Conn., 1967), pp. 13–22, 31–43, 191–99.

11. Richard Eburne, *Plaine Pathway to Plantations . . .* (London, 1624), pp. 23–25; Lockridge, *A New England Town,* pp. 1–22; Arthur H. Buffington, "The Massachusetts Experiment of 1630," *CSM Pubs.* 32 (1933–37): 308–20.

12. For a penetrating discussion of the contradictions in the Calvinist ethic, see Perry Miller, "Declension in a Bible Commonwealth," in Perry Miller, *Nature's Nation* (Cambridge, Mass., 1967), pp. 14–49.

13. Dunn, *Puritans and Yankees,* p. 108; Miller, "Declension in a Bible Commonwealth," p. 30.

14. Timothy Dwight, *Travels in New-England and New York,* 4 vols. (New Haven, Conn., 1821), 1:107; Jameson, ed., *Johnson's Wonder-Working Providence,* p. 84; Marc Lescarbot, *The History of New France,* trans. and ed. W. L. Grant, 3 vols. (Toronto, 1907–14), 2:269; Harry J. Carman, ed., *American Husbandry* (Port Washington, N.Y., 1964), p. 46; George B. Emerson, *A Report on the Trees and Shrubs Growing Naturally in the Forests of Massachusetts,* 4th ed., 2 vols. (Boston, 1887), 1:5; Gilbert Chinard, "The American Philosophical Society and the Early History of Forestry in America," *Proceedings of the American Philosophical Society* 89 (1945): 444–88; F. M. Caulkins, *History of Norwich, Connecticut, from Its Settlement in 1660, to January 1845* (Norwich, Conn., 1845), p. 143; Douglass, *Summary of the British Settlements,* 2:68.

For a scientific statement on the influence of the forest on wind and temperature, see Victor E. Shelford, *The Ecology of North America* (Urbana, Ill., 1963), p. 24. See also Ulysses Prentiss Hedrick, *A History of Agriculture in the State of New York* (New York, 1966), pp. 15–16.

15. Miller, *The New England Mind: The Seventeenth Century*, pp. 207–35; Anne Bradstreet, "As Weary Pilgrim," in Jeannine Hensley, ed., *The Works of Anne Bradstreet* (Cambridge, Mass., 1967), p. 294.

16. "A Briefe Relation of the State of New England" [London, 1689], in Peter Force, ed., *Tracts and Other Papers Relating Principally to the Colonies in North America*, 4 vols. (New York, 1947), vol. 4, no. 11, pp. 7–8.

In 1669 Henry Oldenburg, Secretary of the Royal Society, asked John Winthrop, Jr., if it was true that "they make good gain in N. Engl[an]d by the sale of boards, wainscot, planks, joyners work, coopers-work, carpenters work, ready fram'd?" ("Correspondence of the Founders of the Royal Society with Governor Winthrop of Connecticut," *MHS Procs.* 16 [1878]: 241). In 1674 Carew Reynel wrote that the trade of New England with the West Indies actually hindered the development of English trade with that region (Carew Reynel, *The True English Interest* [London, 1674], p. 91).

17. "Briefe Relation of the State of New England," and "The Revolution in New-England Justified . . ." [Boston, 1691], in Force, ed., *Tracts*, vol. 4, no. 11, pp. 4–5, vol. 4, no. 9, p. 18; "The Resolution entered into by the delegates from the several towns and districts of the Massachusetts-bay . . . laid before the Congress, Sept. 17, 1774" ["Suffolk Resolves"], in Worthington C. Ford et al., eds., *Journals of the Continental Congress, 1774–1789*, 34 vols. (Washington, 1904–37), 1:32.

Appendix A, Shipping Tonnage and the Timber Trade

1. *WJ*, 2:31, 60, 70, 89, 92–93, 126–27, 152–54, 157, 176, 181, 190–91, 201, 204–5, 210, 227–28, 246, 248–50, 252–53, 263, 275–76, 287, 289, 321–23, 325–26, 345–46, 350–51; *Aspinwall Recs.*, pp. 46–47; "Plymouth Records," *MHS Colls.*, 2d ser. 4 (1816): 99–100; *The Letter Book of Peleg Sanford of Newport*,

Merchant, later Governour of Rhode Island, 1666–1699 (Providence, R.I., 1928), p. 70; Isabel MacBeath Calder, *The New Haven Colony* (New Haven, Conn., 1934), pp. 160–61; Charles M. Andrews, *The Colonial Period of American History*, 4 vols. (New Haven, Conn., 1934–38), 2:175–77, 176 n. 3; Joseph B. Felt, *The Annals of Salem from Its First Settlement* (Salem, Mass., 1827), p. 156; Charles Boardman Hawes, *Gloucester, by Land and Sea: The Story of a New England Seacoast Town* (Boston, 1923), pp. 23–25; J. Leander Bishop, *A History of American Manufactures from 1608 to 1860*, 2 vols. (Philadelphia, 1864), 1:39; Marion H. Gottfried, "The First Depression in Massachusetts," *NEQ* 9 (1936): 69–70.

2. "The Names of such ships & masters that have Come in and gone out of our Harbours and Given bond for His Majesty's Customes," Massachusetts Archives, 60:33; "Mass. Shipping Abstracts," pt. 1, vol. 1, pp. 41–76, 93–127; Massachusetts Archives, 7:16–41; Bernard Bailyn and Lotte Bailyn, *Massachusetts Shipping, 1697–1714: A Statistical Study* (Cambridge, Mass., 1959), tables 1 and 4.

It is possible that a few vessels made more than one departure during the period 25 Mar.–29 Sept. 1687 or during the same period in 1688. However, the names of ships and their places of registry are recorded in the "Mass. Shipping Abstracts," and ships with the same names, registries, and tonnages do not appear frequently. In the records for 25 Mar.–29 Sept. 1687 only seven pairs of vessels have identical names and tonnages.

James F. Shepherd and Gary M. Walton, *Shipping, Maritime Trade, and the Economic Development of Colonial North America* (Cambridge, 1972), app. 3, table 8, have calculated the average size of 249 vessels trading in the port of Boston in 1688 at 46.5 tons, 354 vessels in 1716 at 49.6 tons, and 321 vessels in 1753 at 51.7 tons.

3. Vincent T. Harlow, *A History of Barbados, 1625–1685* (Oxford, 1926), pp. 39–41, 43–44, 338–40; Sir Dalby Thomas, *An Historical Account of the Rise and Growth of the West-India Collonies; and of the Great Advantages They are to England, in Respect to Trade* (London, 1690), pp. 15, 18–20; Richard S. Dunn, "The Barbados Census of 1680: Profile of the Richest Colony in English America," *William and Mary Quarterly*, 3d ser. 24 (1969): 11, 16; Richard Ligon, *A True & Exact History of the Island of Barbados* (London, 1690), p. 113; Richard Pares,

Yankees and Creoles: The Trade between North America and the West Indies before the American Revolution (Cambridge, Mass., 1956), pp. 16–18, 24–28, 66–69, 84, 86, 103–6; Carl Bridenbaugh, *Cities in the Wilderness: The First Century of Urban Life in America, 1625–1742* (New York, 1971), pp. 30–34, 178–79, Bernard Bailyn, *New England Merchants in the Seventeenth Century* (New York, 1964), pp. 129–30; Ralph Davis, *The Rise of the English Shipping Industry in the Seventeenth and Eighteenth Centuries* (London, 1962), pp. 9–10, 16; Violet Barbour, "Marine Risks and Insurance in the Seventeenth Century," *Journal of Economic and Business History* 1 (1928–29): 563; Calder, *New Haven Colony*, pp. 160–61; *WJ*, 2:248–50, 263, 275–76, 287.

Soon after the 400-ton *Seafort* sailed on her maiden voyage in the mid 1640s, she ran aground in a storm off Cádiz and broke up. In 1646 a 260-ton vessel launched on the Charles River in Cambridge ran aground and broke up near the spot where the *Seafort* had sunk (*WJ*, 2:248–50).

4. *WJ*, 2:31, 60, 70, 89, 92–93, 126–27, 152–54, 157, 176, 181, 183–87, 190–91, 197, 201, 204–5, 210, 227–28, 246, 248–50, 252–53, 263, 275–76, 287, 321–26, 345–46, 350–51; *Aspinwall Recs.*, pp. 46–47; "Plymouth Records," *MHS Colls.*, 2d ser. 4 (1816): 99–100; *Letter Book of Peleg Sanford*, p. 70; Calder, *New Haven Colony*, pp. 160–61; Andrews, *Colonial Period*, 2:175–77, 176 n. 3; Felt, *Annals of Salem*, p. 156; Hawes, *Gloucester*, pp. 23–25; Bishop, *History of American Manufactures*, 1:39; Gottfried, "First Depression in Massachusetts," pp. 69–70.

The effects of piracy on shipping costs are discussed by Shepherd and Walton, *Shipping, Maritime Trade, and Economic Development*, pp. 81–85.

5. William B. Weeden, *Economic and Social History of New England, 1620–1789*, 2 vols. (Boston, 1890), 1:252; Bailyn and Bailyn, *Massachusetts Shipping*, pp. 23–26, 86–87; William G. Saltonstall, *Ports of the Piscataqua* (Cambridge, Mass., 1941), pp. 12–14; John J. Currier, *Historical Sketch of Ship Building on the Merrimac River* (Newburyport, Mass., 1877), p. 13; Edward Pierce Hamilton, *A History of Milton* (Milton, Mass., 1957), pp. 86–87; Bishop, *History of American Manufactures*, 1:38, 41–42; L. Vernon Briggs, *History of Shipbuilding on North River, Plymouth County, Massachusetts* (Boston, 1889), pp. 214–15, 217, 282–85, 336; Carl C. Cutler, *Mystic: The Story of a Small*

New England Seaport (Mystic, Conn., 1945), pp. 138–39; F. M. Caulkins, *History of New London, Connecticut* (New London, 1895), pp. 12–14, 231–36; *Conn. Recs.*, 3:297.

6. Tonnage figures calculated from Bailyn and Bailyn, *Massachusetts Shipping*, pp. 84–85, table 6. The registered tonnage of New England included only those vessels that crossed the seas or carried goods from one plantation to another. Small coastal vessels were not registered.

7. Bailyn and Bailyn, *Massachusetts Shipping*, p. 53.

Index

Index

Index

Casco Bay (Me.), 108
Charles II, 112, 113
Chimneys, 65
Clarke, Thomas, 113
Clear-cutting, 27
Cleared land, 48, 59, 159 n. 10, 160 n. 11
Clearings, 28–30
Coal, 16–18, 155 n. 39
Conant, Roger, 58
Conservation, 13–14, 125–26
Cooperage, 123
Copper smelting, 124
Cotton, 80–81
Courts, 104, 108
Cradock, Matthew, 58, 69
Craftsmen, 51–52, 63
Cranfield, Edward, 117
Cutts, John, 116

Dalton, Timothy, 103
Dennison, Daniel, 106, 107, 109
Dense woodlands, 33–34
Depression of 1640, 75–76, 77–79
Dover (N.H.), 102, 103, 111, 112
Dudley, Joseph, 117–18, 197 n. 11
Dudley, Thomas, 64
Dwellings, 50, 64–66, 179 n. 23
Dyewood, 94

Eaton, Theophilus, 58
Enclosure, 6
Endecott, John, 58, 197 n. 11
England: need for timber, 10–13, 18–21, 152–53 n. 20; popu-
lation, 10–11, 149 n. 5, 150 n. 9, 153 n. 20; trade with New
England, 85–86, 94. See also Britain
Evelyn, John, 14, 20
Exeter (N.H.), 102, 103, 112, 195 n. 5

Falmouth (Me.), 108
Fences, 62–63

Index